CRIMES OF NEW YORK

STORIES OF CROOKS, KILLERS, AND CORRUPTION FROM THE WORLD'S TOUGHEST CITY

EDITED BY CLINT WILLIS

Thunder's Mouth Press
New York

CRIMES OF NEW YORK:
STORIES OF CROOKS, KILLERS, AND CORRUPTION FROM THE WORLD'S
TOUGHEST CITY

Compilation copyright © 2003 by Clint Willis
Introductions copyright © 2003 by Clint Willis

Adrenaline® and the Adrenaline® logo are trademarks of
Avalon Publishing Group Incorporated, New York, NY.

An Adrenaline Book®

Published by
Thunder's Mouth Press
An Imprint of Avalon Publishing Group Incorporated
161 William Street, 16th floor
New York, NY 10038

Book design: Sue Canavan

frontispiece photo: Foiled Bar Robbery, © Bettmann/Corbis

Library of Congress Cataloging-in-Publication Data is available.

ISBN 1-56025-527-7

Printed in the United States of America

Distributed by Publishers Group West

For
Bob Porter
and
Jane Rosenberg

contents

Introduction

New York for a long time has been a superb breeding place for crime—lots of potential victims and plenty of criminals.

Take a ride on the Staten Island Ferry. There stands the Statue of Liberty, waving them in—the tired, the poor, the huddled masses: perfect victims for the people who got here before them. The new arrivals soon find themselves huddled in New York City's tenements and sweatshops—victims of slum-lords and unscrupulous entrepreneurs. The newcomers generally remain poor and weak for at least a generation or so. Some turn to crime—larceny, murder, drug deals—finding their easiest prey among the poorest and weakest of their neighbors.

New York's role in the financial industry creates opportunities for crime among the city's more established denizens—the sort who live and work in the incredibly expensive buildings that define the city's famous skyline. These thieves can be as rapacious as any street thug. Meanwhile, the city's huge economy—its tax base, its real estate, its workforce—create wonderful opportunities for political corruption. There is so much to steal, and there are so many ways to steal it.

New York also delivers writers worthy to record its criminal life. They are drawn to and nurtured by the city's sheer size, its place in the publishing industry, its literary history, its food and music, its land-scape, its energy—by the sheer variety of experience to witness and record there.

We generally deplore crime because it has victims and because we know that we may be among them. But crime stories are entertaining in part because we identify with the criminals enough to want to know their stories—where they come from, where they go, where they end up. Some of us take a vicarious thrill from the rule-breaking that goes on in crime stories—in part because many of us hate (viscerally if not in principal) the rules that govern our lives.

Think of it: the thousands of state, local, and federal regulations—not to mention extra-legal rules and the by-laws of conscience—that we must obey if we are to make a living, stay out of jail, stay married, retain custody of our children, keep a driver's license, maintain our self-respect . . . All of these things are shockingly contingent upon our willingness to toe certain lines. It may strike us that some criminals are in some unfamiliar way free. A man picks up a bottle and hits another man on the head with it. The wish to know what that feels like may be part of what keeps us reading these stories.

Crime stories (true or otherwise) at least offer a chance to witness and to wonder. They don't always offer explanations; crime isn't always or even often about logic—or else the logic is so obvious as to be unin-teresting. Crime is political in a sense; politics help explain why certain people are poor or desperate or confused enough to break the law. But by the time a person commits a crime, it's no longer about laws—it's a personal matter. The law at that point becomes something technical and hopeful; something that depends upon us for its meaning. That is part of why many of the best writers try to show us the criminal—not merely the crime or its consequence.

Such writers' stories are funny or sad as often as they are shocking. The humorist and reporter St. Clair McKelway once wrote about a conversation he had with a New York judge named John A. Mullen.

The pair decided between themselves that many people who were technically criminals shouldn't be called criminals:

> We thought of a word that can frequently be substituted for the word "criminal", the word "rascal". The definition of it in the Oxford English dictionary is interesting, I think: "Rogue, knave, scamp (often playfully to a child & etc.; *you lucky rascal)*; belonging to the rabble (archaic; the rascal rout, the common people).

McKelway often chose to write about criminals who fit that definition—childlike and relatively harmless thieves and imposters; troublemakers, men and women of the people, characters who in some sense refused or failed to grow up. He admired some of them—men such as Stanley Clifford Weyman, an astonishingly accomplished imposter whose roles included a member of the New York State lunacy commission, Consul General of Rumania, and Lieutenant St. Cyr of the French Navy.

McKelway was part of a generation that wrote or began writing between the two world wars. Those writers produced some of New York's best reporting and writing. Writers like McKelway, Joseph Mitchell, Herbert Asbury, and Meyer Berger wrote for newspapers and magazines like the *Herald Tribune,* the *Times,* and the *New Yorker.*

These writers perfected their technique and tone during the golden era of the human interest story. A typical day for Joseph Mitchell at the World-Telegram included an interview with an Italian bricklayer who looked like the Prince of Wales and had been offered a job in Hollywood; an interview with a boxer who was a countess and who lived at the St. Moritz Hotel; and an interview with a theatrical agent selling racing cockroaches to society people.

> 'I rent a lot of monkeys,' he told me. 'People get lonesome and telephone me to send them a monkey to keep them company. After all, a monkey is a mammal just like us.' I

wrote that story and then I went home. Another day another dollar.

Reading writers like McKelway and Mitchell, it is easy to imagine that antique wrong-doers were gentler or better than contemporary criminals. But any reader of Luc Sante or Herbert Asbury knows that crime in New York wore a brutal face long before the gangs and drug wars of the late 20th century. The trick in any era is to render such brutality in a form that doesn't descend to caricature.

Pete Hamill does it in his piece on Bernhard Goetz. Four young men in 1984 approached Goetz on the subway and asked him for money. Goetz pulled out a gun and shot them all. Hamill quotes liberally from Goetz's taped confession:

> He says that 'I wanted to hurt them as much as I possibly could.' But even in his rage, he could recognize the fallen men as humans: 'I wanted to look at his [Darrell Cabey's] eyes, I don't even want to say what may have been in my mind. And I looked at his eyes . . . there was such *fear.*' It was as if Cabey's fear was the only sign to Goetz of their common humanity. 'You know, the, the, the look had changed. And I started—it was kinda like slowing down . . .'

The Goetz case raised a question at the heart of many stories about crime: Who is the victim? The answer is almost always more complicated than we would like to believe.

We want crime to be an aberration, which it is; we want it to go away, which it shows no sign of doing. We do our best to escape it. We move to fancier neighborhoods if we can; once there, we hire private security guards to escort us from our cars to our front doors. Or we leave the city for the suburbs or even the country, in hopes that crime isn't waiting for us there.

Meanwhile, crime continues to do its part to destroy lives and property and the society meant to protect them. Our prisons overflow with angry, incompetent, and desperate people, many of them the children and perhaps the grandchildren of other criminals.

Meanwhile, we love a good crime story, more or less as we love any good story. Good stories tell us something about the writer and about his subjects—in this case, the criminals and the criminals' victims. We read a good crime story and we see connections; we see ourselves in the criminal and in the victims. We temporarily visit other lives— ruined and anxious ones; violent and passive ones; comic and disastrous ones; lives we have never imagined for ourselves.

The shock we encounter in a good crime story has surprisingly little to do with bad behavior or its sometimes grisly consequences. We can dismiss or laugh at tabloid headlines—*Headless Body Found in Topless Bar*—in part because they don't surprise us. The surprise we encounter in these stories is more fundamental; it's the shock—the repeated shock—of recognition.

—CLINT WILLIS
SERIES EDITOR, ADRENALINE BOOKS

Notes from Underground
by Pete Hamill

When Bernhard Goetz shot four young black men who

approached him on the subway, he was hailed as a crime-

fighting hero and criticized as a racist vigilante. Here dis-

tinguished New York City novelist and journalist Pete Hamill

(born 1935) offers his take on the story.

The slow and tedious processes of justice brought Bernhard Hugo Goetz last week to a fifth-floor courtroom at 111 Centre Street and there, at least, the poor man was safe. Out in the great scary city, the demons of his imagination roamed freely; across the street, many of them were locked away in the cages of The Tombs. But here at the defense table, flanked by his lawyers, protected by a half-dozen armed court officers, the room itself separated by metal detectors from the anarchy of the city, Goetz looked almost serene.

By design or habit, he was dressed as an ordinary citizen: pink cotton shirt and jeans over the frail body, steel-rimmed glasses sliding down the long sharp nose. His hair looked freshly trimmed. You see people like him every day, passing you on the street, riding the subways, neither monstrous nor heroic. From time to time, he whispered to the lawyers. He made a few notes on a yellow pad. His eyes wandered around the courtroom, with its civil service design and the words *In God We Trust* nailed in sans-serif letters above the bench of Judge Stephen G. Crane. Goetz never looked at the spectators or the six rows of reporters. In some curious way, he was himself a kind of spectator.

So when it was time to play the tape-recorded confession that Goetz made to the police in Concord, New Hampshire, on New Year's Eve, 1984, he, too, examined the transcript like a man hoping for revelation. The text itself was extraordinary. Combined with the sound of Goetz's voice—stammering, hyperventilating, querulous, defensive, cold, blurry, calculating—it seemed some terrible invasion of privacy. We have heard this voice before; it belongs to the anonymous narrator of *Notes from Underground*, that enraged brief for the defense.

Goetz furrowed his brow as he listened to this much younger, oddly more innocent version of himself that had ended the long panicky flight out of the IRT in the second floor interview room of police headquarters in Concord. He started by telling his inquisitor, a young detective named Chris Domian, the sort of facts demanded by personnel directors: name, birth date, social security number, address (55 West 14th Street, "in New York City, and that's, uh, that's zip code 10011"). But it's clear from the very beginning that he realized these would be his last anonymous hours.

GOETZ: You see, I'll tell you the truth, and they can do anything they want with me, but I just don't want to, I just don't want to be *paraded* around, I don't want a circus. . . . I wish it were a dream. But it's not. But, you know, it's nothing to be proud of. It's just, just, you know, it just *is*.

Exactly. It wasn't a dream, certainly not a movie; it just was. On December 22, 1984, at about 1:30 in the afternoon, Bernie Goetz boarded a southbound number 2 Seventh Avenue IRT train at 14th Street and his life changed forever. So did the lives of Darrell Cabey, Troy Canty, James Ramseur, and Barry Allen. Within seconds after he boarded the train, they were joined together in a few violent minutes that changed this city. And when you listen to Goetz making his jangled confession, you understand that on that terrible afternoon, there were really five victims.

DOMIAN: Okay, let's start with the person that was, uh, on the right, so to speak, laying down.

GOETZ: Yeah, I think he was the one who talked to me; he was the one who did the talking.

That was Canty. He is now 20, finishing an 18-month drug rehab treatment at Phoenix House. Before he ran into Goetz, he had pleaded guilty to taking $14 from video games in a bar. In his confession, Goetz is trying hard to explain to Domian (and to officer Warren Foote, who joined Domian) not simply what he did, but its context. The resulting transcript reads like a small, eerie play: the man from the big city explaining a dark world of menacing signs and nuances to the baffled outlanders.

GOETZ: I sat, I sat down and just, he was lying on the side, kind of. He, he just turned his face to me and he said, "How are you?" You know, what do you do? 'Cause people joke around in New York a lot, and this and that, and in certain circumstances that can be, that can be a real threat. You see, there's an implication there . . . I looked up and you're not supposed to look at people a lot because it can be interpreted as being impolite—so I just looked at him and I said, "Fine." And I, I looked down. But you kind of keep them in the corner of your eye . . .

DOMIAN: Did he say anything else to you?

GOETZ: Yeah, yeah . . . the train was out of the station for a while and it reached full speed. . . . And he and one of the other fellows got up and they, uh—You see, they were all originally on my right-hand side. But, uh, you know, two stayed on my right-hand side, and he got up and the other guy got up and they came to my left-hand side and. . . . You see, what they said wasn't even so much as important as the look, the *look*. You see the body language. . . . You have to, you know, it's, it's, uh, you know, that's what I call it, *body language*.

That's what started it off: "How are you?" and body language. It just went from there. Goetz remembered: "He [Canty] stood up and the other fellow stood up. And they very casually walked, or sauntered—

whatever you want to call it—over to my left side. And the fellow . . . uh, he said, 'Give me five dollars.' "

This is the moment that helps explain the intensity of the public response to the Goetz story. It is one thing to read with detached amusement about Jean Harris or Claus von Bulow; such tabloid soap operas have little to do with our lives. But for millions of New Yorkers, what happened to Goetz is a very real possibility. Being trapped on the subway by four bad guys demanding not a dime or a quarter but *five dollars* is similar to the nocturne about the burglar beside the bed in the dark. A quarter is panhandling; five dollars is robbery. Such scenarios don't often happen, but you wonder what you would do if they did. For Goetz, it happened.

GOETZ: One of the other fellows, he had in his fur coat, he had his hand or something like this and he put a bulge. . . . And even that isn't a threat. Because the people, you see, they, they know the rules of the game, the rules of the game in New York. And you know, they're very serious about the rules. . . . You see you don't know what it's like to be on the other side of violence. It's, it's like a picture. When it happens to you, you see, you *see* it. . . . People have the craziest image; they see, like Captain Kirk or someone like that, getting attacked by several guys and boom, boom, boom, he beats 'em up and—and two minutes later, he's walking arm and arm in, with a beautiful woman or something like that. And that's not what it is. . . .

Goetz was not Captain Kirk. He was a frail bespectacled young man living in New York and he had learned the rules of the game. He knew what was meant when one of four young black men told him he wanted five dollars.

GOETZ: I looked at his face, and, you know, his eyes were *shiny,* you know. He, he, he was, if you can believe that, his eyes were shiny, he was *enjoying* himself. . . . I know in my mind what they wanted to do was *play* with me. . . . You know, it's kind of like a cat plays with a mouse before, you know. . . .

DOMIAN: After you got that impression, what did you wind up doing?

GOETZ: That's not an impression, that's not an impression. . . .

Throughout the confession, Goetz struggles with what he clearly believes is an impossible task: to explain to his rural auditors the terrors of New York.

GOETZ: . . . You have to think in a cold-blooded way in New York. . . . If you don't . . . think in what society's going to brand it, as being you know, *cold-blooded* and murderous and savage and monstrous . . . I feel it's *irresponsible*. . . . How can you understand that here in New Hampshire? How, how, how can you?

He explains to the two New Hampshire cops that he began, in his mind, to lay down "my pattern of fire." He would shoot from left to right. That was the only thing he could do, he insists, because this act wasn't premeditated: "I never knew those guys were on the train, you know, and like I said, I'm, I'm no good guy or anything like that. But if they had acted a little differently, if they hadn't *cornered* me. . . ." Clearly what he feared most from them was humiliation. And so he decided to shoot them with the unregistered nickle-plated featherweight .38 caliber Smith & Wesson Special that he had shoved inside his pants.

DOMIAN: Your, your intention was to shoot these people?

GOETZ: My intention, at that moment, let me explain: when I saw what they intended for me, my intention was, was worse than shooting.

DOMIAN: Okay. Was it your intention to kill these people?

GOETZ: My intention was to do anything I could do to hurt them. My intention—you know, I know this sounds horrible—but my intention was to murder them, to *hurt* them, to make them suffer as much as possible.

No, he explained, he didn't have a pistol permit, because the New York police department had turned him down. And then recalling all this to the cops in New Hampshire, the core of his rage began to burn. The reason he wanted a pistol permit was because he had been attacked three years before and was left with permanent damage to his knee. The cops caught the man who did it, Goetz said, and two hours and 35 minutes after his arrest, he was back on the street without bail, charged with malicious mischief; Goetz himself claimed he spent six hours and five minutes filing the charges and talking to the bureaucrats in the victim aid program.

"That incident was an education," he said, his voice beginning to tremble. "It taught me that, that the city doesn't care what happens to you. You see, *you* don't know what it's like to be a victim inside."

And he began to explain what it's like to live in an almost permanent state of fear. This can't be sneered away; thousands, perhaps millions of New Yorkers live with this most corrosive emotion. Most of us have adjusted to the state of siege. We are tense, wary, guarded; but most of us function and do not explode. Goetz was different.

GOETZ: . . . I kind of accept my life, as I know it, is finished. But, but, boy, it would be just—to lead a normal life. If, if you can't, I mean, is it too much to ask? . . . To live being afraid is unbearable, you know? It's too much to ask, goddamn it. . . ."

All over the tape, Goetz talks about fear and its denial. "I'm not afraid of dying instantly," he says at one point. "I don't have a family or anything like that. What I'm afraid of is being maimed and of, of these things happening slowly and not knowing what's going to happen from moment to moment. The fear, in this case, the fear is a funny thing. You see, this is really *combat*." He then becomes even more analytical, sounding like a man who had mastered the theory before engaging in practice. "The upper level of your mind, you just turn off. That's, that's the important thing. And you, you *react* . . . your sense of perception changes, your abilities change. Speed is everything, speed is everything."

And so, with speed, he shot Canty, Allen, Cabey, and Manseur. "They had set a trap for me," he tells the cops, "and only they were trapped. It was just so bizarre. It was—I know this is disgusting to say—but it was, it was so easy. I can't believe it. God." He insists that he knew exactly what he was doing when he was doing it. "I don't believe in this insanity stuff. Because you know what you're doing. You cannot do something and not know it. I mean how could I do it and not know it? This is, this is all bullshit. . . . But if you can accept this: I was out of control. . . . Maybe you should always be in control. But if you put people in a situation where they're threatened with mayhem, *several times,* and then if, then if something happens, and if a person acts, turns into a vicious animal—I mean, I mean, you know, how are you supposed, you know, it's, it's, it's, it's, what, *what do you expect,* you know?"

After firing the first shots, dropping Canty, Ramseur, and Allen, he saw Cabey sitting down.

GOETZ: I wasn't sure if I had shot him before, because he just seemed okay. Now, I said I know this sounds, this is gonna sound vicious, and it is. I mean, how else can you describe it? I said, "You seem to be all right. Here's another." Now, you see, what happens is, I was gonna shoot him anyway, I'm sure. I had made up, I mean, in my mind, that I was gonna pull the trigger anyway. But he jerked his right arm. And on reflex, he was shot instantly. You see, that's the whole thing. You're working on reflex. You don't think. . . .

Scattered through the confession there are many other examples of Goetz's fury and rage, which sound as if they too had become reflexes. "If I had more [ammunition] I would have shot them again and again and again." He says that "I wanted to hurt them as much as I possibly could." But even in his rage, he could recognize the fallen men as humans: "I wanted to look at his eyes, I don't even want to say what may have been in my mind. And I looked at his eyes . . . there was such *fear.*" It was as if Cabey's fear was the only sign to Goetz of their common humanity. "You know, the, the, the look had changed. And I started—it was kinda like slowing down. All of a sudden it's like putting on the, screeching of the brakes, and you just start slowing down. . . ."

He talked about the reactions of other passengers, the train slowing down, a conductor coming in and asking what was going on. He talked about jumping out into the tracks after the train stopped in the tunnel, and coming up at Chambers Street and taking a cab home, and then a long drive that night in a rented car to Vermont because "instinctively, somehow I kinda feel like heading north is the way to go if there is a problem."

Goetz stayed in Vermont for a week. And if you can believe the confession, he seems actually to have been happy. What he did in the subway, he thought, would be considered just another New York crime. ". . . When I got back to New York, the stuff was still on the news and people were talking about it. You see, up here people have just forgotten about it. It was one more piece of, excuse me for using the word—one more piece of shit that happened in New York."

Hearing himself say those words, Goetz massaged his temple, and then lifted his glasses and rubbed his eyes. In the end, the eruption that Saturday afternoon on the IRT wasn't just another piece of shit that happened in New York. It was a lot more than that.

Mom, Murder Ain't Polite

by Meyer Berger

Meyer Berger (1898–1959) was a New York Times *reporter for more than 30 years. "Mom, Murder Ain't Polite" is from his collection of articles,* The Eight Million, *originally published in 1942. Berger early on decided to "devote my life to searching out the odd fish and the unfortunates in a city of several millions." That decision led to stories like this one.*

Anna Lonergan came to our house for dinner one night. She brought her fourteen-year-old son. Between the soup and the chicken courses, Anna fell into a dreamy mood and started talking about her brother and her husbands and all the nice fellas she had known and how hardly any were left, now, what with all the shooting in her neighborhood.

The boy grew restless. He said, "Mom, it ain't nice to talk about murder when you're eating. It ain't polite."

Anna's clear white skin ebbed red. She glared at her son. She turned indignantly to us.

"You got an encyclopedia?" she said.

We had the *Britannica.* Anna seemed highly pleased. She ordered the boy to leave the table.

"You go in the next room," she told him in sharp maternal reproof.

"You stay there and read the encyclopedia and you don't get no dessert."

The boy sullenly left the table.

Anna turned back to us happily. "I always do that," she explained. "When he talks back to his mother I make him go out and read the encyclopedia. That's the way to train children."

And Anna eagerly took up again the story of how many men her husbands had killed.

It is not often that Anna yields to the philosophical mood, but sometimes she talks wistfully of what a funny thing life is; how, when she was a little girl in yellow pigtails, she used to trot around the religious-goods store on Barclay Street with the sisters from St. James' because she wanted to be a nun, and how she turned out, instead, to be Queen of Brooklyn's Irishtown Docks.

This mood never lasts very long. Anna would rather tell about the sixteen years' dock war and how she won dower rights to the queenly title through the strong arms and the good trigger work of her two husbands, Wild Bill Lovett and Matty Martin, and her brother Richard ("Peg-Leg") Lonergan. She estimates that before they died (all three of them of bullet wounds) they killed about twenty men between them in order to gain and hold the waterfront leadership and the graft that went with it. This estimate may sound extravagant but it is really conservative. Records in the Medical Examiner's office show, for instance, that in the ten years from 1922 to 1932 there were seventy-eight unsolved murders in the section of Brooklyn called Irishtown—the rough-cobbled area between the Brooklyn Navy Yard and Fulton Ferry, under and around the approaches to the Brooklyn and Manhattan bridges. The prosecuting officials always fretted about this but were never able to do anything about it. The police usually knew who the killer was but they could never get any witnesses, and without witnesses an indictment was not obtainable, much less a trial. Exactly how many of the seventy-eight unsolved murders in that decade are attributable to dock wars, and how many to incidental motives, nobody really knows.

Anna's men were hard-working fellows who kept pretty regular hours. Six mornings a week they would go down to the docks for the stevedores' roll call. They had to be there to make sure that no stevedore was working who was not paying a share of his salary to the dock leadership. Sometimes a stevedore would argue about paying tribute and he would have to be beaten up or maybe his skull would have to be cracked. Men like that were not shot unless they were exceptionally obstinate. But when some superstevedore, with a gang of ten or twelve supporters, would try to take the leadership away from Anna's men, somebody usually got killed.

When Anna claims that Wild Bill, Matty, and Peg-Leg murdered about twenty men between them, she does not count neighborhood killings attributable to such things as honor, bad temper, and misunderstanding. Murders directly attributable to the racket of extorting a portion of stevedores' salaries were discussed at her dinner table, and she remembers most of them distinctly. She recalls only the more spectacular of the family murders that fall within the noncommercial or amateur category. Back in the twenties, every time there was a killing in Irishtown, the newspapers would label it "dock-war murder," but Anna says that was a lot of journalistic prittle-prattle. When Jim Gillen was killed on Jay Street in 1921, for example, his death was attributed to dock trouble, but the motive was something entirely different. Wild Bill Lovett killed Gillen for pulling a cat's tail. "Bill always hated to see anyone hurt an animal," Anna says.

It has been Anna's experience that you become accustomed to murder if you see enough of it. She didn't like it at first, but as time went on it became more or less routine. Sometimes a sensitive ear may detect a bit of pride in Anna's voice as she tells how many times she has gone to the morgue to identify her own dead or the neighbors'. She started when her father was killed by her mother, and went again when Bill got his. When her brother Peg-Leg was shot to death with Aaron Harms and Needles Ferry, his pals, Anna identified the three of them at one time. Later, Charlie Donnelly disputed the dock leadership with Matty Martin, who was Anna's second husband, and she made another trip to the morgue as a friendly gesture to Mrs. Donnelly, who was afraid she couldn't stand the ordeal of identifying her own husband. Eddie McGuire, murdered on the docks on May 16, 1928, was officially identified by Anna, too, and finally she did the honors for Matty, who had been accused (wrongfully, according to Anna) of the McGuire killing. Anna probably has an all-time record for morgue identifications, but she hasn't checked up on it. She never dreams about any of the killings and never cries when she thinks of them. Detectives say the only time they ever saw her cry was when she claimed Peg-Leg's body.

Anna was the first of fifteen children. Her father, John Lonergan, was red-haired, six feet two inches tall, a second-rate prize fighter when he married Mary Brady over on Cherry Hill on the East Side of Manhattan in 1898. There is some family legend that he once sparred with John L. Sullivan, but Anna wouldn't swear to it. Anna was born with a caul, which is supposed to bring good luck, but her Uncle Nelson, who was a captain on one of Jay Gould's yachts, bought it from Anna's mother. Sailors, you know, believe you can't drown if there's a caul aboard ship. Uncle Nelson had three, which he'd picked up here and there, just to make sure. He couldn't swim.

As a little girl, Anna attended St. James' parochial school on the East Side, the same one that Al Smith went to when he was a boy, and Al's wife sponsored Anna's enrollment in the Sacred Heart sodality. Anna admits, though, that the children were sponsored in groups and that she didn't know Mrs. Smith "real well." The Lonergans moved to the Brooklyn waterfront when Anna was about ten years old and took a house on Johnson Street. During this period Anna was extremely devout, trudged everywhere with the sisters, and, to use her own expression, "was in church morning, noon, and night." At about this time, too, she had her first contact with murder. Margaret Doran, one of her classmates, asked her one day after school to visit the Doran home on Pacific Street, in the same neighborhood, and in the basement they stumbled over the body of Margaret's mother. Margaret's pa, a motorman on the Smith Street trolley line, had chopped off Ma Doran's head. Some dock workers found his body in the river next day.

He had jumped off the wharf, after the killing, in a fit of remorse. Anna doesn't remember any other details, and she doesn't think the incident bothered her for any length of time. She says most people have a wrong idea about murder from books and movies, and it doesn't really haunt you and affect your sleep.

Anna is close to forty now, by her own count. She is still fussy about her blonde, bobbed hair, never misses a Saturday appointment at the neighborhood beauty parlor, and is extremely proud of her white hands. She is careful with her fingernails, too. She never uses red nail polish because she thinks it's cheap and vulgar, but she does do a rather professional job on her face with lipstick and eyebrow pencil. Her experience as a Broadway show girl is responsible for that. She danced at Rector's and Churchill's when she was eighteen and had a nonspeaking part with Fay Bainter in *The Kiss Burglar*. Since leaving the stage, she has been shot twice and stabbed once, and when she mentions these things she always crosses herself and thanks God that none of the scars show. Dressed for the street, she is still a good-looking woman. "My mother was beautiful, too," she'll tell new acquaintances. "She was the pitcher of me when she was a girl; a natural blonde, the same as me, only her hair turned gray overnight after Richard [she hates to have her brother called Peg-Leg] got his."

The first casualty in the Lonergan family was Boy, the family's pet spaniel. Boy was a cop hater, like most of the residents of Irishtown. The elder Lonergan had a special trapdoor in his bicycle-repair shop on Bridge Street, leading into a hole in which the dog could hide after he had nipped a patrolman, but one day a mounted officer, quick on the draw, fired a shot at the Lonergan pet and Boy died in what was to become the traditional Lonergan manner.

Anna was out walking with Laura Rich at dusk on April 16, 1923. She was still in the show business then, and so was Laura, who was from Irishtown too. As they passed the bicycle shop, they saw two other Irishtown girls ("tramps," Anna calls them) talking with old man Lonergan and Peg-Leg. Anna told her mother about it when she got home, and then forgot about it.

But Anna's mother didn't forget about it. She went down to the shop, and before she got through telling John Lonergan what she thought of him and the loose women he was entertaining, the cop had to come in off his beat to restore peace and quiet. A half-hour later Mrs. Lonergan went back to the bicycle shop and within a few minutes after she got there, her spouse was dying from bullet wounds. Anna heard about it and rushed down to the store. She pushed her way through the crowd and got in before the cops came. The old man was sprawled out on the floor and Mrs. Lonergan was kneeling over him, screaming. Anna sent for a priest and got her mother into a chair. "Mamma," she said, "what have you done to Papa?"

Peg-Leg wasn't in the store when the old man was killed. He showed up at the station house as his mother was being booked for murder, and tried to take the blame. That's why the rumor got around, later, that he actually committed the murder. Anna admits that Peg-Leg told the desk lieutenant, "The old lady didn't do it; I did," but she says there was no truth in his confession. "It was Mamma who done it," she says explicitly.

The two girls who started the whole business came to John Lonergan's wake and made Anna furious, but she restrained herself until they left her house. Then she went after them with a boy's baseball bat which had been parked in the umbrella stand in the hall for some years. She caught up with one of them, a girl named Kate, and knocked her out cold. Anna thinks now that perhaps it wasn't ladylike, but, as she says, "I was berling mad at the time."

Big Ed Reilly, who was famous in Irishtown as a deliverer of oppressed gunmen and beautiful ladies with homicidal tendencies long before the Hauptmann case, was hired by Bill Lovett as Mrs. Lonergan's attorney. Reilly's oratory at the trial made short work of the case against Mrs. Lonergan. It pictured Anna's mother as the patient drudge, beaten and kicked by her brute of a husband every day of their married life. With a quavering voice the lawyer depicted Mrs. Lonergan moved to great anger when the old man sent Anna home from the bicycle shop bleeding at the mouth because she had asked him to give her money for the family supper. Mrs. Lonergan had gone to the shop to reproach her husband for this and in the course of the argument which resulted the elder Lonergan had pulled a gun. Mrs. Lonergan, naturally, had tried to take it away from him and had shot him, accidentally. Anna was the star witness for her mother. She talked convincingly, and the jurymen seemed sad and turned Mrs. Lonergan loose.

Sometimes when Anna recalls her wedding to Bill Lovett, on July 28, 1923, she grows melancholy. She would have liked a church wedding with a misty veil and long train, and maybe some orange blossoms and organ music, but she had to stand up before City Clerk McCormick in ordinary street clothes. A formal wedding would have been out of place, in the circumstances. The ceremony came off only a month after Anna's mother had been freed of the murder charge; Peg-Leg, her brother, had just been arrested in connection with another killing (the murder of Eddie Hughes in a Sands Street speakeasy), and the bridegroom himself was out on bail on a charge of carrying a concealed weapon.

Anna had known Bill since they had been kids together on Catherine Street on the East Side, but had never thought much of him. He was shy around women and he was short—only five feet seven inches in height—and his face was a peculiar gray, owing to a lung condition. His black hair accentuated the pallor. The family had liked Bill, though, and the elder Lonergan had encouraged the match. Peg-Leg was for it, too, because he and Bill had been in Cumberland Hospital once at the same time—Peg-Leg with a bullet wound he'd acquired in a brawl in a Gold Street speak-easy, and Bill with five bullet wounds inflicted by the Frankie Byrnes gang of Irishtown.

Bill's courtship was almost mute. He used to sit around the Lonergan home by the hour, pretending he was calling on Peg-Leg, and he would stare at Anna. The old man pleaded with Anna to talk to Bill. "I don't talk to fellers who go around shooting people," she said one time.

That made the old man mad. "Your brother shoots people, too," he argued.

"Yeh," said Anna, "and he ought to be ashamed of himself."

Bill finally compelled Anna's admiration, though, by assuming ownership of a loaded .25-caliber automatic that was found on the elder Lonergan when detectives raided a Greenpoint speak-easy where he and Peg-Leg and Bill were having some of their favorite needle beer. "It was only a little gun," Anna says when she tells about it, "but I always thought it was a swell thing for Bill to do."

Bill promised to give up homicide as soon as he and Anna were married. They moved out to Ridgefield Park, New Jersey, to a little house with a garden around it, and Anna buckled down to the mean job of reforming Bill completely. It was even harder than she thought it would be. He was to have gone to work in a Paterson silk mill, but never quite got around to it. He had a few hundred dollars left after the house was furnished, and coasted along on that. They had been married about a month when Bill came home late one night, sat down in a parlor chair, and yanked out his automatic. (Anna had let him keep that one, out of his collection, for self-protection.) He told Anna to get into the far corner of the room. "I want to see if you can take it," he said. She had an idea what was coming, but she started for the corner, hoping he'd change his mind before she got there. He didn't, though. If Anna knows you well enough, she'll take the shoe off her left foot and show you where Bill shot away part of her big toe.

Anna was proud of Bill's marksmanship, of which the toe shooting is an example, but he did embarrass her sometimes by showing off with his automatic. He never did any shooting unless he was very drunk. Once, before they moved to New Jersey, he shot out all the lights in a Smith Street trolley car. Anna was humiliated, to hear her tell it, but she got a laugh out of the passengers. They all looked so scared. Another time, when Anna and Bill were visiting friends in Irishtown, Bill shot two pork chops out of the friend's frying pan. It was good shooting, but it was a social error. They were never invited to that house again. On another occasion, at an Easter Sunday party in Bridge Street, before they were married, their host put on a derby hat and gave an imitation of Charlie Chaplin. It wasn't a good imitation, and Bill fired a shot at the hat. Someone jiggled his arm and the slug caught the host in the shoulder. Bill was all for a second try, but he was talked out of it.

Bill was very proud of Anna and bought her the best clothes he could find. He liked to be seen with her, and was pleased when other men eyed her, but was apt to get nasty if they looked at her too long. He shot one man just for that. It was over on the Chelsea docks, in Manhattan, where he'd gone to visit his father, who was a stevedore there. An inoffensive French chef on a liner stuck his head out of a porthole for a breath of air. Anna came into his line of vision and he let his eyes rest on her for a few seconds. This annoyed Bill. "He thought this Frenchman was trying to make me," Anna explains, "so he gets his gun out and shoots the poor feller's right ear off."

During the courtship period in Brooklyn, Anna could always tell when Bill was primed for a killing. A spot in the center of his pale forehead would grow dark when the urge came on. His stevedore pals knew that spot, too, and would excuse themselves from Bill's presence when they saw it blooming. Still, to hear Anna tell it, Bill wasn't really vicious, because the fiercest dogs would make up to him, and in her opinion that is an infallible sign of something basically gentle in a man's nature. Bill liked babies, too. He proved that the night of March 31, 1920, when he killed Dinny Meehan, who was Irishtown dock leader at the time. As he walked through the Meehan flat on Warren Street, Brooklyn, he stopped in the parlor to pat little Dinny, Jr., on the head before he went into the bedroom and put two slugs into big Dinny. One of the shots ricocheted and wounded Mrs. Meehan, who was sleeping with her husband, but she recovered. Three years later Mrs. Meehan showed Anna the scar as an argument against her marrying Bill, but it didn't change Anna's mind.

Outside of shooting off Anna's big toe to see whether she could take it, Bill made an ideal husband, for a while. He stayed in the Jersey cottage at night and read a lot. Anna says he was a sucker for anything penned by Arthur Brisbane, and for all kinds of history. He was a great Bible reader, too, and could quote long passages from the Scriptures. He didn't care much for the movies, but he knew they were Anna's favorite form of entertainment and he'd take her whenever she asked. Today Anna prefers Wallace Beery and John Barrymore films. She likes Broadway shows, too, but not as much. She seldom comes to Broadway now at all. Stage pathos leaves her cold unless a child is involved; the spectacle of kids getting a dirty deal, on the stage or off, always makes her cry.

Three months after she started to reform Bill, Anna noticed that he wasn't paying much attention to his history books, his solitaire, and two-handed pinochle. He was off form in his checker game, too, and seemed tired of Paterson. He sometimes spoke wistfully of Irishtown. One night, when he couldn't bear the nostalgia, he blurted that he was going to Brooklyn. "Just for a little visit, Doll," he told Anna. She decided to go over, too, and he arranged to meet her later that night near her favorite Irishtown beauty parlor, at Jay and Fulton Streets. When he didn't come, Anna went to his mother's house on Bath Beach and asked Bill's brother George, who was studying for the priesthood, to help her search for Bill. George didn't like the idea, but he agreed to go along. When they had made the rounds of all the waterfront speak-easies and home-brew joints, George suggested they try the Dock-loaders' Club at 25 Bridge Street, but Anna vetoed that. She said Bill had been shot once at that address, and was superstitious about returning to any place where he'd once been hurt. They gave up the search then, but it was at the Dockloaders' Club that Bill was found by the police some hours later, filled with bullets, his head bashed in with a stevedore's bale hook.

Bill was buried in the National Cemetery in Cypress Hills with full military honors. He had served with the Seventy-seventh Division in France and had won the D. S. C. After he got back from the other side, he had been shot on five separate occasions and had been formally arrested seven times (but never tried) for killing people. His death left Anna penniless. The insurance companies had considered him a poor risk. Anna closed the house in New Jersey and moved back to her mother's.

She was rather proud of the long homicidal record of her first husband. A newspaper reporter once asked her how she ever came to marry a man who, during his career, had been officially accused of seven murders. Anna bristled so fiercely that the journalist shrank. "The papers only gave Bill credit for seven," Anna said bitterly. "He killed nearer twenty-seven in Brooklyn." In her indignation, Anna went on to say that Bill never got credit, either, for the half-dozen murders he added to his list during the two years that he was hiding out in Chicago after he had killed Dinny Meehan, the dock leader. The Chicago murders were strictly amateur, though, she says now, and perhaps deserve only a footnote in his record. He did the Chicago jobs as a favor to friends who gave him shelter.

Another thing that stirred Anna to anger was any newspaper reference to her as "gun moll." She has never fired a revolver or automatic, and is a little afraid of them. It isn't that she's a softy. She has taken loaded weapons from many a truculent drunk, and she often had to pick guns up during house cleanings at home. But she has never really used one in her life.

Anna doesn't consider herself tough. As a young girl, she shied away from the more raucous neighborhood elements because the he-men of the Irishtown section along the Brooklyn waterfront didn't conform to her ideals of what true gentlemen should be. She has been arrested only once. When she was fourteen years old, she was shopping one night with some older Irishtown girls when an Italian storekeeper, as she puts it, "made passes at us with his eyes." All Italians—called "ginzoes" by the 'Towners—were poison to an Irish girl like Anna. She fished a slab of liver off the street counter of a butcher shop next door and smacked the shopkeeper's face with it. It splashed his shirt with red stains and he thought he had been stabbed. His screams brought the police, and Anna and her friends were taken to the Poplar Street police station. She might have gone free because she was a minor, but a sort of grim loyalty is one of her virtues, and she gave her age as eighteen. She and her friends were released next day after a night in jail.

After that the only fighting Anna did was in behalf of Peg-Leg, her brother, who was red-haired and pugnacious like her father. Anna loves to recall how Peg-Leg held on to the groceries and change the night he lost his left leg under a Smith Street trolley car. The accident happened when he was stealing a ride on the way back from the store, she remembers, and he was carried into Conley's saloon. He wouldn't get into the ambulance until he had handed the package over to his mother. Anna likes to tell the story because it illustrates what stuff the Lonergans were made of. Papa Lonergan gave the boys free rein as they grew up, but was strict with the girls. Until she was eighteen, Anna had to be in bed every night before the Navy Yard bells bonged at nine o'clock, or feel her father's horny hand. Later, when she was in show business, the curfew didn't apply. The family needed the money. Even Mrs. Lonergan worked, scrubbing offices in the Borough Hall district, to keep the family going.

While Anna was light-footing it on Broadway, Peg-Leg was helping his father run his bicycle shop. They had the Telephone Company trade. In those days, the repair men rode bicycles instead of Fords. Peg-Leg had a lot of interests outside of the shop, too. Despite his wooden leg he managed to get around, and became pretty handy with an automatic. He was a good man in a speak-easy brawl, and got an early start on his long string of homicides. He never went to prison for any of them, but neither did Anna's husband, Bill Lovett, or any other Irishtown trigger men. That seems to puzzle most people when they hear about it, but it's quite simple, as Anna explains it. Most of the killings were done when there were no witnesses around. Even when there were witnesses the cops couldn't get anything out of them. The neighborhood code forbade squealing, and in Irishtown an informer was rated twenty degrees lower than an Italian policeman.

By the time he was twenty, Peg-Leg was a holy terror along the docks and in the Irishtown speak-easies, but Anna will not admit it. She will concede that he killed a lot of men, but will insist that he was good at heart. He took up homicide, she contends, not from choice but by accident. It seems that when Peg-Leg was seventeen, Giuseppe Bonanzio, a Navy Street drug peddler, tried to get him to handle narcotics in the bicycle shop as a sort of sideline. Peg-Leg refused and

Bonanzio pulled a gun. Peg-Leg grabbed the weapon, according to Anna, and it went off. Bonanzio dropped with a bullet in the heart. The killing made Peg-Leg a neighborhood big shot, and pretty soon he was taking on killing jobs for his friends on the docks. "He wasn't a professional killer," Anna says. "He'd just do these jobs to help his friends out."

Peg-Leg figured in so many shootings that the magistrates got sick of seeing his face in court. His official record shows three arrests for assault and three for homicide, but Anna says the records don't begin to reflect his activities. "You can't go by the police records," Anna says.

After Bill died, Peg-Leg teamed up with Matty Martin, who was to be Anna's second husband. Matty was what might be called the coleader of the Irishtown stevedores. With his partner, Charlie ("Cute Charlie") Donnelly, and a gang of supporters, he dominated the docks and exacted tribute from all the dockworkers. Peg-Leg would meet Matty on the docks every day and help him with his work. Then the two of them would go to Anna's house for dinner and relaxation.

It wasn't long before these evenings took on a romantic tinge. Like Bill, Matty went in for mute courtship. Anna has found that rather a common trait among men who do a lot of shooting. They're hard-boiled and fearless among men, but practically tongue-tied around women. "It used to be real pitiful to watch Matty trying to get out a word, every now and then," she remembers. It took every bit of courage he had. Matty was taller than Bill, but, like Bill, he was a heavy drinker. He could hold even more than Bill could, though, and no one could ever tell when he was drunk. Bill had liked publicity, but Matty hated it. When Matty finally proposed to Anna, he persuaded her to get married at Saugerties, New York, so the newspapers wouldn't make a fuss about it. They were married in February, 1924, three months after Bill had been killed and buried. Right after the wedding they returned to Brooklyn to live with Anna's mother in the Bushwick district, which is a long way from the waterfront.

It was Anna's idea the family should move out of Irishtown. She thought people were getting to know too much of the family affairs, what with the publicity that came with every fresh shooting. Besides, she hoped Bushwick would be a safer place for Matty. They moved, but it didn't turn out that way. Two weeks after the wedding, when she was walking down the street with Matty, not far from the house, one of the aspirants for the stevedore crown on the Irishtown docks stepped out of a doorway with a revolver and aimed at Matty. Anna jumped for him, caught his shooting hand, and tried to pull the weapon away from him. One shot went off, and the powder burned Anna's right temple. It left no scar, for which she is grateful. She thinks that if the burn had left a mark people *would* think she was a gunwoman. She never tells the name of the man who tried to shoot Matty, which may be taken as indication that he is still alive.

Anna found that Matty didn't care much for food. He lived on booze most of the time. The only thing he really cared for in the way of solids was home-baked bread. His poor appetite didn't bother her, however. Bill hadn't been much of an eater, either. Matty was more easily domesticated, on the whole, than Bill had been. He preferred tinkering with radios to going out and he bought every new gadget for eliminating static or getting more distance. At one time, he owned and tinkered with five radio sets. None of them worked very well.

The chief reason for Matty's radio tinkering late at night was insomnia. Sometimes, when he did get to sleep, he would wake up screaming. It wasn't conscience, Anna says; Matty's mother said he used to do it even when he was a baby. Besides being an insomniac, Matty was a somnambulist. One hot night, when the Lonergans were asleep on mattresses on the parlor floor, he got up and walked to the rear window. Anna, who happened to be awake, was amazed at the ease with which he stepped between the sleepers in the dark. On another of his walks in his sleep Matty went downstairs, ate everything in the ice-box, and took up the *Brooklyn Daily Eagle* that lay on the table. An hour later Anna went down with her mother to look for him. When Mrs. Lonergan became convinced that Matty wasn't shamming, that he was actually reading in his sleep, she told Anna to get him out of the house. "Take him away," she ordered, terrified. "He gives me the horrors."

Anna and Matty then took up housekeeping in a one-family frame house in the Bushwick district. Anna never liked apartment houses, because she has found apartment-house dwellers nosy. Another advantage of the one-family house was the flower garden. Anna had always been fond of flowers, and she found Matty was, too. He had a "green thumb"—a way with plants—as well as a supple trigger finger. He was tender with guppys, too, and in sentimental moods played the zither well.

Peg-Leg, while Anna and Matty were living in the quiet life in Bushwick, didn't find enough activity or competition on the docks to satisfy his craving for target practice, so he ventured into the Gowanus area for frequent ginzo-baiting expeditions. He focused his attention on the Adonis Social Club, an Italian cabaret in Twentieth Street where Al Capone, as an unknown dance-hall bouncer, had perfected his marksmanship by shooting necks off beer bottles when there was nothing else to do. Peg-Leg and two of his stooges, Needless Ferry and Aaron Harms, swilled and guzzled liberally in the cabaret the night before Christmas, 1925, sneered at Jack ("Stickem") Stabile, the bartender, and insulted Italian patrons individually and in groups. They chased all the Irish girls out, just as they used to do in Fort Greene Park, and told them to "come back with white men." Then Peg-Leg and his friends went on drinking.

On Christmas morning, Anna made another excursion to Kings County Morgue and identified Peg-Leg, Ferry, and Harms. All three had been shot through the back of the head as they stood at the Adonis bar. Detectives made twenty arrests in the case, but ran into the customary thing—none of the men or women who were in the club when the shooting started knew who had fired the shots, and no amount of persuasion by the police, physical or oral, could convince them that they did. Among the twenty prisoners was Capone, and he was turned loose along with the others. Anna says she knows who did the job in the Adonis Club and that she knows who killed Matty and who killed Bill, but she says she won't tell.

Anna arranged Peg-Leg's burial. She was in the habit of taking charge of all family burials. She has always been the family spokesman, too, whenever any member of her family figured in a shooting. She never tells the police much. "The way I look at it," she says, "is this: those who live by the gun, they die by the gun. It's in the hands of God." Anna is extremely religious, and always has been. Through all the shooting and the frequent murders in which her husbands and brother figured, she never missed a Mass. Her mother, who is still living, is just as steady in church attendance. Anna makes special novenas to pray for her mother's health. Her favorite saint is Saint Teresa, the Little Flower, to whom she pleads for safe guidance for her brothers and sisters. "I always pray they'll have good company and not go bad," she says.

Things stayed quiet for Anna a long time after her brother Peg-Leg was buried. Matty was arrested at Peg-Leg's wake for carrying a loaded revolver and did six months on the charge. After he finished his prison term, he went back to the docks, and resumed his coleadership. He would come home from the docks every night around six o'clock and fiddle with his rheostats and verniers, and his life seemed secure and relatively peaceful. He gave Anna all she needed to run the house and a liberal clothing allowance besides. He even took her to the movies once a month, much as he disliked the cinema. But by the end of 1929 Matty's share of the money extorted from the stevedores and truckmen on the waterfront had dropped from an average of two hundred dollars a week to around fifty. The depression had hit shipping hard. Anna noticed, however, that "Cute Charlie" Donnelly, who shared the leadership of the stevedores with Matty, was still able to keep his wife in good clothes and seemed to have as much money as ever. She must have mentioned it to Matty. On the morning of January 29, 1930, Matty had a business conference in the loaders' shack on Dock Street and flatly accused Donnelly of double-crossing him. After the conference, Donnelly was found dead on the floor of the shack. No witnesses. Anna felt sorry for Mrs. Donnelly. She identified the body at the morgue and helped with the funeral plans.

After the Donnelly killing, for which Matty had to make the customary trip before the magistrate to get his usual dismissal, Anna kept hearing rumors that Matty was marked for the next "out." The night of December 13 she had a bad dream, and with it her first and only premonition that death was in the offing. She explains it now as "a funny kind of feeling" and clutches in the general vicinity of her heart when she tells about it. She awakened Matty and told him about the dream, but he wasn't impressed. He didn't come home to dinner the next night, though. A police car called instead, and took Anna to Cumberland Hospital. Matty had been wounded in a De Kalb Avenue speak-easy. He lived two days. When the cops asked him who had shot him, he wouldn't discuss it. They had three men in custody, they told him—were they the ones? "Turn them guys loose," said Matty, and died.

There is every reason to believe that Matty told Anna who had shot him before he died.

Anna is especially proud of the confidence reposed in her by her husbands and their friends in all matters pertaining to homicide. Whenever there was a fresh killing, the men would tell her about it immediately. That wasn't true in the homes of other warring dock loaders. Few women could be trusted as Anna was. She did not, however, get all her information about the murders from her immediate family. The underworld has a system all its own, called "the kite," which brings murder bulletins to those who can be trusted with them. Anna used to get them long before the police or newspapers did. Sometimes they would come by telephone, sometimes by messenger. "It's like a magazine subscription," she says. "You don't ask for it, but it keeps right on coming." Anna has an idea that she is cut in on the kite line because occasional newspaper articles and a mention, now and then, in some book (there's a whole chapter about her, for instance, in *Not Guilty*, the book about Sam Leibowitz) keep her name fresh in the minds of people along the waterfront who are close to the warring stevedore gangs and who get murder news while it's hot.

Anna is quite proud, too, of her popularity at Sing Sing. She has made several trips to the death house to console friends, and all the boys up there seem to like her. The late Leonard Scarnici, bank robber and murderer, was, in spite of being an Italian, one of her friends. After he was put to death in the electric chair, she felt pretty bad about it. "Maybe he buried a man alive up in Connecticut, like they say he did," she said recently, "and maybe he did all the killings they gave him credit for, but I knew him and I still think he had a heart of gold."

Anna lives alone, now, in a little one-family house in the Bushwick section. She devotes a lot of time to keeping the place neat. She is fussy about little details; it makes her uncomfortable if a guest so much as nudges an antimacassar out of place. She keeps about two hundred books in the house, most of them slightly out of date. She has read all of Victoria Cross, and her favorite novel is *One Night of Temptation*, by that author. There is a copy of Herbert Asbury's *Gangs of New York* in her collection, but she keeps it only out of sentiment for Matty, who liked it. Anna never cared for it very much, because it's about tough people. At least that's what she says. In the next breath, though, she's apt to point out that both Bill and Peg-Leg are mentioned in it, as well as her Uncle Yake Brady, who was a noted brawler on Cherry Hill.

Anna doesn't think she will ever marry again, although she has had some attractive offers. She says she may, of course, change her mind any day. There was a report, after Matty died, that she intended to marry Edward (Red) Patterson, a South Brooklyn holdup man who had done time in Sing Sing Prison, but that was not true. Anyway, Patterson is dead now. He was killed in a brawl by Jim Cahill, an ex-cop.

Anna keeps hoping for better times. She has an idea she may find a future in politics, and to get started in the right direction has joined a Democratic club in her neighborhood. She thinks she might be coleader someday. She learned how to smoke at the club, and picked up a passing knowledge of bridge there. She hasn't been near the docks for a long time. She cut down her waterfront visits after one of the lads stabbed her in the left arm because she demanded a cut on the meager, present-day graft. For a time after Matty's death the boys who inherited the water-front leadership saw to it that she got thirty dollars a week, but later they cut that off. "There's only a few of the old crowd left down there, anyways," she says, "and they're a bunch of heels."

The Wily Wilby

by St. Clair McKelway

P.G. Wodehouse once said of St. Clair McKelway (1905–1980) that "nobody tells a story better than he does." McKelway often wrote about imposters. This story about a certain Mr. Wilby was included in McKelway's 1951 book True Tales from the Annals of Crime and Rascality.

One sunny afternoon in the autumn of 1939, the proprietors of a Chevrolet agency in San Francisco were given a disheartening shock by an auditor from General Motors who was making a routine examination of the agency's books. The auditor came out of the accounting department and informed them that ten thousand of the dollars the proprietors thought they had were, as a matter of fact, missing. Leaving the proprietors with their thoughts, the auditor went back into the accounting department and continued his studies. After several days, in the course of which he kept uttering sharp cries of amazement and awe, he came to the proprietors again, with his hands full of bank statements and canceled checks, and with garlands of adding-machine tape around his neck, and told them that their former secretary and treasurer, a man known to them as James W. Ralston, had diverted the ten thousand dollars to his personal bank account and had hidden his defalcations so adroitly and with such originality that it had been a real pleasure to uncover them. The man known as Ralston had resigned several months before and had left the agency after shaking hands all around. He had made no secret of the fact that he was investing his savings in an automobile agency of his own, in the town of Colton, some five hundred miles south of San Francisco and not far from San Diego. He had said that he and his wife were going to settle down there in a little house he had bought. After their conversation with the auditor, the proprietors told an assistant district attorney that Ralston had seemed to them to be a very nice fellow—thirty-five years old, five and a half feet tall, a natty dresser with a gay manner and a sincere way of talking, wavy brown hair graying at the temples, blue eyes, fair complexion. He was picked up the next day in Colton, where he had already come to be regarded as a hard-working, respectable, up-and-coming automobile man. To the officers who took him back to San Francisco, he seemed in no way contrite, and, on the whole, cheerful. Sitting with them on the train, he kept slapping his knee and saying that he'd be damned if he could understand how the General Motors auditor had ever discovered his embezzlement. In jail, he talked shop with the auditor and questioned him closely about that. He paid a lawyer a thousand dollars to handle his case, gave back to his former employers fifteen hundred of the ten thousand dollars he had taken from them, and entered a plea of guilty.

As is customary in such cases, the probation officers tried to find out as much about the prisoner as they could, in order to give the court a report on him before he was sentenced. It turned out that his real name was Ralph Marshall Wilby, that he was a Canadian citizen, and that he had done some embezzling before, both in Canada and in the United States. In his early twenties he had humbugged a Toronto corporation in an unusual fashion while working for it as a bookkeeper. He was employed there under his real name and, using an alias, ingeniously put his other self down on the corporation's books as one of its stockholders. For two years, the corporation faithfully paid him dividends that amounted to several thousand dollars in all. He was cagy enough not to attend stockholders' meetings but, signing his other name, mailed his stock proxies to bona-fide stockholders who he knew belonged to a faction that was in favor of high dividends. After two years of this, Wilby resigned as bookkeeper. As stockholder, however, he continued to receive dividend checks for two more years. Then the corporation discovered what Wilby had been doing to it, and he was arrested, convicted of grand larceny, and sent to a reformatory for a short term. He gave back to the corporation a few hundred of the thousands he had taken from it, but he didn't say he was sorry. He asked many questions about how the corporation had at last come across his defalcations. His behavior at the reformatory was excellent and he was out of it in a year. He then came to this country. Using his real name, he married an American girl, and she lived happily with him until, in 1935, he was caught in the middle of a rather picayune embezzlement in Norfolk, Virginia. The complaint against him there was dropped when the Virginia authorities were assured by the immigration officials that he would be deported to Canada at once. His wife lauded him publicly at the time for his fidelity, generosity, good habits, and sunny disposition. She regretfully obtained an annulment only after he had been sent back to Canada. Wilby then adopted the name Ralston and quickly slipped back over the border, finding a job almost immediately as a bookkeeper at the Chevrolet agency in San Francisco. He was soon made secretary and treasurer, and he then married another American girl. This wife was living happily with him when he was arrested in Colton in 1939. She followed him to San Francisco and, like the first wife, went out of her way to speak highly of him. She had not known he was an embezzler, and when the facts were explained to her, she said, "Well, he's a very fine man except for that one quirk, or whatever it is."

It was discovered while Wilby was awaiting trial in San Francisco that he had played fast and loose with a Buick agency in San Diego a week before his arrest in Colton. The General Motors auditor, who had been impressed by the delicacy of Wilby's methods in San Francisco, was shocked when he found out about Wilby's conduct in San Diego.

Wilby had been crude down there. Under the influence of what he later described as a whim, rather than a quirk, Wilby had driven from Colton to San Diego one day and had there dropped into a Buick agency that he knew was occasionally visited by auditors from General Motors. He had introduced himself as Ralston, said he was an auditor from G.M., checked the books and the cash on hand, and simply stuffed eight hundred dollars of the cash on hand into his hip pocket. He had then driven back to his humdrum life in Colton. The two proprietors of the San Diego agency were looking at each other suspiciously when stories and photographs of the San Francisco embezzler came out in the newspapers. They then went arm in arm to the San Diego prosecutor's office. Wilby was taken from San Francisco to San Diego, where he pleaded guilty without bothering to hire a lawyer. The fact that he hadn't yet been sentenced for the more impressive embezzlement in San Francisco seems to have rattled the Southern California judiciary. The San Francisco case was merged with the one in San Diego, and when the case finally came up, early in 1940, the judge was lenient and perhaps naïve. On Wilby's solemn promise never to return to the United States, the judge, instead of giving him a suspended sentence, put him on probation for ten years and turned him over to the immigration officers. He was shipped off to Canada, and his second wife regretfully applied for an annulment. Three months later, he was asking for a job as an accountant in the offices of a New York corporation that had an extraordinarily complex bookkeeping system and had frequently boasted in its brochures that its disbursements amounted to nearly forty million dollars a year. He got the job, and within a few weeks he had married still another American girl and she was living happily with him in Jackson Heights.

Wilby's preparations for his invasion of the New York commercial field were characteristically bold and imaginative. As soon as the immigration officers set him down in Canada, he began to look around for a new name. What he lived on during this period is not known, but it is assumed by students of his career that he had providently deposited some capital in Canadian banks while he was working and embezzling in California. In any case, he was able to invest some cash in his search for a new name. This time he didn't just want to make one up, as he had done when he chose "Ralston"; he wanted a name that meant something. He therefore placed an advertisement in a number of Canadian and American trade journals. It declared that there was a wonderful opportunity for a good certified public accountant in a big firm, not named, with international connections. Applicants were invited to write, stating qualifications, etc., to Box No. So-and-So. Wilby received many applications. The one he liked best was from a C.P.A. named Alexander Douglas Hume. This Mr. Hume furnished impeccable references; he had worked for a number of New York corporations and he listed them all, giving in each instance the name of at least one executive whom he knew personally and who he was sure would be glad to give him a leg up. Hume was a Canadian citizen and was at that time working as a chartered accountant in Toronto. Wilby wrote to him and asked for more details. Hume supplied them. The two men corresponded for some weeks. Then it began to look as though there was an obstacle in the way of Hume's taking the job that Wilby seemed to be dangling in front of him. Hume confessed to Wilby that he had begun to think seriously of offering his services to the Empire. After all, he said, there was a war on and he was young and able-bodied. In their correspondence, which continued for a month after this letter, they discussed the progress of the war. Wilby said he certainly admired Hume's patriotism, said he wished he were young and fit himself, and so on. Finally, Wilby received a hurried and somewhat emotional letter from Hume, in which he said he had just accepted a lieutenant's commission in the Canadian Army and that he guessed Wilby would not be hearing from him again until the Axis powers had been put in their place. Wilby wrote back offering his congratulations and wishing Hume the best of luck.

It was then that Wilby came to New York. He went to an employment agency in downtown Manhattan that specializes in finding jobs for accountants. He filled out a form, giving his name as Alexander Douglas Hume and listing Hume's New York references. When the head of the employment agency saw the form, he sent for him, because he had known Hume slightly when the latter had worked in New York five years earlier. "Glad to see you after all these years, Hume," the agency man said when Wilby walked into his office. The agency man has recalled over and over since then that the man looked at him, grinned, cried, "Why, of course!" and shook hands cordially. "You've lost weight," the agency man remarked, and Wilby explained that he had been on a diet and was in better shape than he had been in for years. Actually, there was no resemblance whatever between Wilby and Hume, but Wilby rose above that. Using his sincere way of talking, he went on to give the agency man some tips on how to avoid the temptation of potatoes and other starches. Then they settled down to the business on hand. The agency man got out a list of corporations that were looking for first-class accountants, and Wilby mulled it over, asking intelligent questions about the volume of business and the accounting methods of the different firms. He finally chose the William T. Knott Company, and the agency man telephoned that corporation. Wilby went to the Knott offices, on West Thirty-first Street, and was shown right in to the private office of the treasurer, a Mr. Casey. The two men talked for quite a while. Casey was impressed by the applicant's knowledge of bookkeeping and also, as he has remembered again and again, by the man's cheerful, modest, and businesslike manner. Casey picked up a telephone, muttering "Just routine, you know," and called one of the corporations Hume had worked for. He spoke to the officer mentioned in Hume's references and, sure enough, the officer said he remembered Hume well, that he was an excellent accountant and a first-class man all around. "Give him my regards," the officer said, and Casey did. As Hume, Wilby was put to work the next day.

The William T. Knott Company is what is known as a management corporation, and is very busy. It manages sixteen department stores in this country and one in Canada for a parent corporation called Mercantile Stores. Among the many things it has to do is pay for the merchandise these stores buy from manufacturers and jobbers. The department stores check the invoices when the goods are delivered and then send the invoices along to the Knott Company, which pays the manufacturers and jobbers by check. Being a trustworthy and successful management corporation, it is careful about the way it disburses this money. It keeps a list of purchase orders, and these are checked against the invoices. A force of accountants, clerks, typists, and business machines then takes the approved invoices and runs them through a labyrinthine bookkeeping system. At the far end of the labyrinth, there emerge in due time a corresponding number of tastefully embossed bank checks, each one made out, in austere black and white, to such-and-such a manufacturer or jobber for a certain number of dollars and one-hundredths thereof. Once the checks have been signed they are clapped into window envelopes and whisked off to the waiting manufacturers and jobbers by United States mail. The human workers and the business machines all get along fine together in the accounting department of the Knott Company. The human workers are male and female, and the business machines are standard. The machines do many of the more tiresome chores. One machine even goes to the bother of signing the checks. This check-signing machine is exceedingly complicated and mechanically above reproach. Only a privileged few of the human workers are allowed to get anywhere near it, and even for them it won't sign so much as small-fry jobbers' checks unless certain secret perforations and hush-hush notches have been made by various other knowledgeable business machines around the office on certain unmentionable pieces of cardboard, one for each invoice that has been approved for payment. The check-signing machine takes these pieces of cardboard and, if the perforations and notches feel all right to it, signs the checks. When the machine isn't working, some of its most important elements, such as one bearing an engraving of the signature of the treasurer of the corporation, are removed. These are locked up in one corner of the office, and the machine itself is locked up in another corner. The system is just about foolproof.

During 1940, Wilby, under his new name, worked for the Knott

Company as a traveling auditor, going from one department store to another and checking up on their cashiers and bookkeepers. During 1941, he was an accountant in the New York office. All that time, the male and female workers and the standard business machines clicked and snuffled along with hardly a mistake and never a defalcation, and the corporation continued happily to disburse nearly forty million dollars a year by means of its complicated system. In 1942, Wilby was made chief accountant and put in charge of that system. His salary, though it had been increased several times, was only six thousand dollars a year. He nevertheless thought he was in a position to make a fortune, and he was right. During 1942, he took $110,936.81. The corporation didn't miss the money, and the auditors found nothing wrong with the books. Wilby's work seemed more than satisfactory to his employers. They not only thought a lot of his efficiency but were delighted at the way he got along with the people who worked under him. He was always cheerful and relaxed, even when working at top speed and under pressure. He was considerate of the human office force and, even in his high executive position, was not above taking a personal interest in the business machines. He always had time to listen to the probems of the accountants, clerks, and typists, and more than once dazzled a business-machine operator by stepping up to a recalcitrant machine and diagnosing its inner difficulties after a shrewd glance and some sympathetic fingering. The general feeling at the Knott Company was that the new chief accountant had a truly rare and wonderful personality. At the end of his first year in the job, the corporation gave him the title of assistant treasurer, to add to the title of chief accountant, and also gave him a bonus of five hundred dollars, over and above the six thousand dollars he had earned and the $110,936.81 he had stolen.

Wilby thought he was in a position to do even better in 1943 than he had done in 1942, and he was right again. In 1943, he took $275,984.48. At the end of that year, the Knott Company still was feeling no pain, and it showered another five-hundred-dollar bonus on Wilby. Thus, in the two years, Wilby had got twelve thousand dollars in salary, a thousand dollars in bonuses, and $386,921.29 in stolen funds. He saved some of what he earned and all of what he stole, and he had the money where he could get at it any time he wanted it. He had invested some of it in bonds that were readily negotiable, but most of it was in accounts in New York banks.

While he was accumulating this fortune, Wilby and his third wife lived in an apartment in Jackson Heights, for which he paid sixty-five dollars a month, unfurnished. It was fitted out with maple living-room, dining-room, and bedroom sets from Bloomingdale's. Wilby's wife, named Hazel, had been a salesgirl in the women's-wear department at the Knott department store in Cincinnati. He met her and married her in 1940, while he was a traveling auditor for the Knott Company. A cashier in the Cincinnati store had been suspected of dipping into the till to the extent of several hundred dollars, and the management hadn't been able to prove it. Wilby was sent out there to check up on the fellow. It was a whirlwind trip for Wilby. He trapped the cashier, turned him over to the management, met Hazel, and took her to a justice of the peace. She was just twenty-one, good-natured, extremely good-looking, and a few inches taller than the five-and-a-half-foot Wilby.

While Wilby and Hazel were living in Jackson Heights, she did not know that her husband had at his disposal any funds in addition to his salary and bonuses, and she thought his name was Alexander Douglas Hume. She called him Doug. She was his trusting partner in what their neighbors looked upon as a rather dull existence. For a few months after they were married, they went out fairly regularly to a movie, or to dinner in Manhattan, but after Wilby became chief accountant he seemed to be more closely tied to his work than most of the other husbands in Jackson Heights. He brought home a briefcase stuffed with office records and pored over them until late at night. He went on what he said was a business trip almost every week-end, sometimes rushing all the way to the Middle West and back between Friday night and Monday morning. Hazel never accompanied him. She whiled away the lonely weekends in a housewifely manner. She had gone to

Cincinnati from a small town in Oklahoma, was impressed by New York and thoroughly pleased with her husband, and soberly co-operated with him in his determination to live well within his salary and bonuses. They had a joint checking account in a Jackson Heights bank, and Wilby showed her how to keep it straight and how to detect the trouble if the bank ever made a mistake of a dollar or two in its monthly statement. She read *Vogue* and *Harper's Bazaar* and, on the weekends he was away, made clothes for herself, keeping track of the fashions of the day and cutting out and sewing up striking ensembles, for which she is still remembered by her former neighbors. Wilby was proud of her good looks and bragged to his friends at the office about how little money she spent on her clothes. On the rare evenings when the husband had no homework, the Humes would go out for a conservative fling at a neighborhood bar and grill, sometimes in the company of a couple who lived nearby and were their particular friends. These friends noted, to their subsequent amusement, how careful Wilby was with his money. He drank moderately, and when the four of them were together he would pay only for himself and Hazel, saying "Dutch, you know," and leaving a dime for the bartender at the end of the evening. "He wasn't stingy in a mean or unpleasant way, but he never threw any of that money around," these neighbors frequently told other neighbors later on. They found Wilby always sociable and agreeable, and usually jolly and lighthearted. A photograph taken at the time shows him holding the neighbors' baby and grinning, his hair slightly tousled and hanging over his forehead. From her greater height, the beautiful Hazel is looking down at him with an affectionate smile.

One Friday morning, toward the middle of January, 1944, when, in addition to whatever Wilby had saved out of his earnings, he had $386,921.29 at his finger-tips, he stepped out of his private office at the Knott Company and dropped into the private office of Mr. Casey, the treasurer. He told Casey that he was all tired out. The accounts for 1943 were balanced, everything was under control, and he wanted to know if he could have a short vacation. "Just a long week-end," Wilby said. "I thought I'd run up to Canada for the skiing. Take Mrs. Hume along. I could get away tonight and be back by Tuesday." Casey said, "By all means, Doug," and wished him happy landings. Both men chuckled over the joke, and Wilby thanked Casey warmly. They shook hands. That night, Wilby left for Canada, taking along not only Hazel but also a briefcase, which, as she noted, and joshed him about, he kept under his arm or under his pillow the whole time. Hazel thought they really were going to go skiing in Canada.

On the Tuesday Hume was due back, Casey's secretary brought him a telegram that caused a good deal of concern around the office. The telegram had been sent from a small town near Toronto, and it said, "Douglas has suffered broken leg skiing. Will be confined here several weeks. Letter will follow. Hazel Hume." Casey was distressed. Hazel had not said exactly where her husband was confined, but Casey took steps to find out. He wired the manager of the Knott store in Hamilton, a town near Toronto, to check all hospitals, hotels, and nearby resorts to see if he could locate the company's chief accountant and assistant treasurer, and then find out if poor Hume needed anything. The store manager wrote back in a day or two and said he hadn't been able to find Hume, but that he would keep trying. A week went by and there was no further word either on or from the Humes. Then, one day, Casey began to experience a clutching sensation in the pit of his stomach. He sent somebody out to Jackson Heights to see if the Humes had returned. At the same time, he called in the auditors, told them about the skiing trip, and suggested that they get started right away on the annual audit for the year just ended. The man who went out to Jackson Heights found nobody at home in the Hume apartment. The auditors took the bales of Knott Company canceled checks for 1943, unfastened them, and added up the amounts of the checks on a squadron of adding machines. They compared this total with the total withdrawals from the Knott account, at the Fifth Avenue Branch of the National City Bank. The totals were nowhere near the same; the withdrawals were much higher. This could mean only one thing. Somebody had destroyed some canceled checks, and must have had a shady reason for doing so. The auditors rushed into Casey's office with the bad news. After a little while, Casey telephoned the office of District Attorney Frank S. Hogan. Assistant District Attorney George G. Hunter, Jr., of the Frauds Bureau, was assigned to the case, and Hunter called in Joseph M. Gasarch, a lawyer and a C.P.A. who was then a member of the Bureau of Accounting—he is now its head—of the District Attorney's Office. Hunter and Gasarch went over to the Knott Company and talked to the auditors. The facts the auditors had were very meager. There seemed to be a shortage of $275,984.48 in the 1943 accounts, and some canceled checks were missing. There was no legal evidence that the chief accountant and assistant treasurer had taken the money, but it looked as if he probably had. Gasarch, who is a chubby, bald, middle-aged man with a plodding manner and a great enthusiasm for his work, nestled down into what he recognized as a delightful situation and did not entirely emerge from it for over a year.

While the Knott Company's auditors devoted themselves to a study of the accounts for 1943, and began to wonder whether the 1942 accounts were as nearly perfect as they had thought they were when they approved them the winter before, Gasarch noted the amounts of some of the missing canceled checks and went to the files of the Fifth Avenue Branch of the National City Bank. This is a careful branch of a cautious institution, and it makes a point of taking a photograph of the face of every check it pays before it cancels it and sends it back to the depositor. Gasarch got hold of the microfilm photograph of one of the missing canceled checks and found that it had been made out— and duly signed by the Knott check-signing machine—to a firm called Avon Mills, presumably a manufacturer whom the Knott Company had paid for goods purchased by one of its department stores. As the bank hadn't made a photograph of the back of the check, Gasarch couldn't tell who had endorsed this one, or even what city the firm did business in. A bookkeeping entry, however, showed that the check had come in for payment from the Trenton Banking Company, of Trenton, New Jersey. Gasarch went over to Trenton and found that the Avon Mills account had been closed some months before, but the bank officials remembered the man who had opened the account, back in March, 1943, and they had his signature on file. It was "A.D. Hume." Nobody else in Trenton had ever heard of a company called Avon Mills. Deposits in the bank account had come to $67,857.90, which had been transferred to another bank. The Trenton bank had a record of that, too. The money had been transferred to the personal account of A.D. Hume in the National City Bank of New York.

Gasarch slid back to New York and found that the National City Bank had carried an account for A.D. Hume, in the amount of $119,050.13, at the same time it was carrying the Knott Company account, and at the same branch. The Hume account had been closed shortly before the chief accountant and assistant treasurer left for Canada. All this was enough evidence on which to base a warrant for the embezzler's arrest, and the police departments of various Canadian cities were, accordingly, asked to start looking for Alexander Douglas Hume. Assistant District Attorney Hunter instructed Gasarch to go ahead with his investigation and see what more he could find out. It was tough going, and Gasarch enjoyed every moment of it. Following the course of Wilby's manipulations, he has said since, was like tracing the ins and outs of a zigzagging mountain brook that sometimes flows underground. For a while, there would be easy stretches of comprehensible book-juggling, and deep clear pools at the bottom of which he could make out the dim trail of a Knott disbursement leaving the Knott check-signing machine and wriggling into one of Hume's bank accounts. Then all trace of the embezzler and his defalcations would vanish, and there would be a subterranean interlude whose secrets could be explained only by the embezzler himself.

In a short time, Gasarch found that the man known as Hume had stolen the $275,984.48 between March 20th and July 8th of 1943. Exactly how the Knott Company's machines had been maneuvered into writing and signing the checks couldn't be determined, because the fake invoices and the secret pieces of cardboard the embezzler used had disappeared, along with the canceled checks. Gasarch did, however, discover that those checks had gone to Eastern Mills and York

Mills (as well as Avon Mills), which were fictitious firms, operated in Trenton at desk space the embezzler had rented in a broker's office. The operations of these firms consisted entirely of receiving and depositing Knott checks in four Trenton banks. Each of the fictitious firms had had deposits of from sixty-five thousand to seventy-five thousand dollars, and the total of the four accounts corresponded exactly with the shortage in the Knott bank account in New York. All the missing checks for 1943 were thus accounted for. In addition to the large sum deposited in the Fifth Avenue Branch of the National City Bank, the embezzler had put forty-five thousand dollars in another branch of the same bank, and had divided the rest of the money between branches of the Corn Exchange and the Chase National, all in the name of A.D. Hume.

When the embezzler had rented space in Trenton, he bought a beat-up second-hand desk. He did not forget this when, in September of 1943, he closed his mills and transferred to the New York banks the money the Knott Company had unwittingly disbursed. He sent the broker a check for the September rent and, with it, a letter saying he was sorry to have to inform him that he would be "vacating the desk space at the end of this month, as we have decided not to locate permanently in Trenton, at least not at present." He had hired, on a part-time basis, a typist in the broker's office, a Miss Wood, to do the small amount of clerical work he required, and he remembered to speak of her in a complimentary way and to refer, half humorously, half seriously, to his dilapidated desk. "Needless to say," he wrote, "I hate to leave such good company and the excellent work of Miss Wood. And, by the way, if you should learn of anyone desiring the desk—that is, if one should call it that—I certainly would appreciate your arranging an immediate sale for it. Any price will be satisfactory, as it will, of course, be of no use in the future." The broker sold the desk for twelve dollars, sent Wilby a check for that amount, and got another charming note from the man who signed himself A.D. Hume, acknowledging receipt of same.

It wasn't long before the auditors at the Knott Company trooped into the treasurer's office again and told him that the books for 1942 showed a shortage of $110,936.81. They were sure the shortage hadn't been there when they went over the books before, they said. Some canceled checks were missing now, however. Casey told Gasarch about this, and Gasarch, with a nod and a grin, submerged himself in the 1942 situation. The embezzler had made it more difficult for himself, and for Gasarch, that year. He had scattered his fictitious firms all over New England, the Middle West, and the South, instead of establishing them in a convenient industrial center like Trenton, within commuting distance of New York, as he had got around to doing in 1943. In 1942, Wilby had manufacturers and jobbers with palms extended in Boston, Pittsburgh, Cincinnati, Buffalo, Toledo, and Jonesville, South Carolina. Gasarch discovered that the embezzler had rented desk space and had hired part-time secretaries in all those cities, but had not trusted them to do anything except receive his mail and hold it for him, unopened. The only time the embezzler could get around to his desk-space offices was on weekends, and as Gasarch reconstructed some of those weekend trips during 1942, he was amazed that the man's constitution hadn't cracked under the strain.

The defalcations that year occurred between March 9th and November 13th, and during that time dozens of Knott checks went through the Knott check-signing machine and were mailed to such figments of the embezzler's imagination as Bailey Fabrics, the Edstander Company, Emmons Brothers, Godshall Manufacturing Company, Frederick B. Hecht, the Package Delivery Service, the Qu'Appelle Company, and the Wayland Spread Company. When the embezzler knew that a batch of checks was in the mail, he would write or wire his part-time secretaries, telling them to hold his mail for him until noon on Saturday, and if he hadn't picked it up by that time, to leave it with the doorman or the night elevator operator. Rushing out of New York the moment he could get away from the Knott Company on Friday afternoon, he would pick up the mail in one of the towns before Saturday noon and deposit the checks in the account of one of his various firms, and then move on. He would puff into another city in the late hours of Saturday night or on Sunday morning, pick up more checks from the elevator operators and doormen, deposit them in the banks' overnight-deposit chutes, and then hurry back to New York in time to be at his desk at the Knott Company on Monday morning. Nobody there ever saw him looking any less fresh than a daisy.

At a bank in Toledo, the fictitious name George B. Towle had been used for an account into which had flowed some of the embezzled money. The Toledo bank wanted to be sure that this Mr. Towle was a proper man to do business with, and went to the trouble of checking his references. There is a notation on Towle's application for an account with this bank that reads, "Expects to become a client of Wm. T. Knott Co. Gives Mr. Hume as reference." Then, later: "Spoke with Mr. Hume of Wm. T. Knott Co., who stated he knew Mr. Towle for many years; knows Towle to be a legitimate businessman (advertising line) and that Towle expects to connect with Wm. T. Knott soon."

To one of his part-time secretaries in the Middle West, the embezzler wrote at the height of the 1942 embezzlements that he couldn't understand why she had not received the ten dollars he owed her for her previous month's services. He had left a check for her in that amount with the night elevator operator, he said. "Kindly check your records again," he wrote, "and if you have not received it, then I shall check with my bank and see if it has been cashed by the night elevator man in question." What had happened, further correspondence shows, was that the elevator man had forgotten to give the check to the secretary, then remembered it a day or two after she got Wilby's letter. "Delighted that your accounts are now in apple-pie order," the embezzler wrote the secretary when he learned this.

Only one person, as far as Gasarch could determine, ever raised any question about what the chief accountant and assistant treasurer of the Knott Company was doing during those two years. This was Dan True, who handled the accounting department of a Knott store in Butte, Montana. This Mr. True didn't like the looks of certain freight charges that had been debited against his store by the Knott Company, and he wrote to the treasurer of the corporation about it. The treasurer turned the letter over to the chief accountant and assistant treasurer, and True was gently put in his place by a home-office memorandum reading as follows:

Subject: Errors in Control Accounting for Transportation
To: Mr. Dan True.
Copy to: Mr. M.A. Casey—Treasurer, Knott Co.
From: A.D. Hume

On the summary attached to your letter of Nov. 19, directed to Mr. Casey, I find one mistake which has apparently been overlooked, and very largely our fault, in New York. On your summary, there is no balance shown as of July 31. However, if you look at our Trial Balance run, you will find that there was a balance of $6,831.63 but this was not shown on the F-I as a separate figure but included with Merchandise-in-Transit. This policy, for the one month of July, was followed with all stores. We had intended, of course, to follow through by actually transferring the freight balance by post-closing entry to Merchandise-in-Transit and then distributing this into purchases in the following month, thereby clearing the freight account at the end of every month, excepting for any distribution that had to be made during the following month, regardless of whether the account was debit or credit. By adding the July balance to your summary, you will find that the freight overdistributed figure does amount to a small balance in favor of the overdistribution, and that is the way your freight account now stands. With best regards,
A.D. Hume

What the embezzler was saying in that memorandum meant something more to Gasarch than it would to most people, and Gasarch grabbed hold of this relatively small example of what the embezzler had done to the Knott Company's accounts after the money was stolen. It led Gasarch to one of the subterranean places he had hoped to get into. He traced the $6,831.63 mentioned by the good man True all the way through the Knott accounting system and was able to see how (or almost how) the embezzler had made the Knott books balance in spite of his defalcations. All the money that had been stolen had been charged to the department stores, and the charges had been so deftly distributed among the stores, in so many different ways, and with such shrewd knowledge of what accounts could stand being raised a bit here and there, that the stores hadn't noticed it. Gasarch could now understand what had happened when the auditors went over the 1942 books. The embezzler had allowed the auditors to add all the bank statements and the canceled checks, including the ones he had himself endorsed, with the result, of course, that the withdrawals from the Knott bank account tallied with the total of the canceled checks. Then he had destroyed the canceled checks he had endorsed and had altered hundreds of entries in the books, so that, in effect, what the Knott Company had lost to him it got back from the stores, in the form of debits against the stores' accounts, such as the freight account. Gasarch couldn't understand, however, why the embezzler had become panicky in the middle of January, 1944, had run off to Canada, and had then disappeared so mysteriously that the treasurer of the Knott Company had eventually got that queasy feeling in his stomach. If the embezzler had waited until the annual audit for that year was over, and had then destroyed the canceled checks, Gasarch believes the embezzlements would never have been discovered.

While Gasarch was rounding out, as best he could without the embezzler's help, the picture of these two years of brilliant defalcation, the police of Montreal, Toronto, and Ottawa brought to a conclusion the search for Alexander Douglas Hume. They traced him to the European Theatre of Operations and found that, as a major, he was leading a battalion of Canadian troops. The Toronto police wired New York about this, adding, pointedly, that Hume had been in the Canadian Army since 1940. They also sent a photograph of Major Hume, who turned out to be a rather serious-looking chap with a face not at all like Wilby's. Gasarch cheerfully went to work to see if he could find out who it was that had carried out the marvelous Knott Company embezzlements. He once more visited the Fifth Avenue Branch of the National City Bank. There, after days of searching through the bank's records, he found that the man who had called himself Hume had, in May, 1943, made what to this date seems to have been the only patently careless mistake that can be scored against him in connection with the Knott Company embezzlements. He had asked the bank to buy him, with money from his personal account, a draft for fifteen thousand dollars in Canadian funds. In filling out the purchase order, he had directed that the Canadian draft be made out to "Ralph M. Wilby." A bank clerk had written that name down in the blank space provided for the name of the payee and Wilby had then changed his mind and asked that the draft be made out to himself, i.e., to "A.D. Hume." It was the sort of slip any man with more than one name might easily make.

Newspapers almost invariably refer to an embezzler as a man who was "a trusted employee" until he juggled his company's funds. The hackneyed phrase is usually given a moralistic emphasis, evidently with the intention of suggesting that the behavior of the rascally bookkeeper should be regarded as particularly odious because the man's employers had never dreamed that he might be unreliable. When the first news stories appeared in the New York papers about Ralph Marshall Wilby's embezzlement of $386,921.29 from the Knott Company, he was described as "a trusted employee" over and over again. All the stories made a point of rubbing that in. In Wilby's case, as in the cases of most embezzlers in these times, the cliché was inaccurate and its use indicates an old-fashioned and romantic idea of the relationship between bookkeepers and the people who employ them. The ugly truth is that the higher a bookkeeper climbs in the accounting department of a firm, the lower the estimate of his trustworthiness becomes in the minds and hearts of his employers. Although Wilby had worked for the Knott corporation for four years, had been given several increases in salary and two bonuses, and had reached the position of chief accountant and assistant treasurer before he put his stolen fortune in a briefcase, went to Canada, and disappeared, his employers, it turned out, hadn't trusted him in the first place. One of Wilby's best friends at the Knott corporation, and seemingly one of his greatest admirers, was the company's treasurer, Mr. Casey. It was Casey who had encouraged and aided Wilby's progress from the position of traveling auditor to that of chief accountant and assistant treasurer. Yet this same Mr. Casey, acting for the corporation in what a romanticist would have to consider an abominably gelid manner, had bet the Travelers Insurance Company (which insures all kinds of people besides travelers) that Wilby would someday steal some of the corporation's funds. The Travelers Insurance Company had bet that Wilby wouldn't. This wager was represented by a bond of three hundred thousand dollars, the terms of which were that the Knott corporation would pay the Travelers Insurance Company an annual premium of a good many thousands of dollars as long as its chief accountant and assistant treasurer didn't steal any money from the corporation. If he did steal any money, the Travelers Insurance Company would reimburse the corporation for what he had stolen, up to the sum of three hundred thousand dollars.

The fact that Wilby's employers had bet against him in this manner and that the Travelers Insurance Company stood to lose the three hundred thousand dollars unless Wilby could be hunted down and persuaded to return the larger part of the money he had embezzled from the Knott corporation was one of two circumstances that made his disappearance even briefer than it might have been. The second circumstance was that Wilby's third wife, Hazel, was a very pretty girl. That was one reason Wilby had married her. A New York probation officer wrote of Wilby after he had been brought back to New York, "He is a man who could easily be lost in a crowd, having neither the physique nor the personality to give him distinction." Hazel, on the other hand, had a physique, if not a personality, that gave her distinction. She attracted attention wherever she went, and was totally unable to get lost in a crowd.

The search for the man thought to be Alexander Douglas Hume was put into the hands of Fred Hains, a capable detective attached to the staff of District Attorney Frank S. Hogan. Hains, who has since become a lieutenant, has an easygoing manner, an active brain, and a worldly outlook. Before doing anything else, he wired the police departments of Montreal, Toronto, and Ottawa detailed descriptions of Hume and his pretty wife, and also gave them information about Hume's life as it was summarized on his employment record. It didn't look like much of a case to Hains. He is aware of, and rather entertained by, the fact that there is hardly any place in the world a crook can go now where somebody won't recognize him, provided photographs of him are distributed with sufficient largess. He knew that in this embezzlement case the Travelers Insurance Company would be anxious to put up all the money needed for a wide distribution of photographs. The company, however, had not been able to find a photograph of Hume.

Hains went out to Jackson Heights and talked to the superintendent of the apartment house there in which the Humes had lived. He discovered that Hazel had returned to Jackson Heights on January 19, 1944, the day after Mr. Casey had received the telegram informing him that Hume had broken his leg skiing. She had told the superintendent that she and her husband were going to settle in Canada, and had paid the rent for the two months the lease of the apartment had to run. Then she had packed a couple of trunks and had the furniture crated and moved out. The superintendent said she had seemed to be in a hurry but hadn't looked worried and certainly hadn't acted furtive. Adding this information to what he had been told about the Humes by people at the Knott Company, Hains surmised (correctly) that she wasn't aware that her husband had stolen a fortune. This meant that she probably would be moving around freely, wherever she was, and that her husband probably would be moving around with her. Hains talked to the Humes' best friends, a couple in Jackson Heights. As he had hoped, they had taken a snapshot of the Humes. They found it and gave it to him. The superintendent remembered that the Railway Express had come for the trunks and the furniture. Hains learned from the express company that these had been shipped to Hazel's parents, in Oklahoma. He took down their names and the name of the town in which they lived. He telephoned the sheriff of the town and asked him to arrange to have all mail addressed to Hazel's parents closely watched by the post office.

After a few days, the Toronto police wired that they had a line on Hume. Then, a day or two later, the Toronto police dug up a photograph of the real Alexander Douglas Hume and sent it to Hains. Hains was able to see at a glance that this wasn't the man who had stolen the money from the Knott corporation. Before he had time to let Toronto know about that, Toronto sent him the news that Alexander Douglas Hume had been in the Canadian Army since 1940. Hains laughed, and began to like the looks of the case. He knew now that he was after a man who had somehow been able to obtain the employment record of an honest certified public accountant, had posed as this C.P.A. in New York for four years, and had, in addition, stolen nearly four hundred thousand dollars while competently holding down the job of chief accountant and assistant treasurer of a big corporation.

It was a week or so later that the embezzler's actual name was discovered by Gasarch, and Hains then learned very quickly that Wilby had a record as an embezzler in California and in Ontario. The Travelers Insurance Company delightedly made thousands of copies of the snapshot of the Wilbys that Hains had found in Jackson Heights, and began mailing them to police departments, hotels, railroads, airports, and its branch offices all over the United States and Canada, along with the information that the man in the photograph was wanted for the Knott embezzlement.

Hains and a fellow-detective, George Salyka, then set out for Oklahoma. In the town where Hazel's parents lived, they picked up from the sheriff a letter Hazel had written them after she closed up the apartment in Jackson Heights. It said that she was returning to Toronto immediately, that she and her husband were going to stay in Canada permanently, and that they were thinking of going out to British Columbia, where he had some relatives. She asked her parents to keep the furniture for a while, until she and her husband had decided where they were going to settle down. Her husband had inherited a small fortune from a great-aunt, she said, and he wanted to look around British Columbia for a good business in which to invest some of this money. Hains communicated the gist of this to Ottawa, Toronto, Montreal, and Vancouver, and was about to return to New York when his office there relayed to him a wire from the police chief of Victoria, the capital of British Columbia, that said his men had just missed Wilby at the Empress Hotel and expected to catch up with him in a day or two.

As Hazel later testified in court in New York, Wilby had by that time told her that his real name was Wilby but had not told her that he was an embezzler. When they reached Toronto, Wilby told her he had a confession to make. In his youth, he said, he had been deported from the United States because he had gone over the border without signing the proper papers. He had accordingly found it necessary to adopt an alias when he returned to the United States later. He had inherited a small fortune from a great-aunt who had died in England, and had increased it by playing the stock market, but had not paid any income tax on it. He was afraid to stay in the United States any longer, because he might be sent to jail for violating the income-tax law, and he had therefore brought his fortune with him in his briefcase, in cash and bonds. He asked Hazel to return to Jackson Heights, close up the apartment, store the furniture, and rejoin him in Toronto, after which they would go out to British Columbia, visit his relatives, find a business to invest in, and live comfortably for the rest of their lives. A trusting girl but not a dumb one, Hazel was afraid that her husband might be arrested and taken back to the United States. Wilby reassured her on this point in a characteristically businesslike manner. He took her to a solicitor in Toronto and asked the solicitor's opinion as to whether he could be extradited for not paying an income tax. The solicitor told him he could not. Hazel asked the solicitor a great many questions and soon felt fine about the whole thing. A Canadian citizen, the solicitor told her, could be extradited only for a really serious offense, such as murder or grand larceny. Wilby paid the solicitor a small fee. Hazel came to New York, closed up the apartment, and went back to Toronto. The Wilbys then traveled, in easy stages, across the continent to Victoria. Wilby readopted his real name, and Hazel began to call him Ralph instead of Doug.

By the time the Wilbys reached Victoria, the photographs that were being mailed out by the Travelers Insurance Company had been circulated in eastern Canada, but they had not reached British Columbia. In the meantime, Hazel was noticed in a crowd in the lobby of the Empress Hotel by a photographer on the Victoria *Times* named Flash Strickland. He noticed her simply because she was beautiful. He uttered a low, British Columbian whistle and gaped at her. A girl in the society department of the same newspaper happened to come into the lobby at that instant, in search of news items. She asked the photographer what he was gaping at. He indicated Mrs. Wilby, who was getting into an elevator by then. The reporter went over to the desk, asked who the beautiful girl was, and copied down the name from the register—"Mrs. Ralph M. Wilby, Hamilton." Hamilton, a city near Toronto, was Wilby's home town. An item appeared next day in the Victoria *Times* to the effect that Ralph M. Wilby, of Hamilton, and his attractive young wife were at the Empress Hotel. A few days later, a Toronto paper picked up the item. A stenographer in the Toronto office of the Travelers Insurance Company saw it and recognized the name of the embezzler whose photograph had come in from New York. She told her boss, who told the Toronto police, who told the Victoria police. When the Victoria police got to the Empress Hotel, the Wilbys had checked out. They had gone to visit Wilby's relatives, just outside town. When they returned to Victoria, a few days later, and checked into the Empress Hotel again, Wilby was arrested. That happened on the fifty-eighth day after he had left New York for the long weekend.

Hains received this news without surprise. The Travelers Insurance Company was happy, but only momentarily. The Victoria police wired the following day that when Wilby was searched he had only a few coins in his pockets, and that no money or bonds were found in the Wilbys' baggage, and no bankbooks. Gasarch was glad Wilby had been caught, because he hoped that he would be able to have a talk with him and find out some of the things he wanted to know about the finer points of his embezzling methods. Assistant District Attorney Hunter had obtained an indictment against Wilby by this time for grand larceny, and he went to Victoria to start extradition proceedings. The Canadian law requires that before a prisoner can be extradited, sufficient evidence be presented to convince the presiding judge, for all practical purposes, of his guilt. Gasarch went along with Hunter, as an expert witness for the prosecution. Hains and Salyka went along, too, to bring Wilby back to New York.

It took four months and cost the State of New York at least ten thousand dollars to get Wilby out of Canada. He hired the best solicitors and barristers that money could buy. One of them was a former Attorney General of British Columbia. Wilby had buried some of the stolen money in tin cans in the back yard of a house he had bought on the outskirts of Vancouver, and he had buried some more of it along a highway near Victoria. Hazel later testified, in New York, that she had dug some of this money out of the ground with her own hands and given it to the Canadian attorneys. The Canadian attorneys, still later, asserted that they hadn't dreamed it was stolen money, and nobody was ever able to persuade them to give any of it back, either to the Knott corporation or to the Travelers Insurance Company. Exactly how much they received has never been established. The extraordinary vigor with which they fought for Wilby indicates that they were being well paid or else that their devotion to him was a fine and touching thing. They appeared in court on Wilby's behalf on twenty-three occasions, obtained three writs of habeas corpus for him, appealed when the courts refused to sustain the writs, and were preparing an additional appeal to the Privy Council in London, when Hains and Salyka, taking advantage of a momentary hiatus between writs of habeas corpus, at last managed to grab Wilby and bring him back to Seattle in a small fishing vessel. They had almost got him out of Canada between writs once before that, but Wilby had raised an outcry while he was under their custody in a hotel and had persuaded Canadian police to take him away from the New York detectives. By the time the Canadian police were persuaded that Wilby was not being kidnapped, his attorneys had obtained another writ. Hunter, along with a Canadian barrister the New York District Attorney's office had retained, fought Wilby's lawyers with determination, and even brilliance, but, as Hunter wrote, "such strange things have happened that we cannot count on anything." Wilby conducted himself all this time with the self-righteous dignity of a man of consequence who is being unjustly persecuted. He did not deny having stolen the money, but he was convinced that he shouldn't be extradited for that. He was standoffish with the New York detectives during the short periods they had him in custody between writs. Casey, the Knott treasurer, went to Victoria and talked to Wilby in jail, and Wilby was outraged when Casey asked him please to give up the battle, come back to New York, and straighten out the Knott books. "The books are in a mess, you know," Casey said to Wilby mildly. Wilby told him indignantly that the books were *not* in a mess—that they were in perfect balance, since every penny he had stolen had been carefully charged off to the department stores. On the train back to New York from Seattle, Wilby relaxed somewhat with the detectives and played gin rummy with them for small stakes. "He's a lot of fun to be with, in many ways," Hains said later.

Locked up in the Tombs, Wilby refused for weeks to tell Gasarch what he wanted to know, and also refused to tell the Travelers Insurance Company whether he had any of the stolen money left and, if so, where he had hidden it. He hired an attorney with what the attorney says he hopes was not stolen money, and he finally persuaded Wilby to plead guilty. Before Wilby did so, however, he made a bargain with the Travelers Insurance Company that was as original as his methods of embezzlement. He offered to tell the company where it could find around three hundred thousand dollars of the stolen money if it would give him ten thousand dollars for himself. The company took this up with various surety companies, representing various banks, all of which might have had to assume responsibility for Wilby's fraudulent checks and therefore stood to gain if Wilby returned three hundred thousand dollars of the stolen money. Wilby's argument was that he had had ten thousand dollars of his own money when he went to Canada, in addition to the stolen money. He had, of course, stolen $386,921.29, but, he said, he had given about eighty thousand dollars of it to his Canadian barristers and solicitors. Nobody could find out whether this was true or not, but Wilby was in a strong position to bargain, because he was offering three hundred thousand dollars for ten thousand dollars. The Travelers Insurance Company and the surety companies, all of which were to reduce their losses on a complicated percentage basis through any of the stolen money that was returned, mulled over Wilby's proposition for several weeks and finally accepted it. After Wilby had been given a certified check for ten thousand dollars, he told an attorney for the Travelers Insurance Company where what remained of the stolen money was, and the attorney went to Canada and dug it up. It came to three hundred and three thousand dollars.

In a co-operative mood now, Wilby not only talked to Gasarch and gave Casey and other Knott people useful tips on how the tangled books of the corporation could be straightened out but also wrote, while in the Tombs awaiting sentence, a ten-thousand-word document that discussed, with the cool detachment of Napoleon's review of the battle of Waterloo, the ups and downs of his two years of embezzling from Knott. The first third of this statement of Wilby's was a masterly explanation of what the Knott accounting system was and how it worked. It told how the department stores managed by Knott sent in their invoices for goods purchased—these invoices are "aprons" in accountancy terminology—and how these aprons were put through the human workers and the business machines so that, at the other end of the system, checks for the manufacturers and jobbers emerged from the Knott check-signing machine. Wilby mentioned by name the various Knott employees who were in charge of sub-departments of the accounting department, and told what their duties were and how well they performed them. Then he quietly started a new paragraph, to explain how he did what he did to the Knott corporation, like this:

As to my defalcations, no fixed course was followed throughout excepting in the year 1943, when they followed a more or less similar routine. During 1942, the methods differed largely from those used in 1943.

In 1943, the course was, to a large extent, as follows: At some time before or after a batch of original aprons had been received from the department stores and distributed by Miss Catala, I would insert a further apron or aprons payable to "my" companies and would correct the accompanying listing by either running a new adding machine tape or making penciled corrections on the original listing that the store had prepared. On other occasions, I took an apron that was payable to some vendor from the originals sent out by the stores and assuming, for example, that this apron was for $235, and payable to John Doe Co., I would add a "6" in front of this amount, thus making the corrected amount "6235" and would erase the name of the original vendor and insert the name of "my own" company. This made changing the store's listing comparatively easy. Then, of course, I would make a further apron just exactly as the store had originally made it and either add it to that day's aprons and listing, or else to a following day's.

So there were several methods by which the aprons payable to "my" companies were supplemented into the various stores' original aprons and listings, but it all adds up to the same thing, that they were included without any difficulties.

As I mentioned before, sometimes they were added before Miss Catala received the mail, which was no trouble, as it was merely a matter of taking an envelope from her desk before her arrival in the morning, or getting it from the mailing department before the distribution was made to Miss Catala's desk on the pretense that I was anxious to get some store's reports. As original aprons were coming in from every store on each day, one just couldn't avoid getting an envelope with some of these original apron insertion. If my step was taken after the coding, original aprons were in the course of being mailed before the addition of aprons to "my" companies.

If this act was after the control clerk had noted the original total, I would merely change her figures upon my apron insertion. If my step was taken after the coding, I would have to correct the control figures and would code the apron myself. As I could handle practically the functions of every accounting employee, whatever method followed presented no great difficulties. As soon as the apron was added to a store's listing, "my" apron thereafter followed a normal course, which I naturally permitted, up to a certain point.

The number of settlement checks issued and mailed by Knott averages between 600 and 700 daily. Many more settlement checks, as a rule, are outgoing on Fridays from Knott's than on other days. I had learned from experience that checks mailed by Knott on Friday evenings did not reach "my" offices or post-office boxes by early Saturday mornings, when I went to make bank deposits for "my" companies. But Saturday mornings were practically the only occasions on which I could arrange to be in Trenton, or the other cities, during banking hours, and unless I could actually gain possession of "my" checks on Friday at the Knott office, it meant a delay of one week in "my" deposits. This was contrary to my policy of getting the deposits in the banks just as soon as possible and to withdraw the funds as soon as it appeared to be safe, without arousing suspicion and, of course, always allowing sufficient time for their complete clearance.

Therefore, always on Fridays, and generally on every other day also, I would arrange to get those checks payable to "my" companies just before the final functions were completed by the Knott office staff, and would complete these functions myself and then pocket the checks so that I could take them with me for the earliest possible Saturday deposit. There were two or three other reasons why I invariably tried to follow this plan of completing "my" checks myself and gaining possession of them before they left the Knott office.

One of the other reasons was that during the year of 1942, I allowed several of "my" checks to be completely handled by the Knott staff and thereafter my earliest chance to pocket these checks was after they had reached the mailing room. I took these from the mailing room, but they were missed, as their count and the number as per the scratch pad notation was not in agreement. This discrepancy was reported to the audit department head, Miss Murphy, and she, in turn, criticized her clerk, who had inserted the checks in the envelopes and had counted and taken them to the mailing room. Miss Murphy had believed that this clerk was careless and even considered removing her from that capacity. Thereafter, I never resorted to such practice again, because I hated to see the clerk get in trouble through no fault of her own.

There was one method which would have been the easiest course of all—this being to have a notation made on the check, at some point of its preparation, that it was to be given to Mr. Hume upon its completion. But I considered such policy much too risky, just in case some question might be asked or raised about the check during its preparation, and consistently being a sizable amount, this was quite possible, so I did not wish to have my name associated with any of "my" checks whatsoever so far as the Knott office was concerned.

Another reason for my favoring and arranging to complete the functions of "my" checks, and then pocketing them, was that, one time early in 1943, I had allowed one or two checks to be completed in all functions by the accounting staff and to be mailed out by the company, as was the normal course for all other checks. But one of these letters bearing a check to "my" Avon Mills never reached Trenton until one or two Saturdays following the week it should have been there in the ordinary course of events. I was literally sick with worrying—naturally imagining everything. This envelope finally arrived, bearing the notation that it had been sent to Chicago, Ill., in error by the post-office department, though it had been correctly addressed. The mistake troubled me sufficiently that I did not allow any more checks to be completed and mailed by the office and the mailing staff of Knott's, though I did mail such checks myself.

Wilby proved to everybody's satisfaction, in his written statement and in conversations with Gasarch and with people from the Knott Company, that he had worked entirely without confederates. None of the human workers in the Knott accounting department were blamed because Wilby had done what he had done. Some of the business machines were criticized, however, and were later taken apart and put together again, after certain newly devised safeguards, which Wilby's methods seemed to make advisable, had been added. But it was felt by people who know and work with such machines that if the machines had been able to talk, as well as think, they would have spoken to somebody about Wilby long before his disappearance caused the corporation to suspect that he had not been honest with it.

Wilby, it turned out, might have gone on stealing from the Knott corporation in 1944, and for years afterward, as he had done in 1943 and 1942, if it had not been for the Federal Bureau of Investigation. The connection of the F.B.I. with the Wilby case has not been mentioned in the published chronicles of J. Edgar Hoover and his G-men, but it was the F.B.I. that caused Wilby to leave the Knott corporation when he did.

Wilby had covered up his defalcations with such impeccable technique that he would probably never have been suspected of wrongdoing if he had stayed around to steal some more in 1944, or if he had at least waited until the annual audit of the corporation's books was completed, in the winter of 1944, and had then just resigned after shaking hands all around. Instead, he left in a hurry. As he explained in the document he wrote in the Tombs, he had outwitted everybody but he had not been able to foresee the interest of the F.B.I. in his operations. The F.B.I. had no suspicion that he was an embezzler. It thought it was on the trail of a Nazi Fifth Columnist, and had done everything but alert Walter Winchell for a scoop. Wilby had taken no precautions against that kind of thinking. Something of a philosopher, he has possibly reflected, in the years since all these things happened, that the three circumstances that led to his downfall make a crazy pattern, sort of like life. In Hazel's beauty there was truth; the fact that the Knott corporation had mistrusted him all along had about it a flavor of irony; and the F.B.I. contributed a comic ingredient.

In 1942, Wilby related in his confession, he had some Knott checks sent to a fictitious jobber in St. Louis, to whom he had given the name Frederick B. Hecht. It never occurred to him that the fact that it was a German name was going to get him into trouble with anybody. That's what happened, however. In those days, the F.B.I. checked up on all sorts of bank accounts all over the country, and especially those in German names. An F.B.I. man going over the records of Wilby's St. Louis bank came across the Hecht account and asked the bank who Hecht was. The bank knew only that a number of Knott Company checks had been deposited in the account. It sent a man to New York to inquire of the Knott Company about Hecht. He was referred to Wilby, who requested time to look into the matter. "I busied myself towards being able to present the proper invoices for Hecht at my next meeting with the bank's representative," Wilby explained later in the statement. He drew up some new fake invoices, having destroyed the old fake invoices, and thought he had convinced the bank that Hecht was a legitimate jobber who was not engaged in un-American activities, but eighteen months later the F.B.I. still had the Hecht account on its mind. One evening in December, 1943, an earnest young F.B.I. man came out to Jackson Heights to see the Knott corporation's chief accountant and assistant treasurer about it. The F.B.I. man told Wilby frankly that he hadn't been able to find Hecht anywhere. He was positive that Hecht was a Nazi Fifth Columnist, he said, and he asked Wilby if he couldn't think of some clues that might lead to the discovery of Hecht. "I gave some false clues to the F.B.I. man about Hecht," Wilby wrote. "In the next two or three weeks, the F.B.I. man called on me at the Knott office on two further occasions to obtain further information about Hecht. I continued to furnish misleading advice, though I realized that the time for a showdown was rapidly approaching." Wilby did not wait for the showdown.

There was an extended hearing before Judge John A. Mullen, in the Court of General Sessions, when Wilby appeared for sentence, on February 1, 1945. Wilby's New York attorney argued persuasively for leniency, pointing out that the amount of money Wilby had restored represented something of a record. Judge Mullen, however, pointed out that this had been made possible only by the fact that the amount of money Wilby had stolen also represented something of a record.

Hazel testified at length and convinced Judge Mullen, as she convinced everybody else, that until Wilby was arrested she had not known he was an embezzler. "When I married my husband," Hazel said, "I didn't know how much money he had. The reason for that, I asked him one time and very politely he refused to answer my question. I thought perhaps I was being a little too inquisitive, and, therefore, I never asked him again. I knew nothing about his financial affairs."

"I know," Judge Mullen put in. "My probation report indicates that she did not have any reason to believe that her husband had ever taken any money, because it was not spent on her and it wasn't spent on anybody else."

Hazel was asked when it was that her husband had told her he had come into a substantial sum of money, and she said it was on the train going to Canada.

"How did the subject come up on that occasion—do you remember?" the Judge asked.

"Yes, I do," Hazel said. "He was carrying a little brown brief case and out of just one of those questions I said, rather jokingly, 'What have you got in there?' And at the time I don't remember exactly what he said, but, as I recall, he said, 'Well, that consists of our worldly wealth' or some little remark like that."

"And what did you say—anything?"

"Well, I said, 'Don't leave it lying around. You'd better take good care of it.' "

Later on in the hearing, Wilby's attorney made a rambling speech about Wilby's earlier embezzlements and emphasized the fact that Wilby had always lived economically and was highly regarded by all three of his wives. "I am trying at least to indicate what went through Wilby's mind," he concluded.

"That, I am afraid, we will never know," Judge Mullen said.

The Judge had weighed the facts in the case with a good deal of care before this hearing, and he weighed them some more before he pronounced sentence. The facts were not easy to weigh. Wilby's attitude toward embezzlement seems to have been the only flaw in an otherwise perfectly sterling character. He had never been charged with breaking any statutes except those having to do with embezzlement. Embezzlement is a statutory felony both in the United States and in England these days, but Judge Mullen was aware that before the sixteenth century it was not a crime in English law, because it was not regarded as an offense against the people. In those days, it was thought to be laughable rather than criminal and was not to be judged the same way theft was, because the embezzler merely takes money that he has been hired to handle. The only recourse the owner of embezzled funds had, under English law, was to sue the absconding bookkeeper in the civil courts. King Henry VIII, who had himself been humbugged by embezzlers, promulgated the first anti-embezzlement statute in 1592. New York revised its anti-embezzlement statutes as late as 1942 to plug up some loopholes that had offered advantages to certain types of embezzlers. Judge Mullen was also aware that embezzlement is still not generally regarded as a crime against the people, and that courts often give embezzlers suspended sentences or very short prison terms if they make restitution of the funds they have stolen. He was aware that the Knott corporation had lost nothing, because Wilby had restored three hundred and three thousand dollars of the stolen money and the Travelers Insurance Company bond had easily covered the additional $83,921.29. The Travelers Insurance Company had lost something, but, on the other hand, its premium rates allow for just such losses, and it had not suffered any more that year than in any other year, and had shown a handsome profit in spite of Wilby. The same was true of the surety companies and the banks. Wilby, however, had cost the people of the State of New York at least ten thousand dollars just to get him out of Canada, and the fact that firms like the Knott Company must pay for large bonds for employees like Wilby means that this additional expense is passed along to the consumer. Judge Mullen is a jurist who does not believe in punishment except when it can serve as a deterrent. He couldn't help feeling that if Wilby, with the ten thousand dollars in his pocket that he had gotten from the Travelers Insurance Company, was given a suspended sentence, or even an especially light sentence, he would be a foolish man if he didn't go right on embezzling for the rest of his life. Judge Mullen therefore sentenced him to from five to seven years in Sing Sing. Wilby's behavior there has been good and he will be out soon. Like her two predecessors, Hazel applied for an annulment and got it. She became a model for a while, married again, and is living happily in New York. When Wilby leaves Sing Sing, the immigration officers intend to ship him back to Canada at once.

The Persecution of
the Reverend Dr. Dix

by Herbert Asbury

*Newpaperman Herbert Asbury (1891–1963) wrote books
about America's urban underworld. His work was out of
print and largely forgotten until the recent reissue of* The
Gangs of New York, *which Martin Scorsese made into a
2002 movie (see page 71). With any luck, more readers
will now discover other examples of Asbury's work, such as
this short piece.*

On a frosty morning in February 1880 the Reverend Dr.
Morgan Dix, rector of Trinity Church, left his breakfast
sausages to answer a ring at the doorbell of the rectory in
No. 27 West Twenty-fifth Street. His visitor was a clerical
gentleman, who presented a card which proclaimed that he represented a select academy devoted to the education of the female young.
He had come, he said, in response to a note ostensibly signed by Dr.
Dix, and was prepared to quote favorable terms for the care and
training of the three little girls whom, according to the bogus letter, the
rector wished to place in such an institution. Explaining that a distressing mistake had been made, the bewildered clergyman returned to
his sausages, but it is of record that he never ate them, for scarcely
had the clerical gentleman departed than another arrived. Thereafter
they came in droves, more than a score calling before nightfall. And

mingled with them were many representatives of Bible societies, religious and secular publishing houses, and all sorts of manufacturing
and wholesale establishments, all of which had received letters saying
that Dr. Dix wished to inspect samples and hear prices before pur-
chasing large quantities of supplies for various charitable organiza-
tions under his control. And when no one else was ringing the rectory
bell, the postman was clamoring for admittance with huge sacks of letters and postcards from firms which had not sent salesmen. Next day
the procession of callers continued, and the mail was augmented by
grave and sorrowful communications from leading Episcopal bishops
and clergymen throughout the East, who had received curt notes, to
which the signature of the rector had been forged, reprimanding them
for not having answered Dr. Dix's letters. The tone of many of the letters from the bishops and divines was anything but Christian, and several hinted that perhaps the distinguished rector of Trinity should
consult a physician.

On February 21, 1880, Dr. Dix received an anonymous letter, the
writer of which said he would do his part toward making the rector's
celebration of Washington's Birthday a memorable occasion, and that
he had notified the old-clothes-women of Baxter Street and Park Row
(then Chatham Street) to call at the rectory and negotiate for the purchase of Mrs. Dix's entire wardrobe. He enclosed a pair of soiled stock-
ings which he suggested could be worn by the rector's wife after the
sale. This time Dr. Dix arose early, and so was able to fortify himself
with sausages and wheatcakes before a rickety wagon, almost wholly
occupied by a very fat woman and drawn by a forlorn little horse over
whose back a small boy flapped the reins, rattled through Twenty-fifth
Street and stopped before the parsonage. The fat woman descended by
placing her hands upon the horse's haunches and oozing out of the
wagon. Striding ponderously up the steps, she whanged the doorbell.
When Dr. Dix appeared, she shrilly demanded that the clothing be
produced, shouting that whatever the clergyman had for sale was
worthless and that she would lose money on it. Dr. Dix attempted to
explain, but abandoned the task as hopeless when another woman,

with a sack over her shoulder, rushed through the gate and elbowed the first caller away from the door, while down the street a great clatter announced the coming of three others, who dragged hand-carts after them.

The rector retreated, slamming and barring his door, and the women settled down on the stoop to wait, convinced that Dr. Dix merely wanted to haggle. The old-clothes-dealers continued to arrive throughout the morning, and by noon the lawn of the rectory was filled with the excited clamor of twenty-eight women and twelve fretful children, most of whom were fighting, while the tumult was increased by the yells and gibes of street gamins who lined the picket fence and flung stones at the visitors. Several neighbors who attempted to enter the rectory and console the distressed clergyman were set upon by the women, who insisted upon bargaining for the clothing upon their backs. When one man refused to sell his elegant cloak, it was torn from his shoulders. Dr. Dix finally called the police, and late in the afternoon the women and children were driven from the yard by a squad of patrolmen.

But scarcely had the clatter of the carts and wagons died away than a carriage whirled round the corner from Fifth Avenue, raced through Twenty-fifth Street, and drew up in front of the rectory. One of the city's leading physicians leaped out and dashed into the house, only to emerge a few moments later very indignant. He had received an urgent call that Dr. Dix had gone into an epileptic fit and was dying. Similar messages had been left at the offices of some thirty other doctors, and it was after midnight when the last of them had come and gone. Dr. Dix slept fitfully that night, and before breakfast was awakened by a half-dozen shoemakers who had been notified to call at the rectory and measure some children for shoes. Before lunch at least fifty men and women who had advertised for work appeared. They had received notes advising them that jobs were to be had from Dr. Dix. The after-noon was quiet, except for a large influx of mail, but about dusk a score of the most prominent clergymen of New York presented them-selves at the rectory, having received invitations, to which the rector's name had been forged, to dine with Dr. and Mrs. Dix and meet the Bishops of York and Exeter.

Next morning the business houses of Lord & Taylor, A.T. Stewart & Company, Stern Brothers, Arnold Constable & Company, and others received curt letters, also supposedly signed by Dr. Dix, saying that the rector had turned their impertinent communications over to his lawyer for immediate legal action. Since no such communications, of course, had ever been written to Dr. Dix, officials of these firms were greatly excited and hurriedly sent emissaries to the rectory to assure the clergyman of their undying respect and esteem. This trouble had scarcely been disposed of when Dr. Dix received a letter signed "Gentleman Joe," who said that the annoyances would cease if the rector would pay him a thousand dollars. Dr. Dix was instructed, if he was willing to make the payment, to publish in the New York *Herald* two days later a personal saying: "Gentleman Joe: All right." This letter offered the first clue to the identity of the tormentor, and Dr. Dix promptly implored the aid of the Central Office, as the Detective Bureau was then called. The best minds of the police began to grapple with the problem, but none of the detectives knew anyone called "Gentleman Joe." Upon their advice Dr. Dix inserted the advertisement as directed, but in the same issue of the paper were two others exactly similar to it, obviously published by the persecutor. Gentleman Joe paid no attention to Dr. Dix's personal, but for the next few days he let the rector alone and turned his attention to a score of other prominent citizens, all devout church members and temperance workers, to whom he sent tart and threatening letters signed with the names of disreputable saloon-keepers and demanding payment of long overdue bills for beer and whiskey. These insulting missives were given to lawyers, who collected many fat retainers before they were found to be bogus.

On March 17, 1880 Dr. Dix received another letter from Gentleman Joe, who said that unless fifteen hundred dollars was sent to a designated place, the rectory would again be besieged on the following Friday. Detectives took possession of the house on that day, and the clergyman locked himself in his office and refused to see any one but members of his family. Early in the morning there came to the rectory a lawyer with a letter to which Mrs. Dix's name had been forged, and which said that she wished to consult with him about a divorce. Twenty other lawyers called during the day on like errands, bearing exactly similar missives, as well as an agent for a steamship line with two tickets to Havana, and a score of persons who had advertised for lost or stolen property. They had been notified that their belongings were being held for them at the rectory. During the next three days at least a hundred persons appeared in response to summonses of various sorts, and about a week later an indignant stranger forced his way into the rectory, accused the astonished Dr. Dix of being too friendly with his wife, and threatened to cane the clergyman unless he immediately made a public apology. Next day the rector received a letter from Gentleman Joe saying that he had thoroughly enjoyed his visit, and boasting of his ability as an actor.

The police made extraordinary efforts to capture Dr. Dix's persecutor, assigning every detective on the force to the case and invoking the aid of the Post Office. Gentleman Joe had gone to the expense of procuring stationery engraved with "Trinity Parsonage, 27 West Twenty-fifth Street," but the printer could not be found; and the police also failed when detectives were stationed at mailboxes throughout the city to open the receptacles whenever a letter was mailed and compare the handwriting with that known to be Gentleman Joe's. But it was not until a clergyman of another denomination mentioned that he had seen a former Trinity Sunday-school teacher who rejoiced in the elegant cognomen of Edward Eugene Fairfax Williamson that the police finally pounced upon the rascal's trail. They at once suspected Williamson because, having been unmasked as a person of low character, he had been expelled from Trinity when he scorned reformation and boasted of his amorous experiences in Turkey and other Eastern countries.

In the Post Office the police found a card upon which Williamson had written a request that his mail be forwarded to the Hotel Windsor, at Fifth Avenue and Forty-sixth Street. His chirography was the same as that of the letters signed "Gentleman Joe." At the Windsor the detectives found that Williamson had left for Baltimore on the day his handwriting was discovered in the Post Office. He was traced to Barnum's Hotel in that city, and thence to a private boarding-house, where he was arrested. He told the police that he had not annoyed Dr. Dix through personal animus, but that he was impelled solely by a craving for amusement and had selected the rector of Trinity because of his importance as a citizen.

Upon his trial in New York he was convicted of attempting to blackmail the Reverend Dr. Dix and of accusing the clergyman of what modern journalism blushingly refers to as "a statutory offense." He was sentenced to Sing Sing Prison, where he died.

The police were unable to learn very much about Gentleman Joe's career and never knew whether he was simply a sneak-thief and a petty criminal with a tendency toward the sensational, or the equivalent of the modern master mind, and a thief and crook of unusual adroitness. They connected him with only a few petty thefts and swindles, and apparently he never worked, yet he always had plenty of money, and in both Pittsburgh and New York, where he lived during his two visits to the United States, he moved in good society. In New York, indeed, he became well known in literary circles, publishing considerable poetry and producing a play which was well received. However, it was later discovered that these literary works had been written by a nun in a New Orleans convent, though it was never known how Gentleman Joe obtained them.

Gentleman Joe first swam into the ken of the police in 1868, when he traveled extensively in Europe as an English gentleman and was involved in several minor crimes. In 1870 he came to New York, where he lived for two years, publishing his poetry and becoming a teacher in Trinity Sunday school. His only disclosed criminal exploit during this period was the theft of a quantity of gold pens, stationery, and other small articles from a shop opposite the Gilsey House, at Broadway and Twenty-ninth Street. After his expulsion from Trinity Sunday school Gentleman Joe went to Europe, and was next heard of when he was sent to Newgate Prison to serve a year for tormenting a Hebrew gentleman in London, in much the same fashion as he later persecuted Dr. Dix. Upon his release from Newgate, in 1875, he returned to the United States and lived in Pittsburgh for several years, swindling a few jewelry firms out of small amounts. He then came to New York and began annoying Dr. Dix. The police always regarded him as a very mysterious person and suspected that he was the ne'er-do-well younger son of a prominent English family and that he received remittances from his relatives. Apparently he had devoted his life to the commission of small crimes, not for the purpose of gain, but simply to amuse himself. His most pronounced characteristics while leading a comparatively honest life in New York were a fondness for notoriety and sensation and a great delight in writing letters. Of this last exercise he must have been very fond indeed, for during his persecution of Dr. Dix he penned more than three hundred, all elegantly phrased and displaying considerable education.

from The Gangs of New York
by Herbert Asbury

Herbert Asbury's most famous book, The Gangs of New York, is a work of social history. This selection examines New York City's underworld during the 25 years or so that followed the Civil War.

At the close of the Civil War, while the statesmen of Tammany Hall dipped greedy fingers into the city's money chests, New York entered upon an unparalleled era of wickedness; so demoralized were the police by political chicanery and by widespread corruption within their own ranks that they were unable to enforce even a semblance of respect for the law. For more than twenty-five years the criminal classes revelled in an orgy of vice and crime; and the metropolis, then comprising only Manhattan Island, richly deserved the title of "the modern Gomorrah," which is said to have been first applied by Rev. T. DeWitt Talmage in a sermon in the Brooklyn Tabernacle during the middle seventies. Both the Rev. Talmage and the Rev. Henry Ward Beecher, pastor of Plymouth Church in Brooklyn, made frequent pilgrimages to Manhattan and visited the shrines of wickedness under escort of Central Office detectives, acquiring sermon material which they employed in the point-with-horror manner still used so effectively by modern clergymen.

Before the War the dives, dance halls, and houses of ill-fame were largely confined to the Five Points, the Bowery and Water, Cherry and other streets along the East River water front in the old Fourth Ward. But scarcely had the South laid down its arms at Appomattox than hundreds of bagnios, with red lanterns gleaming from the windows or dangling from beams on the porches, appeared throughout the city. They operated without molestation so long as the owners paid the assessments imposed by their political overlords, and even advertised with great boldness in the newspapers and by printed circular. The most celebrated single group of these places was the Sisters' Row in West Twenty-fifth Street, near Seventh Avenue, where seven adjoining houses were opened in the sixties by seven sisters who had come to New York from a small New England village to seek their fortunes, and had fallen into ways of sin. These were the most expensive bordellos in the city, and were conducted with great style and ceremony. On certain days of the month no gentleman was admitted unless he wore evening dress and carried a bouquet of flowers, and the inmates were advertised as cultured and pleasing companions, accomplished on the piano and guitar and familiar with the charms and graces of correct social intercourse. The proceeds of Christmas Eve were always given to charity. Another noted resort was Josephine Woods', in Eighth Street near Broadway, where a grand blind man's bluff party was held every New Year's Eve, and open house was kept throughout New Year's Day in imitation of the prevailing custom in more refined society.

In a speech at Cooper Union in January, 1866, Bishop Simpson of the Methodist Episcopal Church made the startling and discouraging announcement that prostitutes were as numerous in New York as Methodists, and later, in a sermon in St. Paul's M.E. Church, fixed the number at twenty thousand, approximately one-fortieth of the population. John A. Kennedy, Superintendent of Police, vigorously denied the truth of the Bishop's statements, and said that although he had no figures on the Methodists, who had not come under his jurisdiction, the records of the police force showed that there were but 3,300 public prostitutes in the city, distributed among 621 houses and ninety-nine assignation hotels, and including 747 waiter girls employed in concert saloons and dance halls. However, Bishop Simpson and other reformers produced considerable proof, and it is quite likely that his figures more nearly approached the truth than those of the Superintendent, for the latter dealt only with the professional aspects of the problem, and, moreover, did not include the thousands of street women who swarmed the thoroughfares of the city. Originally women of this class were known as night-walkers, for they were seldom seen on the streets before dusk, but as they became bolder they were called street-walkers.

Many of the worst of the dives with which New York was infested during these days of iniquity, and which were utilized as rendezvous by the gangs of criminals and the hordes of fallen women, were in the area between Twenty-fourth and Fortieth Streets and Fifth and Seventh Avenues, a region of such utter depravity that horrified reformers referred to it as Satan's Circus. As late as 1885 it was estimated that at least half of the buildings in the district were devoted to some form of wickedness, while Sixth avenue, then the wildest and gayest thoroughfare in the city, was lined with brothels, saloons and all-night dance halls, and was constantly thronged by a motley crowd seeking diversion and dissipation. This area was a part of the old Twenty-ninth police precinct, which ran from Fourteenth to Forty-second Streets and from Fourth to Seventh Avenues, and was the original Tenderloin, so named by Captain, later Inspector, Alexander S. Williams. After long and unrewarded toil in outlying districts, Captain Williams was transferred to the command of the Twenty-ninth in 1876. A few days later a friend, meeting him on Broadway and noting his expansive smile, asked the cause of his merriment.

"Well," said Williams, "I've been transferred. I've had nothing but chuck steak for a long time, and now I'm going to get a little of the tenderloin."

Perhaps the most famous of the dives which came under Williams' jurisdiction was the old Haymarket, in Sixth Avenue just south of Thirtieth Street. Because of its long life—it survived several closings and was in active operation until late in 1913—the Haymarket became widely known throughout the United States, and was a favorite place for the plucking of yokels who ventured into the metropolis to see the sights of the great city. The house was opened as a variety theater soon after the Civil War, and was named after a similar playhouse in London. But it was unable to compete with such celebrated theaters as the Tivoli in Eighth Street and Tony Pastor's in Fourteenth Street, and was closed about the first of December, 1878. However, within a few weeks it was remodeled and reopened as a dance hall, which it remained to the end of its days.

The Haymarket was housed in a three-story brick and frame building, which by day was dismal and repulsive, for it was painted a dull and sulphurous yellow and showed no signs of life. But with the coming of dusk, as the performers in Satan's Circus assembled for their nightly promenade of Sixth avenue, the shutters were removed and lights blazed from every window, while from huge iron hooks before the main entrance hung a sign, "Haymarket—Grand Soiree Dansant." Women were admitted free, but men paid twenty-five cents each for the privilege of dancing, drinking and otherwise disporting themselves within the resort. The galleries and boxes which had extended around three sides of the main floor when the house was a theater were retained, and off them were built small cubicles in which, at the height of the Haymarket's glory, women habitues danced the cancan and gave exhibitions similar to the French peep shows. The descriptive title of "circus," which is now generally applied to such displays in this country, is said to have originated in the Haymarket. The dictionary defines the cancan as "a rollicking French dance, accompanied by indecorous or extravagant gestures," but it appears to have been much more than rollicking as performed in the old Haymarket, especially during the early morning hours when the place was hazy with smoke and the tables and floors filled with drunken revellers, among whom lush workers and pickpockets plied nimble fingers. In more recent years the cancan has given way to the hoochy-coochy and other forms of muscle dancing, which first became popular with the appearance of the original Little Egypt at the Chicago World's Fair.

The French Madame's, in Thirty-first Street near Sixth Avenue, took its name from the nationality of its proprietor, an obese, bewhiskered female who sat throughout the night on a high stool near the cashier's cage. She acted as her own bouncer, and acquired great renown for the manner in which she wielded a bludgeon, and for the quickness with which she seized obstreperous women customers by the hair and flung them into the street. While the resort was ostensibly a restaurant, practically no food except black coffee was sold, although a big business was done in wines and liquors. The place was much frequented by the street women, who readily accepted offers to dance the cancan, which was performed in small chambers above the dining-room. For a dollar they danced nude, and for an additional small fee gave exhibitions similar to those provided in the booths of the Haymarket. Resorts similar to the French Madame's, except that they had small dance floors, were the Idlewile in Sixth Avenue near Thirty-first Street, and the Strand, a few doors south, which was operated by Dan Kerrigan, a member of the Tammany Hall General Committee during the late seventies. The Rev. T. DeWitt Talmage spent an evening in each of these places in 1878, and raised such a furore with his sermons that the police, upon orders from Mayor Cooper, closed them to women for a period of several months.

Other famous dives of the Satan's Circus district were the Cremorne, in Thirty-second Street west of Sixth Avenue; Egyptian Hall in Thirty-fourth Street, east of Sixth Avenue; Sailors' Hall in Thirtieth Street, which was frequented principally by Negroes; Buckingham Palace in Twenty-seventh Street, noted for its masked balls; Tom Gould's in Thirty-first Street, a drinking dive with rooms for rent upstairs, and the Star and Garter, an establishment of a slightly higher class which was opened at Sixth Avenue and Thirtieth Street in 1878 by Ed Coffee, a famous sportsman of the period. The Star and Garter enjoyed an immediate success, largely because of the popularity of the head bartender,

Billy Patterson, a rotund and jovial genius who was one of the really great drink mixers of the age. It was his boast that he did not have an enemy in the world, and that he could concoct a drink which would make any man his abject admirer; it was a great honor to have Billy Patterson, in person, prepare a beverage. When he was finally struck down by a mysterious assailant who attacked him with a slung-shot one night as he left the side door of the Star and Garter, the circumstance caused so much comment throughout Satan's Circus that it gave rise to the famous query, "Who struck Billy Patterson?"

The Cremorne occupied the basement of a building in Thirty-second Street just west of Sixth Avenue, and was regarded by the police as one of the most abandoned dives of the period. The origin of its name is unknown, but it is likely that, in common with many other resorts of the district, it was named for a London dance-hall or barroom. The street entrance led directly to the bar, at the end of which, behind a large and handsomely carved desk, sat the manager, a huge, pompous, unapproachable personage whose great walrus mustaches and luxuriant beard gave him the sobriquet of Don Whiskerandos. Beyond the manager swinging doors opened into a large room, garishly decorated with paintings and statues noted more for nudity than artistic merit, where men and women sat together at tables and drank to the accompaniment of music from a squeaky violin, a booming bull fiddle and a rattling piano. The women here, as in most of the other resorts, received a commission on all drinks; small brass checks were given them for mixed beverages and straight liquors, and when wine was bought by their friends they saved the corks. Drinks for ladies were twenty cents, but gentlemen paid the standard price of fifteen cents or two for a quarter. Next door to the Cremorne was another establishment which bore the same name, but it was a mission conducted by Jerry McAuley, a reformed gambler and drunkard whose name has been immortalized by the present McAuley Mission in Water Street, where religion and sandwiches are now available nightly for the bums of the water front. Befuddled customers of the dive frequently wandered into McAuley's Cremorne by mistake, whereupon he promptly locked the doors and preached to the roisterers before he would permit them to resume their round of dissipation.

A new type of resort, the concert saloon, appeared in New York in 1860, when a Philadelphian opened the Melodeon in the old Chinese Assembly Rooms in lower Broadway. These places soon became very popular, and within a few years there were at least two hundred of them scattered throughout the lower part of the city. They provided dancing and liquor, but the principal attractions were the waiter girls and the low, and frequently lewd, theatrical performances, although some of the cheaper establishments, especially those along the Bowery, offered as entertainment only a piano virtuoso, who was always drunk and was called Professor.

The most celebrated of these resorts was that operated by Harry Hill in West Houston Street east of Broadway. For many years Hill's place was rightly considered one of the sights of the metropolis, to which visiting clergymen repaired to gather material for sermons on the iniquities of Gotham. It occupied the whole of a sprawling, dingy, two-story frame house, which had two front entrances, a small door for ladies, who were admitted free, and a larger one for gentlemen, who paid twenty cents. Before the main doorway a huge red and blue lantern shed its rays against a gigantic sign-board which leaned against the side of the house, and upon which were lettered half a dozen lines of doggerel, composed by Hill and inviting the wayfarer to partake of

> Punches and juleps, cobblers and smashes,
> To make the tongue waggle with wit's merry flashes.

Harry Hill prided himself on his religious habits, and went to church regularly every Sunday, and to prayer meeting on Wednesday night; and frequently donated large sums to charity, as evidence of his willingness to co-operate in good works. He was an inveterate poet, and once a week mounted the stage and gave a recital of his output, while the other activities of the resort ceased, not even drinks being served until the master had finished. It is distressing to note that on this night the attendance was generally very slim. The rules of the house were written in rhyme, and were prominently displayed upon the walls. "The pith of these rules is," says a contemporary writer, "no loud talking; no profanity; no obscene or indecent expressions will be allowed; no one drunken, no one violating decency, will be permitted to remain in the room; no man can sit and allow a woman to stand; all men must call for refreshments as soon as they arrive, and the call must be repeated after each dance; if a man does not dance he must leave. Mr. Hill himself is a man about fifty years of age, small, stocky and muscular, a complete type of the pugilist. He keeps the peace of his own concern, and does not hesitate to knock any man down, or throw him out of the door, if he breaks the rules of the establishment. He attends closely to all departments of the trade. He is at the bar; in the hall, where the dancers must be kept on the floor; at the stage, where the low comedies and broad farces are played. He keeps the roughs and bullies in order; he keeps jealous women from tearing out each other's eyes. With burly face and stocky form, he can be seen in all parts of the hall, shouting out, 'Order! Order! Less noise there! Attention! Girls, be quiet!' And these he shouts all evening."

The dance hall proper had originally been a series of small rooms, which had been made into one by the removal of partitions. There was no regular bar on the main floor, but on one side of the long hall was a counter over which drinks were served, and from which they were distributed by the waiter girls after they had been brought up from the basement, where the more disreputable of Hill's customers spent their evenings in sorry debauch. On the other side of the room was the stage, with a tall box for the Punch and Judy show which was then a popular form of entertainment. Hill's place was a favorite resort of pugilists, and he frequently varied his theatrical entertainment with a prize fight. It was there that John L. Sullivan made his first New York appearance on March 31, 1881, when he defeated Steve Taylor in two and one-half minutes.

Harry Hill competed, on more or less even terms, with such celebrated downtown hells as the American Mabille at Bleecker Street and Broadway, the Black and Tan in the basement of No. 153 Bleecker Street, and Billy McGlory's Armory Hall at No. 158 Hester Street. The American Mabille, which was named for the Jardin de Mabille in Paris, was owned by Theodore Allen, better known as The Allen, member of a family which was originally devoutly Methodist but later notoriously criminal. Three of his brothers, Wesley, Martin, and William, were professional burglars, while a fourth, John, ran a gambling house. The Allen is said to have owned more than half a dozen resorts, and financed gambling houses and places of ill-fame. He was also a friend and patron of the gang leaders, and planned and participated in a large number of bank and store burglaries. He finally killed a gambler and disappeared from the scene. His resort occupied the basement and first floor of the Bleecker Street house, with a dance hall in the basement and the concert saloon upstairs, where dissolute women in gaudy tights danced and sang ribald songs.

The Black and Tan was operated by Frank Stephenson, a tall, slim man with a curiously bloodless face. Contemporary writers marked his resemblance to a corpse; his face was almost as white as snow and his cheeks were sunken, while his eyebrows and hair were black as ink. His eyes were deep set, and very keen and piercing. It was his custom to sit bolt upright in a high chair in the center of his resort, and remain there for hours without displaying any other sign of life than the baleful glitter of his eyes. His establishment was largely frequented by Negroes, but the women were all white and appear to have been quite abandoned. Four bartenders served drinks over a long counter, and behind each was a long dirk and a bludgeon which were frequently used to silence fractious customers. The closing hours of the Black and Tan, as of the other principal resorts, were enlivened by the cancan and licentious displays. For many years one of the regular frequenters of the Black and Tan was an old woman known as Crazy Lou, who was said to have been a daughter of a wealthy Boston merchant. At the age of seventeen she was seduced, and coming to New York to seek the author of her shame, fell into the hands of procurers, who sold her to one of the Seven Sisters in West Twenty-fifth Street. When her beauty faded she was dismissed, and thereafter became a frequenter of the Haymarket, the Cremorne, Harry Hill's, Billy McGlory's and finally the Black and Tan. In her old age she lived on scrapings from garbage pails, and the few pennies she could beg or earn by selling flowers. But each evening she went regularly to the Black and Tan, arriving promptly at midnight and remaining for exactly two hours. She wore a faded, ragged shawl, and always sat at a certain table in a corner, where Stephenson in person served her with a huge tumbler of whiskey which cost her nothing. This she sipped until the time came for her to leave. But one night she failed to appear, and the next morning her body was found floating in the East River. Stephenson expressed his sorrow by setting a glass of whiskey on her accustomed table each night at midnight for a month, permitting no one to sit there until two o'clock in the morning.

All of these dives were havens of grace compared to Billy McGlory's Armory Hall at No. 158 Hester Street, for McGlory's was probably the most vicious resort New York has ever seen. McGlory was born in a Five Points tenement before that district had been regenerated by the Five Points Mission and the House of Industry, and was reared in an atmosphere of vice and crime. In his youth he fought with and captained such famous gangs as the Forty Thieves and the Chichesters, but in the late seventies removed to Hester Street, where he opened his dance hall and drinking den in the midst of a squalid tenement district which fairly swarmed with criminals and harlots. Armory Hall became the favorite haunt of the gangsters of the Fourth and Sixth Wards and the Bowery, and of the thieves, pickpockets, procurers and knockout drop artists who flourished throughout the city. Scarcely a night passed that the resort was not the scene of half a dozen gory fights; and it was not unusual to see a drugged and drunken reveller, his pockets turned inside out by the harpies who had fawned upon him but a few minutes before, dragged from a table by one of McGlory's capable bouncers and lugged into the street, where his pockets were searched anew by the lush workers. Frequently the latter stripped the victim of his clothing and left him naked in the gutter. The thugs who kept the peace of McGlory's were all graduates of the Five Points and water front gangs, and included some of the most expert rough-and-tumble fighters of the period; throughout the night they strode menacingly about the dive, armed with pistols, knives, brass knuckles, and bludgeons which they delighted to use.

McGlory's place was entered from the street through a dingy double doorway, which led into a long, narrow passageway with walls painted a dead black, unrelieved by a gas light or splash of color. Fifty feet down the passage was the bar-room, and beyond that the dance hall with chairs and tables for some seven hundred persons. A balcony ran around two sides of the hall, with small boxes partitioned off by heavy curtains and reserved for the best customers, generally parties of out-of-town men who appeared to be willing to spend considerable money. In these boxes were given exhibitions even more degraded than at the Haymarket. Drinks were served by waiter girls, but as an added attraction McGlory also employed half a dozen male degenerates who wore feminine clothing and circulated through the crowd, singing and dancing. Music was provided by a piano, a cornet and a violin. A night in McGlory's was thus described by a writer for the *Cincinnati Enquirer,* who went slumming, or as it was then called, elephant hunting, among the dives of New York in the early eighties:

> There are five hundred men in the immense hall. There are a hundred females—it would be mockery to call them women. The first we hear of them is when half a dozen invade our box, plump themselves on our laps and begin to beg that we put quarters in their stockings for luck. There are some shapely limbs generously and immodestly shown in connection with this invitation. One young woman startles the crowd by announcing that she will dance the cancan for half a dollar. The music starts up just then, and she determines to do the cancan and risk the collection afterward. She seizes her skirts between her limbs with one

hand, kicks away a chair or two, and is soon throwing her feet in the air in a way that endangers every hat in the box. The men about the hall are all craning their necks to get a sight of what is going on in the box, as they hear the cries of "Hoop-la!" from the girls there.

Some of my companions have been drawn into one of the little boxes adjoining ours. They come back now to tell of what depravity was exhibited to them for a fee. . . . It is getting late. Across the balcony a girl is hugging her fellow in a maudlin and hysterical manner. Another girl is hanging with her arms around the neck of one of the creatures I described some time ago. His companion joins him—a moon-faced fellow—and they come around to our box and ogle us. They talk in simpering, dudish tones, and bestow the most lackadaisical glances on different members of our party. . . . Billy McGlory himself is at the bar, to the left of the entrance, and we go and take a look at him. He is a typical New York saloon keeper—nothing more, nothing less. A medium sized man, he is neither fleshy nor spare; he has black hair and mustache, and a piercing black eye. He shakes hands around as if we were obedient subjects come to pay homage to a king. . . . I have not told the half, no, nor the tenth, of what we saw at his place. It cannot be told. . . . There is beastliness and depravity under his roof compared with which no chapter in the world's history is equal.

Many of the most depraved of the downtown dives were in the vicinity of Police Headquarters at No. 300 Mulberry Street. Half a block from Headquarters was a gambling house which catered only to policemen, and at No. 100 Mott Street, a short distance away, was a saloon kept by Mike Kerrigan, better known as Johnny Dobbs, who served an apprenticeship with the river pirates of the Fourth Ward and then became a celebrated bank robber and fence. Dobbs is said to have handled more than $2,000,000 in stolen money, of which probably one-third went to him as his share of various adventures. But he ran through it, and eventually, in the middle nineties, was found unconscious in the gutter, and died in the alcoholic ward of Bellevue Hospital a few days later. It was Johnny Dobbs who, when asked why the crooks flocked to the neighborhood of Police Headquarters, replied, "The nearer the church the closer to God."

Tom Bray operated a similar resort at No. 22 Thompson Street, but he was a more intelligent man than Dobbs, and banked his money, so that when he died he left an estate of more than $200,000. The House of Lords and the Bunch of Grapes, neighboring dives at Houston and Crosby Streets, were much frequented by English thieves and confidence men. Among them were such famous crooks as Chelsea George, Gentleman Joe, Cockney Ward and London Izzy Lazarus, who was killed by Barney Friery in a dispute over the division of a plug hat full of jewelry, which London Izzy had stolen from a jewelry store after smashing the show window with a brick. The St. Bernard Hotel at Prince and Mercer Streets was one of The Allen's resorts, and along Broadway from Chambers to Houston Streets were at least fifty basement drinking dens, of which the Dew Drop Inn was the most famous. At Broadway and Houston street, near Harry Hill's concert saloon, was Patsy Egan's dive, where Reddy the Blacksmith, a celebrated Bowery Boy, killed Wild Jimmy Hagerty, a Philadelphia gangster who had tried to make Reddy the Blacksmith stand on his head. Reddy was a brother to Mary Varley, a notorious shoplifter, confidence woman and fence, who kept a house in James Street.

Peter Mitchell amassed more than $350,000 in two years, from the profits of a saloon and assignation house at Wooster and Prince Streets, but hanged himself to a whiskey tap before he could spend his fortune. He is said to have become religious in his middle age, and thereafter was afflicted with remorse over the way he had acquired his fortune. Johnny Camphine kept one of the most notorious dives in the city at Mercer and Houston Streets, and in lieu of whiskey commonly sold colored camphine, or rectified oil of turpentine, which had its legitimate uses as a solvent for varnishes and as a fuel for lamps. It has been said that at least a hundred men were driven insane by drinking Johnny Camphine's beverage, and over a long period an average of two men a night were taken out of the place, howling with delirium tremens. Within a few doors of Johnny Camphine's place was a resort owned by a thief and gang leader called Big Nose Bunker, who was accounted one of the great brawlers and rough-and-tumble fighters of his time. But at last he became embroiled in a fight with a water front gangster who chopped off four of his fingers and stabbed him six times in the stomach. Big Nose carried his fingers to the police station in a paper bag and asked that a surgeon be sent for to sew them on, but before an ambulance could arrive he collapsed and died. There was great sorrow throughout the underworld.

The reputation of the Bowery and the Five Points did not suffer from the fame of the resorts around Headquarters and in Satan's Circus along Sixth Avenue. Owney Geogheghan operated his celebrated dive at No. 105 Bowery, and next door at No. 103 was the Windsor Palace, owned by an Englishman and named in honor of the residence of Their Britannic Majesties. Both of these places were hells of exceptional fragrance, wherein raw whiskey was sold for ten cents a drink and crowds of lush workers, pickpockets and blackjack artists waited for a visitor to fall unconscious so they could rob him. Murders were frequent in both Geogheghan's and the Palace. Gunther's Pavillion was another celebrated Bowery dive, and Bismarck Hall, at Pearl and Chatham Streets, was noted for its annex, a series of cave-like rooms under the sidewalk, which were used for immoral purposes. The Hall acquired further renown when the Grand Duke Alexis of Russia visited it in the seventies and recognized one of the waiter girls as a Russian countess who had fallen into misfortune. The legend goes that he bought her freedom from the owner of the dive, to whom she had bound herself for a term of years, and took her back to Russia. Accounts of the incident do not divulge her name. Bismarck Hall and the House of Commons, nearby, were also the haunts of a Bowery character called Ludwig the Bloodsucker, who quaffed human blood as if it were wine. Ludwig was a very squat, swarthy German, with an enormous head crowned with a shock of bristly black hair. Huge bunches of hair grew out of his ears, and his unusual appearance was accentuated by another tuft which sprouted from the end of his nose.

Milligan's Hell was at No. 115 Broome Street, and on Center Street, near the Tombs, Boiled Oysters Malloy ran a basement resort called the Ruins, where three drinks of terrible whiskey were sold for a dime. Mush Riley added to the fame of the district with a dive only a few doors away. Riley acquired his nickname because of a fondness for corn meal mush dipped in hot brandy. He once gave an elaborate dinner to Dan Noble, Mike Byrnes, Dutch Heinrichs and other famous criminals, and served a Newfoundland dog as the *pièce de résistance*, a fact unknown to his guests until they had eaten heartily and praised the unusual flavor of the roast. Noble was chief of a gang of bank robbers and burglars, and to insure the success of his operations cannily obtained places for twenty of his men on the police force. They stood guard for their fellow criminals, and received shares out of the common funds. Noble finally reformed and invested his money in apartment houses.

The dives which flourished around Police Headquarters and along the Bowery were favorite resorts of the pickpockets, sneaks, panel thieves, badger game experts, lush workers, and knock-out-drop artists who operated in great numbers throughout the city. They also offered excellent business opportunities to the gangs of banco, confidence, and green goods men, for this was the period when countrymen actually bought gold bricks and counterfeit money, and were easy prey for the accomplished city slickers. The gold brick game, perhaps the most celebrated of all swindles, is supposed to have been invented by Reed Waddell, who was born in Springfield, Illinois, a few years before the Civil War. Waddell was a member of a prosperous and highly respectable family, but the gambling fever was in his veins, and even in his boyhood he acquired considerable local fame because of his willingness to take chances and the recklessness with which he played for high stakes. His family soon cast him off, and in 1880, when he was but twenty-one, he appeared in New York with the first gold brick ever offered for sale. Waddell's brick was of lead, but he had it triple gold-plated with a rough finish, and in the center sunk a slug of solid gold. It was marked in the manner of a regulation brick from the United States Assayer's office, with the letters "U.S." at one end and below them the name of the assayer. Underneath the name appeared the weight and fineness of the supposed chunk of bullion. When Waddell caught a sucker he was taken to an accomplice who posed as an assayer, with an office and all necessary equipment to delude the victim. This man tested the brick, and if the prospect was still dubious Waddell impulsively dug out the slug of real gold and suggested that the dupe himself take it to a jeweller. The latter's test, of course, showed the slug to be actually of precious metal, and in ninety-nine cases out of a hundred the sale was completed. Waddell sold his first brick for four thousand dollars, and thereafter never sold one for less than three thousand five hundred dollars. Sometimes he obtained twice that amount. In ten years he is said to have made more than $250,000 by the sale of gold bricks and green goods, for he branched out into the latter scheme after a few years of concentrated effort on the bricks. The green goods swindle, which was also called the sawdust game, first made its appearance in New York in 1869. It required two operators, who simply sold the victim a package of genuine money and then exchanged it for a bundle of worthless sheets of green or brown paper, or, if the currency was packed in a satchel, for another bag filled with sawdust. The green goods man first obtained the names of people who were regular subscribers to lotteries and various gift book concerns, and agents were sent over the country to look up the most promising. In due time those chosen for the sacrifice received one of several circular letters which were in general use, of which the following was the most popular:

• • •

Dear Sir: I will confide to you through this circular a secret by which you can make a speedy fortune. I have on hand a large amount of counterfeit notes of the following denominations: $1, $2, $5, $10 and $20. I guarantee every note to be perfect, as it is examined carefully by me as soon as finished, and if not strictly perfect is immediately destroyed. Of course it would be perfectly foolish to send out poor work, and it would not only get my customers into trouble, but would break up my business and ruin me. So, for personal safety, I am compelled to issue nothing that will not compare with the genuine. I furnish you with my goods at the following low price, which will be found as reasonable as the nature of my business will allow:

For $1,200 in my goods (assorted) I charge	$100
For $2,500 in my goods (assorted) I charge	200
For $5,000 in my goods (assorted) I charge	350
For $10,000 in my goods (assorted) I charge	600

These circulars, as well as follow-up letters and other literature, were sent boldly through the mails. Some of the green goods swindlers prepared elaborate booklets, illustrated with photographs of bank notes, which the prospective victim was told were counterfeit.

In time Reed Waddell extended his operations to Europe, and was killed in Paris in March, 1895, during a dispute over the division of earnings with Tom O'Brien, a banco man whose only peers were Joseph Lewis, better known as Hungry Joe, and Charles P. Miller, who was called King of the Banco Men. Miller began his career as capper for a New Orleans gambling house, but came to New York when he had saved thirty-five thousand dollars, and opened a small house of chance which was notorious as a skinning dive. Within a few years he was chief of a gang of banco and green goods men who worked principally in the Astor House and the Fifth Avenue Hotel. Miller's headquarters were a lamp-post on the southwest corner of Broadway and Twenty-eighth

Street, against which he could generally be found leaning. In later years the term barico was confused by hurried writers with Buncombe or bunkum, and so degenerated into bunco, and was applied indiscriminately to every type of swindler; but originally it referred only to the operator of banco, an adaptation of the old English gambling pastime of eight dice cloth. Banco was introduced into the United States by a noted sharper who played it with great success in the western gold fields, and brought it into New York about 1860, after he had been driven out of San Francisco by the Vigilantes. Sometimes it was also called lottery. A variation of it was recently introduced in Chicago, but it has been unheard of in New York for many years.

The game was played either with dice or cards. If the former, a layout of fourteen spaces was used, but if the latter the layout contained forty-three spaces. Of these forty-two were numbered, thirteen contained stars also, and one was blank. Twenty-nine of the numbers represented prizes ranging from two dollars, to five thousand dollars, depending upon the size of the bank. The cards were numbered from one to six, and eight were dealt to each player. The numbers were then counted, the total representing the number of the prize drawn on the layout. If the victim drew a star number, which had no prize, he was allowed to draw again on putting up a specified sum of money. He was usually permitted to win at first, and eventually the bank owed him from one hundred dollars to five thousand dollars. He was then dealt a hand which totaled twenty-seven, the number of the conditional prize, the condition being that he stake a sum equal to the amount owed him and draw again. Then, of course, he drew a blank or star number and lost all he had put up. The banco steerer, who performed an office similar to that of capper for a gambling house, lost also, and it was his duty to cause such an uproar that the woes of the victim were overwhelmed. The swindle sounds a bit silly to our modern ears, but it was much in vogue for years throughout the United States and many of the banco men amassed fortunes. Hungry Joe, Tom O'Brien and Miller specialized in bankers, wealthy merchants, and other people of prominence, for not only did they have more money to lose, but were less apt to complain to the police. Hungry Joe scraped acquaintance with Oscar Wilde when the English author visited the United States on a lecture tour, and after dining with him several times at the Hotel Brunswick, inveigled him into a banco game. Wilde lost five thousand dollars, and gave Hungry Joe a check on the Park National Bank, but stopped payment when he learned that he had been swindled. Hungry Joe's own boastful account of the affair, however, was that he took one thousand five hundred dollars in cash from the writer.

The late sixties also saw the beginning of the reprehensible practice of using knock-out drops to deaden the senses of a victim while the thieves picked his pockets or appropriated his jewelry. Laudanum had occasionally been employed by the crimps of the old Fourth Ward water front to drug a sailor so he could be shanghaied without too much protest, but no effective use of drugs for the sole purpose of robbery was made in New York until a California crook, Peter Sawyer, appeared in 1866, and aroused such a furore in police and criminal circles that the former honored him by calling the practitioners of his art peter players. At first Sawyer used nothing more deleterious than snuff, which he dropped into his victim's beer or whiskey, but later he and other peter players came to depend principally on hydrate of chloral. Occasionally they used morphine. Since Prohibition bootleg liquor has generally been found to be sufficiently efficacious.

The medicinal dose of hydrate of chloral is from fifteen to twenty grains, but from thirty to forty grains were used for knock-out purposes. The drug was compounded in the proportion of one grain to a drop, and a teaspoonful was commonly employed to dose a glass of beer. The action of the drug is to decrease the action of the heart, and an overdose is apt to cause paralysis of the heart and lungs. Few men can stand a larger dose than thirty grains, but occasionally the old time peter players were compelled to give up to sixty grains to a victim who had been drinking heavily.

The practice of using knock-out drops became so popular that large gangs of both men and women thieves were formed, and employed no other method to prepare a victim for robbery. They generally worked in pairs, and while one distracted the attention of the dupe the other dropped the poison into his beverage. For many years the police seldom arrested a street walker who did not have chloral or morphine in her purse or secreted in the lining of her muff. The largest and most successful of the knock-out gangs maintained a headquarters in a dive in Worth Street near Chatham Square, at the southern end of the Bowery, employing street boys to trail well-dressed men who ventured into the territory and notify members of the gang when the visitors appeared to be ready for the final touches. More than a score of men amassed fortunes from the sale of small vials of chloral at two dollars each, but eventually the bulk of the business fell into the hands of Diamond Charley, a notorious Bowery character whose shirt front blazed with precious stones in the manner of the later but respectable Diamond Jim Brady. Each evening at dusk Diamond Charley sent out a dozen salesmen carrying small satchels packed with vials of chloral, which they sold openly in the dives and on the street corners. They also offered a small morphine pill which could be hidden under a finger ring, but it would not dissolve readily and was never in great demand. Soon after he had obtained a monopoly Diamond Charley increased the price of chloral to five dollars and then to ten dollars a vial, to the great indignation of the users of the drops, for the cost of manufacturing a dose was not more than six cents. Thereafter many of the thieves compounded their own mixtures, and in their eagerness for quick action added other poisons to the chloral, frequently with fatal consequences which worried no one except the police and the victim's relatives.

Knock-out drops were also used with great success by the cadets and procurers, who conducted their business with the utmost brazenness. Many of the former were organized into associations, and maintained club rooms, where they met for discussion of business problems; while the latter frequently operated from elaborate offices. Red Light Lizzie, perhaps the most famous procurer of her time, employed half a dozen men and women to travel through the small villages of New York and adjacent states, and lure young women into the metropolis with promises of employment; and several young men received salaries from her for enticing girls into dives and plying them with drugged liquor. Red Light Lizzie herself owned half a dozen houses of ill-fame, but she supplied other places as well, and each month sent a circular letter to her clients. Her principal rival was Hester Jane Haskins, also called Jane the Grabber, who became notorious as an abductor of young girls for immoral purposes. She came at length to specialize in young women of good families, and the disappearance of so many aroused such a commotion that in the middle seventies Jane the Grabber was arrested by Captain Charles McDonnell and sent to prison.

The procurers also obtained many recruits from the flower and news girls who were about the streets in great numbers. Many of these, some no more than children, were prostitutes on their own account, and there were half a dozen places of assignation which catered solely to them. The owner of one such establishment advertised that her place was frequented by flower girls under sixteen years of age; another kept nine small girls, ranging in age from nine to fifteen, in the back room of an oyster saloon near the corner of Chatham Street, now Park Row, and William Street. It was the custom of these girls to approach a man in the street, and instead of asking him to purchase flowers or newspapers, hail him with "Give me a penny, mister?" For several years this was the common salutation of the street girls, and the manner in which the more dissolute of the flower and news vendors made known their calling.

Many of the girls were also members of the panel and badger game gangs which abounded throughout the vice area. These methods of thievery were brought to great perfection by the gang captained by Shang Draper, who kept a saloon in Sixth avenue between Twenty-ninth and Thirteenth Streets. Draper is said to have employed thirty women on salary to entice drunken men into a house in the vicinity of Prince and Wooster Streets, where they were victimized by the badger game or robbed by thieves who crept into the room through hidden panels cut into the wall, and stole the victim's valuables while his attention was distracted. Draper's gang was finally broken up by Captain John H. McCullagh, although he continued to operate his saloon until late in 1883, when Johnny Irving was killed in a pistol duel with Johnny Walsh, better known as Johnny the Mick, who was immediately shot to death by Irving's friend, Billy Porter. Irving and Walsh were captains of rival gangs of sneak thieves and pickpockets, and there had been bad blood between them for many years. Draper himself was also a famous bank robber, and was implicated in the celebrated robbery of the Manhattan Savings Institution, as well as many other crimes.

from Low Life: Lures and Snares of Old New York

by Luc Sante

Luc Sante's (born 1954) 1991 book about New York City circa 1840–1920 calls to mind the earlier work of Herbert Asbury. Sante read and admired Asbury's The Gangs of New York *when the book was an out-of-print cult classic. This selection from* Low Life *is about the coppers who patrolled the city's streets, knocking heads and protecting property owners.*

The history of the New York police is not a particularly illustrious one, at least in the nineteenth and early twentieth centuries, as throughout the period the law-enforcement agents of the city continually and recurrently demonstrated corruption, complacency, confusion, sloth, and brutality. Conventionally defined, the police existed to keep the peace, to protect the population, to enforce the laws that had been passed for the common good of all. In truth, however, the police were squeezed by the city's power structure into a position where peace was a relative term, where protection of one part of the population was carried out at the expense of another, and where the meaning of laws shifted according to whoever was in a position to interpret them. Thus, the police became a repressive and profit-gathering force halfway between gangsters and politicians, having to serve as interpreters between the two. They were expected to be stern

and benevolent at once, or perhaps stern with the poor and benevolent to what was held as the respectable part of society, and this con-
tradiction led to the extremes of viciousness and indolence. They were
intended to be the pure element in a system that was corrupt from top
to bottom, while simultaneously being underpaid, expected to render
financial homage to those who did them favors and to enforce the
terms of the graft passed between other levels of society. At times they
seemed like gangsters in uniform, and at times, particularly in the
slums, like a capricious local government in which they combined
the legislative, executive, and judicial branches. Cops felt that they
had the choice of inspiring jokes or inspiring fear, of starvation or
extortion, of being treated as servants by the rich or as the enemy by
the poor, of upholding moral standards or of upholding the standards
temporarily raised at the whim of power and fashion. It is not terribly
surprising that, in each case, most cops chose the latter option.

For the first two centuries or so of the city's existence the police
were managed under the lines of the old Dutch constabulary. There
was no outward means of distinguishing them, but in the small city
of the time they were known to one and all. Jacob Hays, who served
as High Constable in the early nineteenth century, was the first to
devise a method of identification for the police, assigning them five-
pointed stars—brass ones for patrolmen, silver stars for lieutenants
and captains, and a gold star for the office of Commissioner. Sergeants
were given a copper star, hence the ancient refrain "Tell it to the
copper." Mayor James Harper (1844–45) introduced uniforms to the
force, featuring long coats distinguished by brass buttons. These outfits got their premiere at the Bowery Theater fire of 1845, but the
b'hoys laughed at them, saying the cops were trying to imitate London
bobbies, and the uniforms faded away for another decade, although
some compromise was reached by putting leather badges on the cops'
hats. Cops were then called "leatherheads," immediately resulting in
the phrase "as lazy as a leatherhead." In those days, the police had
little effect on the gangs and little impact on the slums. Their major
function was to enforce laws of nicety for the benefit of the upper

classes. Hence, they spent their time arresting drunks, "lewd women," beggars unless they were disabled, persons sleeping outdoors or in public places, persons driving in the streets in excess of five miles an hour. They also forced street peddlers to obtain licenses. For all this, cops were paid $500 a year.

Policemen were appointed by aldermen and assistant aldermen until 1853, when the legislature formed the Board of Police Commissions, made up of the mayor, the city recorder, and the city judge. The only major difference this made was to determine who would get the graft. The average patrolman paid a $40 bribe to the captain of the precinct he desired to work in, and another $150 to $200 to the politician of his choice. Captains, who were paid up to $1,000 a year, were expected to pay out a minimum of $200 for their appointment. Although it would be decades before reform sweeps and boards of inquiry began to look into the complex economics of the city's system of graft, it should be clear that an investment on such a scale would necessarily require that the profit potential of the job should offset its expense. In addition, cops were expected to serve as bagmen and go-betweens, handling payoffs from businessmen to their superiors, and from their superiors, in turn, to politicians. Joke laws ostensibly governing the duties of the police were passed at various times. In 1846 the first rules of departmental conduct were established, embodied in a ninety-page document that few read and no one, apparently, followed; in 1853 an attempt was made to prohibit cops from taking part in partisan political activities, but nothing came of it.

In the same year the state legislature, alarmed by the degree to which the city had become an independent, semi-feudal regime under Mayor Fernando Wood, passed an act forming a Metropolitan Police Force, which would have jurisdiction over Manhattan, Brooklyn, the Bronx, Staten Island, and Westchester County. Governor Horatio Seymour established a new Police Board, and Frederick Talmage, a former City Recorder, was named Superintendent of the force. Wood was ordered to disband his Municipal Police Force, but he refused. Matters were deadlocked in practice and in the courts until 1857, when the

Supreme Court ruled the act forming the new force to be constitutional. Wood continued to stand firm, backed by Municipal Superintendent G.W. Matsell. The powerful Captain George W. Walling, who
had formed the Strong Arm Squad and begun the practice of using
plainclothesmen, went over to the Metropolitan camp and began orga-
nizing a force. In June, a month after the Supreme Court's decision,
both Daniel D. Conover, who had been appointed by Governor John
A. King, and Charles Devlin, who had been appointed by Wood for a
rumored fee of $50,000, simultaneously attempted to assume the
office of State Commissioner. Wood had his cops eject Conover, who
in turn obtained a warrant for Wood's arrest. Walling went to serve it,
and physically seized Wood and began dragging him out of City Hall,
but was intercepted at the door by a party of Municipal cops, who
pried him loose from Wood and threw him out. Then a detachment of
fifty Metropolitans, in frock coats and plug hats, came marching down
Chambers Street from their White Street headquarters, intent on cap-
turing Wood. They were met by the Municipals on the front steps of
City Hall and a half-hour riot ensued. Before the Metropolitans were
turned away, fifty-two cops had been hurt, one of them permanently
invalided. Finally, some Metropolitans spotted the Seventh Regiment
of the National Guard boarding a boat for Boston and persuaded them
to delay their departure. As the troops surrounded City Hall, their
commander, Major General Charles Sandford, marched into Wood's
office. When Wood looked out the window and saw the military presence, he backed down and let himself be arrested. This did not end the
turmoil, however; for the rest of that summer the city was in a state of
chaos. Whenever a cop of one force made an arrest, a cop of the other
would set the culprit free, and the competing forces routinely raided
each other's station houses and freed en masse the prisoners in each
other's jails. In the fall the Court of Appeals affirmed the Supreme
Court's decision, and Wood was finally compelled to disband his
Municipal force. Around the same time the cops who had been injured
in the City Hall riot sued Wood personally for damages, and they were
awarded $850 apiece by the court, but Wood never paid, and the city

finally had to settle the matter with funds from its treasury. Ultimately, control of the police force was restored to the city by the 1870 charter finagled by the Tweed Ring.

The police force, as it was established in the Tweed years, covered Manhattan and the Bronx, the forces of the other boroughs being amalgamated after those boroughs were annexed in 1898. In the 1870s the force had four commissioners, who included the evergreen Matsell along with three professional politicians. The Superintendent was John Kelso, who, predictably enough, was the brother-in-law of a prominent person, while below him served four inspectors, thirty-two captains, sixty-four roundsmen (a designation more or less inter-changeable with lieutenant), 128 sergeants, and 2,085 miscellaneous patrolmen, detectives, doorkeepers, and the like. Each of the thirty-two precincts was headed by a captain; each had two platoons headed by roundsmen, and each platoon was divided into two sections headed by sergeants.

The duties of patrolmen were principally to keep a mental file of the population on their beat; to watch all visitors and intruders; to examine all doors, windows, and gates for proper locks and signs of tampering; and to be aware of all whorehouses and gambling houses and report the identities of parties frequenting them. They were appar-ently most assiduous at noticing the condition of locks, having in one decade spotted 40,000 houses left open at night. The principal crimes they were assigned to watch out for were public intoxication, mal-treatment of animals, interference with telegraph wires, the conducting of dogfights, cockfights, and prizefights, as well as of theatrical enter-tainments on Sundays, and potential and actual riots. They were not permitted to engage in casual conversation, even with each other. In the winter they were clothed in navy-blue frock coats and trousers, and in summer in sack coats and pants of navy flannel; on their heads they wore glazed caps (later in the decade these were experimentally replaced by high-crowned derbies in winter and Panama straws in summer, these in turn giving way to the high helmets that lasted until caps were restored in the teens). They were armed with revolvers and with billyclubs, which took the form of "day sticks" and the longer "night sticks." These were used not only to threaten potential derelicts and work over suspected malefactors but to summon their colleagues by means of sharp raps on the pavement. They were assigned complex schedules of duty and reserve that frequently kept them on their feet for thirty-six hours at a stretch, never fell the same way two days in succession, and gave them one day and one night off in every eight-day rotation. They went on foot except in the shantytown and semi-rural uptown precincts, where they rode horses. Their pay was meager; from the $500 annual salary of the 1840s, the starting wage had only gotten up to $800 by 1901, and out of this amount cops had to disburse for their own uniforms and equipment and they were additionally expected to contribute to police associations and to politically favored charities.

The motto banner of the 1870s was boldly emblazoned "Faithful Unto Death," and featured vignettes of cops at their various duties: chasing runaway carriage horses, being assaulted by thugs on the street, quelling a riot, arresting a footpad at night, guiding lost children, saving an old woman from a fire, saving a drowning man from a boat, standing up in court, and, rather mysteriously, laying hands on a man sitting peacefully in front of a stove. They did, apparently, restore 7,300 lost children in a nine-year period. This nevertheless failed to endear them to their charges in the poorer areas. A writer of the 1880s observed a representative scene:

> One Fourth of July morning, a few years ago, the writer of these pages was coming up Third avenue on a street car. Looking down East 35th street a singular sight presented itself. A platoon of police formed across the street was slowly retreating backward, with revolvers drawn and pointed, while two of their number held on to a rough looking prisoner, whom they carried along with them. Following them was a mob of several hundred ruffians, yelling, cursing, and occasionally throwing stones. Wishing to see the result, I sprang from the car and hurried to a

livery stable just opposite the Police station in 35th street, and about a hundred yards from Third avenue, from which I could see the whole affair. The police retreated slowly across Third avenue, and to the station house, into which they quickly disappeared with their prisoner. A cheer went up from the mob, and the ruffians thronged about the station as of intending to attack it. Immediately the doors were thrown open and the entire force on duty at the station dashed into the street, armed with their long night clubs and headed by their Captain. "Give them the locusts, men," came in sharp, ringing tones from the Captain, and without a word the force dashed at the mob, striking heads, arms, and shoulders, and in less time than it takes me to relate it, the ruffians were fleeing down the street and dispersing in all directions. Not all escaped, however, for each officer returned to the station with an ugly looking prisoner in his grasp.

Indiscriminate use of the night stick remained a police hallmark. Cornelius Willemse, who became a cop at the turn of the century after having worked as a bouncer and lunch man in Bowery saloons (he was originally refused entry to the force by then Commissioner Theodore Roosevelt on the grounds that "No one connected in the faintest way with the liquor traffic will ever be a policeman"), relates in his memoirs that he and his fellow recruits were lectured by a police instructor, Michael Smith:

"Men, when you get your nightsticks, they're intended to be used on thieves and crooks, but don't use them on inoffensive citizens. By no means strike a man on the head. The insane asylums are filled with men whose condition has been caused by a skull injury. Strike them over the arms and legs, unless you're dealing with real bad crooks. Then it doesn't make any difference whether they go to the insane asylum or to jail. They're enemies of society and our common foe.

"Protect the good people and treat the crooks rough. Thereby

you'll have the respect of your superiors and the citizens of New York. If there's danger, take a chance. The police of New York have a reputation you've got to uphold. Policemen make mistakes. They're human beings like everybody else, but we have no use for a coward. When you're in battle, and you'll be in plenty, go to work with your nightstick, but be sure to keep your back against a wall so they can't jump you from behind.

"You'll meet a lot of drunks who are poor, hard-working men. Don't lock them up. If they show fight, there are certain parts of the body where you won't break any bones. Don't lose your head when one of these fellows calls you names and you can make a great many friends on your post by giving them a square deal. Make a good friend of every business man and a bitter enemy of every crook, and you'll be a success on your post. If every policeman would do that, there'd be very little crime."

These pious sentiments were immediately contradicted by a desk sergeant, who reprimanded Willemse for bringing in suspects without working them over with his stick, but gave him a chance to square things by taking the culprits down to the station-house cellar. "There's more religion in the end of a nightstick," the sergeant told him, "than in any sermon preached to the likes of them." The victims of these tactics retaliated in various ways. Youth gangs in San Juan Hill at the turn of the century had a trick of extinguishing the gas lamps on a block, opening the coal chutes and sewer covers, and then yelling for the police, who would rush in and fall into the traps, resulting in injuries that were sometimes quite serious. The same stunt might be tried with a rope or wire stretched across the dark street, and there was the ever-popular option of pelting the cops with bottles and bricks from the rooftops.

The brutally long stretches of duty and reserve continued. Until 1902, when a three-platoon roster was inaugurated in the precincts, cops on reserve were confined to the station houses, where they could rest on cots in a dormitory. A typical such room held forty beds, placed eighteen inches apart, with scant ventilation and no shower facilities. The major perquisite was beer, sent up in cans from a saloon below by means of a clothesline. The station force was a social unit having much in common with a gang or a fraternity. Rookies, called "Goo Goos," were mercilessly hazed. The cops in the latter half of the nineteenth and for much of the early twentieth century were almost exclusively Irish. Germans, who were called "Dutch," and Anglo-Saxons, called "Narrow-backs," had a very hard time breaking into the ranks, and it was virtually impossible for members of other ethnic groups.

When cops made an arrest, the persons they had booked would be taken into holding pens in the station houses, these cells generally being adjacent to the homeless shelters (until Roosevelt eliminated the latter) in basements or annexes. The city's major prison, to which they would be removed in a closed wagon called a Black Maria, was the Tombs, situated on the block bounded by Centre and Elm (later Lafayette), Franklin and Leonard Streets, on the site of the island within the Collect Pond which had been used to stage whippings and hangings. The prison's official name was the Halls of Justice, but it had been modeled after an Egyptian mausoleum illustrated in the book of *Travels* published by John L. Stevens of Hoboken. It was built between 1835 and 1838, with subsequent additions over the years, and the whole thing was eventually condemned in 1938, though its last vestiges were not torn down until 1974. It was designed to hold some 350 prisoners, but the number constantly increased, until it held several thousands toward the end. It had an inner building and an outer building, separated by a yard in which executions were held and linked by a Bridge of Sighs, so called because it constituted the last walk for condemned prisoners. The executioner was always masked and anonymous; the longest-term holder of the office in the nineteenth century was known only to have once been a butcher's apprentice, and he was called Monsieur New York, or, more simply, George. Only officials and political patrons were invited to witness the hangings, but the public crowded onto the top floor of a neighboring building and craned their necks to look over the wall. The Tombs complex also included a women's prison, a boys' prison, a police court (one of several in the city), and a court of special sessions. There were minimum-security cells and infirmary cells, and a capacious vagrant and drunk tank on the Franklin Street side, known as Bummers' Hall. Prisoners were allowed to bring in their own furniture and carpets, presuming, of course, that they could afford to do so; in the front of the building were six cells reserved for the very rich. The main part of the Tombs was reserved for serious criminals (persons convicted of murder, armed robbery, felonious assault, and the like). It was the site of many successful escapes over the years, via windows, delivery wagons, forged passes, and disguises.

The city's federal prison was the Ludlow Street Jail, in which parties bound on federal charges were held in transit, including soldiers and National Guardsmen accused of crimes, but the place was most commonly used by creditors, who would have debtors locked up there on the pretext that they appeared ready to skip town. By the 1920s it was familiarly referred to as Alimony Jail. Petty criminals of all other sorts—petty thieves, drug addicts, morals offenders—were sent to Blackwell's Island. This long, narrow, 120-acre strip of land in the East River was bought by the city from the Blackwell family in 1829. A complex of social-welfare institutions was built there in addition to the prison, including an almshouse, a workhouse, pavilions for the insane, and a set of hospitals. It was renamed Welfare Island in 1929, and more recently Roosevelt Island when it was turned over to private developers, a transaction which left only two hospitals, as well as the ruins of some of the other buildings. The Blackwell's Island prison, sheltered from public view, was a grim and unsanitary place, always overcrowded, and noted for its various tortures, prominent among which were the "cooler" cells, the dousings by means of 120-pound-pressure fire hoses, and the "water drop cure." It was frequently the site of riots. Among famous prisoners incarcerated there at various times were Boss Tweed, Mme. Restell, Emma Goldman, the birth-control advocate Ethel Byrne, and Mae West, jailed for staging her play *Sex* in 1929.

Corruption was always a fact of police life, and it rose to extraordinary heights in the last three decades of the nineteenth century. Under the Tweed Ring, the police force was an amalgam of fiefdoms, each precinct at the mercy of its captain, who, more often than not, ran it as an extortion ring for his personal benefit. Individual policemen were cut off from profits and ceased to care. The *Evening Telegram* assessed the situation in 1875:

> *The rank and file of President [Commissioner] Matsell's "best police in the world" are rapidly drifting into a state of utter demoralization, if we are to judge by the alarming increase in the member of burglaries, highway robberies, and petty thefts, as well as the reports of outrages perpetrated by these model guardians of the public peace in various precincts of the city . . . Burglars now roam the city at will, enter residences, stores and offices and pillage them under the very eye of the police; river thieves boldly board vessels at the piers within sight of a uniformed officer's post, commit piracies and when resistance is offered use the knife and slung shot upon their victims and escape; highwaymen's friends will inveigle an officer into a corner grocery and while he is there canvassing with his boon companions the respective merits of Morrissey and Fox, Disbecker and Smith [John Morrissey and the other three Police Commissioners], the partner of his entertainers is at his post committing highway robbery or picking pockets . . .*

Despite the hysterical language and rather antiquated imagery, the picture presented in this account is not far from the truth. According to another account, the year 1868 saw 5,423 criminal cases, booked at station houses, vanish before reaching court. The breakup of the Tweed Ring and the resulting investigation of 1875 instilled a temporary fever of rectitude. Inspector Thomas Byrnes, who became chief of the Detective Bureau in 1880, was a genuinely tough cop, who did not appear corrupt, although, on the other hand, he had little respect for the constitutional rights of suspects and was more than inclined toward dividing the human race into "criminal" and "respectable" classes. His achievements include the establishment of the Rogues' Gallery and the broadcast of photographs and information on criminals nationwide, as well as the establishment of the Dead Line, an invisible barrier that bounded the area between Fulton and Greenwich Streets, the Battery, and the East River. Any known crook found within this zone, which included the financial district, was subject to immediate arrest.

The same period saw the rise of Patrolman Alexander S. Williams, who was seemingly of the same mold as Byrnes. Assigned to clean up the gangs in the vicinity of Broadway and Houston Street in the late 1860s, he began his offensive by hunting down the two toughest specimens and hurling them through the window of the Florence Saloon. In 1871 he was made captain of the 21st Precinct, which oversaw the Gas House District, and there he broke up the first incarnation of the Gas House Gang. He also first gave shape to the motto rephrased by Patrolman Willemse's mentor: "There is more law in the end of a policeman's nightstick than in a decision of the Supreme Court." After this, he acquired the sobriquet "Clubber," was named Inspector, and was presented with the Tenderloin on a plate. There he prospered, and the extent of his success was only suggested by the investigations of the 1894 Lexow Committee and the 1897 Mazet Committee. Captain Max Schmittberger, who later became a Chief Inspector, testified that he had collected tribute from gamblers and pimps and paid it personally to Williams. One madame, who owned a chain of brothels, testified that she paid Williams $30,000 annually for protection, while other madames with smaller operations said that they had paid initial fees of $500 apiece when they opened their houses and a retainer varying between $25 and $50 per house thereafter. Streetwalkers came forward and told how they paid for permission to practice their trade, while thieves submitted that they had paid him a percentage of their takings. More than six hundred policy shops paid Williams $15 a month each, while pool rooms contributed as much as $300, and the higher-class gambling joints even more. Williams also had an interest in a brand of whiskey, which he forced saloonkeepers to sell. It was revealed that Williams owned an estate in Cos Cob, Connecticut, whose dock alone was valued at $39,000, as well as a town house in the city and a yacht. His explanation to the investigators was that he had made his fortune through speculating on real estate in Japan. Lexow and Mazet ultimately took no action against him. He resigned, however, and went into the insurance business, dying a multimillionaire in 1910. During the investigation he coined his second most famous line. When asked why he had made no effort to close down the whorehouses in his district, he replied, "Because they were kind of fashionable at the time."

The Lexow investigation also proved the end of Byrnes, a man who, it was noted, did not bother to investigate robberies if the victims failed to offer a substantial reward. Although he had never earned a salary greater than $5,000 a year, he somehow had amassed $350,000 in real estate and a fortune, held in his wife's name, of $292,000. When asked about this, he said that they were the result of "gratuities" paid him by Wall Street businessmen.

William S. "Big Bill" Devery was a more straightforward case. Known for his personal motto, "Hear, see, and say nothin', eat, drink, and pay nothin'," and for beginning many of his sentences with the phrase "Touchin' on and appertainin' to," Devery was a classic East Side clubhouse man, with connections that reached deep into the Democratic Party. It was well known that he was corrupt; he in fact admitted as much quite readily. In common with some reformers of his day, he believed in the establishment of vice districts, where fees could be regulated by the police; he blamed widespread corruption on the dispersal of the old East Side brothel concentration. His payoff routine was ingenious: his bagman was a tailor, and anyone who owed Devery or wished for a favor from him would go to the tailor and order a suit, leaving a deposit of, say, $1,000. He was also intimately involved in police hiring and promotion. In 1892 the *Mail and Express* reported that it cost $300 to become a patrolman, $1,400 to advance to sergeant, and $14,000 to be made captain, although a certain Captain

Creedon testified before Lexow that his rank had in fact cost him $15,000, while Captain Schmittberger complained that the prices were inflated, since at the precinct level the Tenderloin was only worth $200 a month in graft. Devery was dismissed from the force in 1894 and indicted for extortion, but was acquitted two years later, and his badge was restored by the Supreme Court. The Police Commission attempted to try him again but was restrained by an order from the high court. He was appointed Inspector in 1898, and six months later was made Chief of Police, a title he tainted so thoroughly that it was abolished after his resignation in 1901.

The less exalted Lieutenant Charles H. Becker of the Gambling Squad, who was eventually executed for ordering the murder of the gambler Herman "Beansy" Rosenthal, may have been called the "crookedest cop who ever stood behind a shield," but in light of his predecessors, such a superlative must be viewed relatively. He made his mark, however, by combining corruption with unrelieved brutality, a distinction he seems to have shared only with Williams among his illustrious forerunners. No doubt, many cops on the beat level pursued this combination of activities, but for the most part, cops of the period who were not ambitious enough to hoist themselves into the upper ranks of profit were simply attempting to get by, and so sought modest graft. In the small time, graft came in two classes, clean and dirty. The "dirty" label applied to shakedowns of gamblers, pimps, and whores, and petty extortions of liquor dealers and saloonkeepers. Clean graft, which was much more common, was essentially a victimless crime and took in the general category of donations from businessmen—for overlooking construction and vehicle violations, for example; for recovering lost and stolen property; and for finding open doors in lofts and stores and locking them. Clean graft also covered the moonlighting practice of cops who spent their days off standing guard in front of the better gambling houses. Cops spent even more time cadging free meals and drinks in restaurants and saloons, engaging in what were referred to as "joke thefts" (mostly of food), and cooping, which even today is police parlance for sneaking off somewhere to take a nap. "Did you ever see policemen semaphore to each other?" asks Willemse. "Two arms extended means you did not see him, one arm pointed means you have seen him and he is going in the direction his hand points. Arms akimbo, means he's in a coop and won't be out or has sent word everything is all right."

The time-honored image of the rotund Clancy picking his apple from the groceryman's crate, allowing himself to be pacified by stew and ale at the corner saloon, gently arresting prostitutes to make his quota and then letting them go out a side door on a technicality, too dreamy and dopey and benevolent to notice the crooks hauling entire sets of furniture out of the showroom, perhaps even watching their cart horse for them while they are thus occupied, is one of those clichés that have endured because they are based on fact. The ordinary foot-soldier cop of the time was very often cut from the mold of the civil-service loafer, a sinner more by omission and complacency than by active intention. Nevertheless, this same character was capable of being casually brutal to non-criminals who did not speak English—for example, to blacks, to street peddlers and hoboes—and, as has been illustrated, found it most convenient to ask questions with his stick. The overwhelming impression is that cops were simply not much good to anyone who did not have the wherewithal to hire them as private day laborers or night watchmen.

from Plunkitt of Tammany Hall
by George Washington Plunkitt
and William L. Riordon

George Washington Plunkitt was a ward boss for Tammany

Hall, the corrupt political organization that dominated city

politics during the late 19th and early 20th centuries.

Plunkitt's meeting with New York Evening Post reporter

William L. Riordon (1861–1909) led to a series of inter-

views, which Riordan turned into a book. Plunkitt here

makes the case for "honest graft".

Everybody is talkin' these days about Tammany men growin' rich on graft, but nobody thinks of drawin' the distinction between honest graft and dishonest graft. There's all the difference in the world between the two. Yes, many of our men have grown rich in politics. I have myself. I've made a big fortune out of the game, and I'm gettin' richer every day, but I've not gone in for dishonest graft—blackmailin' gamblers, saloonkeepers, disorderly people, etc.—and neither has any of the men who have made big fortunes in politics.

There's an honest graft, and I'm an example of how it works. I might sum up the whole thing by sayin': "I seen my opportunities and I took 'em."

Just let me explain by examples. My party's in power in the city, and it's goin' to undertake a lot of public improvements. Well, I'm tipped off, say, that they're going to lay out a new park at a certain place.

I see my opportunity and I take it. I go to that place and I buy up all the land I can in the neighborhood. Then the board of this or that makes its plan public, and there is a rush to get my land, which nobody cared particular for before.

Ain't it perfectly honest to charge a good price and make a profit on my investment and foresight? Of course, it is. Well, that's honest graft.

Or supposin' it's a new bridge they're goin' to build. I get tipped off and I buy as much property as I can that has to be taken for approaches. I sell at my own price later on and drop some more money in the bank.

Wouldn't you? It's just like lookin' ahead in Wall Street or in the coffee or cotton market. It's honest graft, and I'm lookin' for it every day in the year. I will tell you frankly that I've got a good lot of it, too.

I'll tell you of one case. They were goin' to fix up a big park, no matter where. I got on to it, and went lookin' about for land in that neighborhood.

I could get nothin' at a bargain but a big piece of swamp, but I took it fast enough and held on to it. What turned out was just what I counted on. They couldn't make the park complete without Plunkitt's swamp, and they had to pay a good price for it. Anything dishonest in that?

Up in the watershed I made some money, too. I bought up several bits of land there some years ago and made a pretty good guess that they would be bought up for water purposes later by the city.

Somehow, I always guessed about right, and shouldn't I enjoy the profit of my foresight? It was rather amusin' when the condemnation commissioners came along and found piece after piece of the land in the name of George Plunkitt of the Fifteenth Assembly District, New York City. They wondered how I knew just what to buy. The answer is—I seen my opportunity and I took it. I haven't confined myself to land; anything that pays is in my line.

For instance, the city is repavin' a street and has several hundred thousand old granite blocks to sell. I am on hand to buy, and I know just what they are worth.

How? Never mind that. I had a sort of monopoly of this business for a while, but once a newspaper tried to do me. It got some outside men to come over from Brooklyn and New Jersey to bid against me.

Was I done? Not much. I went to each of the men and said: "How many of these 250,000 stories do you want?" One said 20,000, and another wanted 15,000, and other wanted 10,000. I said: "All right, let me bid for the lot, and I'll give each of you all you want for nothin'."

They agreed, of course. Then the auctioneer yelled: "How much am I bid for these 250,000 fine pavin' stones?"

"Two dollars and fifty cents," says I.

"Two dollars and fifty cents!" screamed the auctioneer. "Oh, that's a joke! Give me a real bid."

He found the bid was real enough. My rivals stood silent. I got the lot for $2.50 and gave them their share. That's how the attempt to do Plunkitt ended, and that's how all such attempts end.

I've told you how I got rich by honest graft. Now, let me tell you that most politicians who are accused of robbin' the city get rich the same way.

They didn't steal a dollar from the city treasury. They just seen their opportunities and took them. That is why, when a reform administration comes in and spends a half million dollars in tryin' to find the public robberies they talked about in the campaign, they don't find them.

The books are always all right. The money in the city treasury is all right. Everything is all right. All they can show is that the Tammany heads of departments looked after their friends, within the law, and gave them what opportunities they could to make honest graft. Now, let me tell you that's never goin' to hurt Tammany with the people. Every good man looks after his friends, and any man who doesn't isn't likely to be popular. If I have a good thing to hand out in private life, I give it to a friend. Why shouldn't I do the same in public life?

Another kind of honest graft. Tammany has raised a good many salaries. There was an awful howl by the reformers, but don't you know that Tammany gains ten votes for every one it lost by salary raisin'?

The Wall Street banker thinks it shameful to raise a department clerk's salary from $1500 to $1800 a year, but every man who draws a salary himself says: "That's all right. I wish it was me." And he feels very much like votin' the Tammany ticket on election day, just out of sympathy.

Tammany was beat in 1901 because the people were deceived into believin' that it worked dishonest graft. They didn't draw a distinction between dishonest and honest graft, but they saw that some Tammany men grew rich, and supposed they had been robbin' the city treasury or levyin' blackmail on disorderly houses, or workin' in with the gamblers and lawbreakers.

As a matter of policy, if nothing else, why should the Tammany leaders go into such dirty business, when there is so much honest graft lyin' around when they are in power? Did you ever consider that?

Now, in conclusion, I want to say that I don't own a dishonest dollar. If my worst enemy was given the job of writin' my epitaph when I'm gone, he couldn't do more than write:

"George W. Plunkitt. He Seen His Opportunities, and He Took 'Em."

The civil service gang is always howlin' about candidates and officeholders puttin' up money for campaigns and about corporations chippin' in. They might as well howl about givin' contributions to churches. A political organization has to have money for its business as well as a church, and who has more right to put up than the men who get the good things that are goin'? Take, for instance, a great political concern like Tammany Hall. It does missionary work like a church, it's got big expenses and it's got to be supported by the faithful. If a corporation sends in a check to help the good work of the Tammany Society, why shouldn't we take it like other missionary societies? Of course, the day may come when we'll reject the money of the rich as tainted, but it hadn't come when I left Tammany Hall at 11:25 a.m. today.

Not long ago some newspapers had fits because the Assemblyman from my district said he had put up $500 when he was nominated for the Assembly last year. Every politician in town laughed at these papers. I don't think there was even a Citizens' Union man who didn't know that candidates of both parties have to chip in for campaign expenses. The sums they pay are accordin' to their salaries and the length of their terms of office, if elected.

Even candidates for the Supreme Court have to fall in line. A Supreme Court Judge in New York County gets $17,500 a year, and he's expected, when nominated, to help along the good cause with a year's salary. Why not? He has fourteen years on the bench ahead of him, and ten thousand other lawyers would be willin' to put up twice as much to be in his shoes. Now, I ain't sayin' that we sell nominations. That's a different thing altogether. There's no auction and no regular biddin'. The man is picked out and somehow he gets to understand what's expected of him in the way of a contribution, and he ponies up—all from gratitude to the organization that honored him, see?

Let me tell you an instance that shows the difference between sellin' nominations and arrangin' them in the way I described. A few years ago a Republican district leader controlled the nomination for Congress in his Congressional district. Four men wanted it. At first the leader asked for bids privately, but decided at last that the best thing to do was to get the four men together in the back room of a certain saloon and have an open auction. When he had his men lined up, he got on a chair, told about the value of the goods for sale, and asked for bids in regular auctioneer style. The highest bidder got the nomination for $5000. Now, that wasn't right at all. These things ought to be always fixed up nice and quiet.

As to officeholders, they would be ingrates if they didn't contribute to the organization that put them in office. They needn't be assessed. That would be against the law. But they know what's expected of them, and if they happen to forget they can be reminded polite and courteous. Dan Donegan, who used to be the Wiskinkie of the Tammany Society, and received contributions from grateful officeholders, had a pleasant way of remindin'. If a man forgot his duty to the organization that made him, Dan would call on the man, smile as sweet as you please and say: "You haven't been round at the Hall lately, have you?" If the man tried to slide around the question, Dan would say: "It's gettin' awful cold." Then he would have a fit of shiverin' and walk away. What could be more polite and, at the same time, more to the point? No force, no threats—only a little shiverin' which any man is liable to even in summer.

Just here, I want to charge one more crime to the infamous civil service law. It has made men turn ungrateful. A dozen years ago, when there wasn't much civil service business in the city government, and when the administration could turn out almost any man holdin' office, Dan's shiver took effect every time and there was no ingratitude in the city departments. But when the civil service law came in and all the clerks got lead-pipe cinches on their jobs, ingratitude spread right away. Dan shivered and shook till his bones rattled, but many of the city employees only laughed at him. One day, I remember, he tackled a clerk in the Public Works Department, who used to give up pretty regular, and, after the usual question, began to shiver. The clerk smiled. Dan shook till his hat fell off. The clerk took ten cents out of his pocket, handed it to Dan and said: "Poor man! Go and get a drink to warm yourself up." Wasn't that shameful? And yet, if it hadn't been for the civil service law, that clerk would be contributin' right along to this day.

The civil service law don't cover everything, however. There's lots of good jobs outside its clutch, and the men that get them are grateful every time. I'm not speakin' of Tammany Hall alone, remember! It's the same with the Republican Federal and State officeholders, and every organization that has or has had jobs to give out—except, of course, the Citizens' Union. The Cits held office only a couple of years and, knowin' that they would never be in again, each Cit officeholder held on for dear life to every dollar that came his way.

Some people say they can't understand what becomes of all the money that's collected for campaigns. They would understand fast enough if they were district leaders. There's never been half enough money to go around. Besides the expenses for meetin's, bands and all that, there's the bigger bill for the district workers who get men to the polls. These workers are mostly men who want to serve their country but can't get jobs in the city departments on account of the civil service law. They do the next best thing by keepin' track of the voters and seein' that they come to the polls and vote the right way. Some of these deservin' citizens have to make enough on registration and election days to keep them the rest of the year. Isn't it right that they should get a share of the campaign money?

Just remember that there's thirty-five Assembly districts in New York County, and thirty-six district leaders reachin' out for the Tammany dough-bag for somethin' to keep up the patriotism of ten thousand workers, and you wouldn't wonder that the cry for more, more, is goin' up from every district organization now and forevermore. Amen.

from Rogues' Gallery
by Thomas Byrnes

Inspector Thomas Byrnes (1842–1910) was chief of New York City's detectives in the late 1800s. He was closely acquainted with many of the day's leading rogues, from sneak thieves and pickpockets to forgers and murderers. Byrnes' 1886 book described the criminals' methods and profiled some 400 of the worst lawbreakers.

METHODS OF PROFESSIONAL CRIMINALS OF AMERICA

BANK BURGLARS

The ways of making a livelihood by crime are many, and the number of men and women who live by their wits in all large cities reaches into the thousands. Some of the criminals are really very clever in their own peculiar line, and are constantly turning their thieving qualities to the utmost pecuniary account. Robbery is now classed as a profession, and in the place of the awkward and hang-dog looking thief we have today the intelligent and thoughtful rogue. There seems to be a strange fascination about crime that draws men of brains, and with their eyes wide open, into its meshes. Many people, and especially those whose knowledge of criminal life is purely theoretical, or derived from novels, imagine that persons entering criminal pursuits are governed by what they have been previously, and that a criminal pursuit once adopted is, as a rule, adhered to; or, in other words, a man once a pickpocket is always a pickpocket; or another, once a burglar is always a burglar. Hardly any supposition could be more erroneous. Primarily there are, of course, predisposing influences which have a certain effect in governing choice.

A man of education, refined habits, and possibly a minimum of courage, would not be likely to adopt the criminal walks requiring brute force and nerve. Such a one would be far more likely to become a forger or counterfeiter than a highway robber. Still, under certain circumstances—opportunity and the particular mode of working of those who were his tutors in crime—he might be either, foreign as they would be to his nature. Criminal occupation, however, is, like everything else, progressive. Two things stand in the way of the beginner in crime attaching himself to what he may view—taking them in the criminal's own light—as the higher walks of predatory industry, the top rungs of the criminal ladder. The first is, naturally, lack of experience and skill; the second, lack of confidence in him or knowledge of him by the older and more practiced hands, whose co-operation would be necessary.

Hence, if he cannot strike out for himself by the force of his own genius some new line of forgery, confidence operations, embezzlements, or others of the class of crimes dependent upon brains, adroitness, and address for their success, he must enter on the broad level as a general thief—one of the class who will steal anything that they can get away with, from a needle to a ship's anchor. From that level he may rise, partly by the force of his own increased knowledge of the practice of crime, partly by his natural adaptability for especial methods of preying upon the community, partly by the advice and cooperation of older criminals with whom he comes in contact, whether at liberty or doing time in a prison. From a petty general sneak thief he may become one of a gang of pickpockets, and from a pickpocket, in course of time, may suddenly come to the front with distinction even as a first-class bank burglar.

Cracksmen of this class head the list of mechanical thieves. It requires rare qualities in a criminal to become an expert bank-safe robber. Thieves of this high grade stand unrivaled among their kind. The professional bank burglar must have patience, intelligence, mechanical knowledge, industry, determination, fertility of resources, and courage—all in high degree. But, even if he possess all these, they cannot be utilized unless he can find suitable associates or gain admission to one of the already organized gangs. Sometimes the arrest of a single man out of a gang will put a stop to the operations of the remainder for a long time, simply because they need another man, and can find nobody they can trust. Bank burglars have been known to spend years in preparation—gleaning necessary information of the habits of bank officials, forming advantageous acquaintances, and making approaches to the coveted treasure all the time, but with the patience to wait until the iron is fully hot before striking a blow.

The construction of a massive bank safe, provided, as they now are, with electric alarms, combination and time locks, and other protective appliances, is such, that none but a mechanical genius can discover its weak points and attack it successfully. There is not a safe in use today that is absolutely burglar-proof, notwithstanding the fact that many manufacturers advertise and guarantee those of their build as such. Every now and then safe makers quietly alter the internal construction of their vaults, and these changes are brought about by the doings of some scientific robber. Just as soon as the safe builder becomes aware of the fact that burglars have unearthed a defect in vaults of his make, he sets his mechanics at work upon some new design, in the hope of thwarting thieves and making his vaults the more secure.

The wrecking of every safe, therefore, reveals a blemish, and necessitates alterations, which, of course, later on, make the work of the vault-opener more difficult. Hundreds of safes are turned out of the factories in the several cities weekly, and a calculating burglar, when he has discovered a defect in a certain pattern, will delay exposing his secret to the manufacturer until thousands of the seemingly strong, yet frail, vaults have been made and are in use. That insures him something to operate upon, for he well knows that after his first success, and the fact is reported at the safe factory, improvements will be in order.

The proficiency attained by our bank burglars, and the apparently comparative ease with which they secure the contents of massive vaults, is the result of constant and careful study of the subject. All the resources, ingenuity and cunning of the cracksman who makes bank-wrecking a specialty are put to the test in an undertaking of that sort, and plans follow plans until one is matured which circumstances may warrant as safe, feasible, and profitable. Then the accomplishment of the nefarious scheme only depends upon nerve, daring, and mechanical tools.

Some burglars make their own outfit, but almost any blacksmith will make any tool he is called upon for, if its construction is within his capacity, without asking any questions about the uses to which it is to be put, provided he gets his price for it. It is, of course, more than probable that he guesses the use for which it is intended, but that, he thinks, is not his business. The making of such implements is, as a rule, confined to those mechanics who are actually in league with the criminals who expect to use them. The heavy and unwieldy tools of years ago have been abandoned by the modern bank robber, with his new inventions. While some bank thieves use the spirit lamp and blow-pipe to soften the hardened metals and take the temper out of the steel vault doors or cases, others use only a small diamond-pointed drill. Then again, others, who do not care to spend time manipulating the intricate combination, use simple sort of machines, technically called the "drag" and "jackscrew." The former, simple as it looks, is extremely powerful—and so quiet. By means of a bit a hole is bored through a safe door; a nut is set "inside"; the point of the screw passes through the nut, which rests inside the surface that has been bored; then the screw is turned by a long handle, which two men can operate. As the screw turns, the nut is forced forward, farther and farther. It is a power that hardly any construction of a safe can resist. Either the back or the front must give way.

The "jackscrew" is rigged so that by turning it will noiselessly force into the crack of a safe door a succession of steel wedges; first, one as thin as a knife-blade; soon, one as thick as your hand; and they increase in size until the hinges give way. Where the size or location of the safe or vault to be forced precludes the use of these machines, and an explosion becomes necessary, dynamite and nitro-glycerine are used with the greatest skill, and with such art in the deadening of sound that sometimes an explosion which rends asunder a huge safe cannot be heard twenty yards away from the room in which it takes place.

The patient safe robber is aware of several ingenious ways of picking combination locks. In following their nefarious calling these men attain a delicacy of feeling by which they are able to determine to a nicety the exact distance necessary to raise each tumbler of the lock. The burglar masters a combination with almost mathematical accuracy, and manipulates its complex machinery with the same dexterity and precision that a music-teacher touches the keys of a piano. He is trained to detect one false note in a swelling chorus produced by the click of reverberating ratchets within the lock, and marks the period and duration of the drops. When they come across some new kind of lock, they will manage to get possession of one, whatever its cost, and whatever roundabout means may be necessary to get hold of it, and, taking it apart, will study its construction until they know its strong and weak points, and how to master it, just as well as its inventor or maker could. They are always on the alert to utilize for their purposes every new appliance of power.

The combination-safe picker is the cleverest of all the fraternity of lock workers. His is a life of study and careful experimenting. He proceeds to fathom the mystery of a new and intricate piece of mechanism with the same enthusiastic, yet patient, attention and study that actuates a scientist in search of more useful knowledge. Having acquired mastery over any combination, the burglar guards his secret jealously. Gaining access to the bank or building, he can tell at once the character of the combination he has to deal with, and that with him is tantamount to opening the safe or vault. Having rifled the safe of its contents, he closes the door, and begins to make arrangements to deceive the officials of the institution and the detectives. The crevices of the door are closed with putty, with the exception of a small orifice in the upper or horizontal crevice, through which powder is blown into the safe by means of a small bellows. The hole is then closed, a slow fuse which is inserted into the crack is set fire to, and the building is vacated. Half an hour or so later the fuse ignites the powder, and the safe door is shattered from its strong fastenings.

For fifteen years the manner in which a celebrated combination lock was picked by thieves was involved in mystery, during which time many honest bank employees suffered in reputation, and not a few were unjustly incarcerated. The criminals who operated so mysteriously upon the safes never took all the money or valuables. In many cases they helped themselves to but a small percentage of the proceeds, and it was this ruse that threw the officials off their guard and brought the employees into disrepute. The burglars familiarized themselves with the make and patterns of the locks, and then bored a hole within a short distance of where a spindle held the tumblers. With the use of a common knitting-needle the tumblers were dropped and the safe door opened.

The secret of another ingenious method of opening safes at last leaked out. The paying teller of an Eastern bank having been absent at lunch, returned earlier than was his wont and discovered a strange man on his knees tampering with the dial of the combination. The man turned out to be "Shell" Hamilton, one of the Mark Shinburn gang. His arrest was the means of leading to the knowledge of the fact that the gang had been systematically picking a patent combination lock by removing the dial and placing a piece of paper behind it, so that when the safe was opened the combination registered its secret upon the paper. The thieves next watched their opportunity to gain possession of the paper, and the difficulty was at once overcome of opening the safe and gaining possession of its valuable contents.

Every gang of bank burglars has its recognized leader, whose word is law. He is a man of brains, possessed of some executive ability, sleek and crafty. The care with which, perhaps for years before the consummation of a crime, he arranges the plans for getting at the vault, illustrates the keenness of his perception and his depth of thought. Every little detail is considered and followed, so as to allay suspicion and permit him to get the closer to his prize. Bank burglaries invariably date back, and in some cases it has been known that the interior drawings of the building and plans of the vaults made at the time of their erection have for twenty years passed through the hands of several gangs as the sole legacy of some crafty leader. If provided with such important information, when, at last, the plundering of some institution is intended, the standing of the concern and the value of the securities kept in the vault must first be ascertained. Should these prove satisfactory, the conspiracy gets under way. Next, some inquiries are necessary as to the mechanical part of the work to be done. The name of the maker of the vault, the size of the lock by which it is protected, and if electric appliances guard it, must all be known, and are very easily learned.

The burglars generally hire a store adjoining the institution, from which they can operate the better, and in some instances they have gone so far as to rent the basement of the bank, or rooms overhead. They may fit up the place as an oyster saloon, billiard room, shoemaker's, barber's or tailor's shop, or start a dental establishment. The leader of the gang will for a long time employ none but the best workmen, sell A1 goods, pay his rent regularly, seem anxious for custom, be pleasant to all, and make himself a most desirable tenant; and his landlord has in several instances been the very president of the bank that this bland and good-natured tenant was secretly plotting against.

The leader of the burglars, after a few weeks' steady attention to business, will pass much of his spare time in conversation with the bank clerks, and thereby manages to gain their confidence. Being a rather good judge of human nature, he is thus able to survey the institution, secure all the inside information he desires, and probably gain an important ally in his nefarious undertaking. If he can tamper with or corrupt one of the clerks or watchmen, then the job is plain sailing. As soon, however, as the scheme becomes known to an outsider, the leader, fearing treachery, hastens matters as rapidly as possible. Should the mechanical part of the work have been figured down, and the combination be at the mercy of the robbers, the final work is generally completed between Saturday night and Sunday morning.

By cutting through the dividing partition wall, ceiling, or floor, the bank burglar and his assistants find no difficulty in getting into the bank. Then the wrecking of the vault begins, and in a short time the treasure that it contains is in the possession of the cracksmen. The task complete, the burglars carry their booty into the adjoining store, or perhaps the basement below the ransacked institution, and at the proper time remove it to a much safer place. When it is discovered that the bank vault was really not as secure as it was supposed to be, the affable business man who ran the oyster saloon or billiard room next door, or made change in the barber's or shoemaker's shop in the basement, or superintended the drawing of teeth overhead, has suddenly abandoned his expensive fixtures and light stock, and has left for parts unknown. He has realized thousands for every dollar that he invested, and in most cases he leaves in the lurch the mean tool who betrayed his trust in the hope that he would reap a rich reward by revealing to a professional robber the secrets of the institution where he was employed.

Some bank burglars devote most of their time and attention to the cashier of the bank that they have made up their minds to rob. They track him to his home, gain access to his sleeping-room at night, either by collusion with one of the servants, picking the door-locks or springing a window and gaining the keys, and take impressions in wax. Duplicates are easily made from these casts, and at the first opportunity the bank can be safely plundered. Should, however, the cashier be disturbed by the intrusion of the cracksmen into his apartment, the burglars would be forced to make an attempt upon the bank that night. Securing possession of the keys by threats, a couple of men would be left to guard the cashier while the other members of the band would proceed to the bank and rob it. In several instances the desperate robbers, under threats of instant death, have compelled the cashier whom they have surprised to accompany them to the bank and open the vault, so that they could rifle it.

BANK SNEAK THIEVES

For many years bank sneak thieving flourished to an alarming extent in New York City, and under the old detective systems it seemed impossible to put a stop to that form of robbery. Notorious thieves in those days were permitted to loiter about the street, and on more than one occasion it was alleged that well filled cash boxes disappeared from bankers' safes while detectives were on watch outside. It was also openly insinuated that there was collusion between the police and the rogues, and numerous changes were made, but it was afterwards discovered that the accusations were groundless. While it may have been true that the detectives in some cases were not as vigilant as they might have been, subsequent developments have demonstrated that the financial quarter of the city was in the past but poorly protected. Well known thieves no longer haunt that prescribed locality, and since the establishment of a sub-detective bureau in Wall Street, six years ago, not a dollar has been stolen from any of the wealthy concerns in the great money centre by professional criminals. The inauguration also of a patrol service by experienced detectives during business hours, and the connecting by telephone of all the banking institutions have been the means of putting a stop to the operations of that particular class of rogues known as bank sneak thieves. Still, in the other cities of the country, where these precautions which have proved such a great preventive against the perpetration of crime have not been adopted, these thieves succeed in carrying on their depredations and reap rich rewards. Bank sneak thieves are all men of education, pleasing address, good personal appearance, and are faultless in their attire. With astonishing coolness these determined fellows commit the most daring thefts. The handful of successful rogues who have attained such exalted rank in the criminal profession despise the thousands of other robbers who live by the commission of small crimes. Aware of their superiority, these men are overbearing when chance brings them in contact with thieves of a lower degree. This is most noticeable in their manner of conducting themselves while serving out sentence in prison. As their exploits must necessarily occur in daylight and in public places, these robbers are really more daring than the bank burglar, who prefers to work under cover of night. The bank sneak is not an adept with the pick-lock, but great presence of mind, a quick eye, and wonderful nerve are the essentials he must possess to become a success.

Generally not more than three or four of these thieves are engaged in any robbery, and each of them has his allotted part to perform in the conspiracy. One may be a careful lookout, another must be an interesting conversationalist, and the third, generally a small-sized man, is the sneak, who stealthily steals behind the counter and captures the cash box or a bundle of bonds. While some robberies are carried out in a few minutes after the conception of the scheme, others have been planned months beforehand. The rogues who prowl about bankers' and brokers' offices day after day are ever on the watch for an opportunity to make a daring dash for plunder. Their appearance is so like that of the honest merchant or stock speculator that they have no difficulty in deceiving those who have no suspicion as to their real character or calling. They have also a faculty of worming themselves into the best society, and they spend their evenings in the lobbies of the leading hotels or other places where those foremost in financial circles are in the habit of assembling to discuss the events of the day. Information gathered in chance chats afterwards proves of valuable assistance to the cunning sneak thief in the carrying out of his operations. It is during those brief conversations that the robbers ascertain the topic that will most interest their intended victim. All men have their hobbies, and just as soon as the bank thief becomes aware of the fact that a certain banker, broker, paying teller or cashier has a failing for discussing any one thing in particular, they devote considerable time studying the subject until they are able to talk upon it properly and interestingly. This is one of the preliminary steps in a planned robbery. Next the thieves make themselves familiar with the manner in which business is conducted in the bank or office they are plotting to pillage. They never neglect any point, no matter how small it may be. The exact time that the clerks are in the habit of leaving their desks for dinner, the restaurants they dine at, and the time they are allowed for meals, are all noted. These are necessary for the success of the undertaking, and when at last all the plans have been perfected, the prize is captured at a time when there are but few persons in the banking institution. There have been exceptions to this rule, however, and cash boxes have been successfully spirited away just at the moment of the receipt of some astounding financial intelligence, and while the office was thronged with merchants and brokers discussing the startling news. Thefts of that sort require but a moment, and have been executed as rapidly as the occasion presents itself.

Here is a genuine instance of the great presence of mind of these criminals, from the record of one of the leading and most successful sneak thieves: There was a heated discussion in a broker's office one day about the location of a town in Ohio. The noted robber slipped into the place just in time to overhear several of the gentlemen declaring that the town was in different counties in that state. While the argument progressed the thief hit upon a plan that would enable him to capture the cash box, which temptingly rested in the safe, the door of which was open. He left as quickly as possible, and, meeting his confederate outside, sent him to a stationery store, telling him to buy several maps, and one especially showing the counties and towns in Ohio. Then the rogue returned to the broker's office to await his opportunity. A few minutes later he was followed by his companion in the role of a map peddler. Being at first told that no maps were wanted, the cunning accomplice, in a loud voice, said:

"Can I show you a new map, giving the boundaries of all the towns and counties in Ohio?"

The appeal was overheard by one of the men who had been involved in the recent discussion. He told the peddler to stop, at the same time saying, "Now, boys, I'll bet whatever you like that the town is in the county I said, and as chance has brought us a map, the bets can be settled without delay." Several bets were made, and for a few minutes the broker's office was in a much greater state of excitement than it ever had been before, even in panic days. As the peddler slowly unrolled his bundle of maps the brokers and the clerks gathered about him, anxious to learn the result. The sneak took advantage of the excitement and made his way, unnoticed, to the safe. He captured the cash box, containing $20,000, and escaped with it while his confederate was selling the map.

Another professional sneak, known as a man of great coolness and determination, and possessed of no small degree of courage, is credited with having entered a bank early in the morning and going behind the desk, divested himself of his coat, and, donning a duster, installed himself as clerk. He coolly waited there some time watching for a chance to seize a roll of greenbacks, bonds, or anything valuable that he could lay his hands on. One of the clerks requested the intruder to leave, but the wily thief retorted by telling the former to mind his own business, and also intimating that as soon as his friend, the president, arrived, he would have what he pleased to call a meddlesome fellow punished. The clerk, however, insisted upon the rogue's vacating the desk, and he finally did so under protest. In a seemingly high state of indignation the robber left the place, and later on the cashier, to his surprise, discovered that he had suddenly and mysteriously become $15,000 short. Of course the thief never called a second time to explain the mystery.

A bundle of bonds vanished from one of the rooms in a Safe Deposit vault in an Eastern city, recently, and the theft was not discovered until three months after the robbery had been committed. One of the depositors had called at the place for the purpose of clipping off his coupons. He had taken his box out of the compartment in which it was kept, and had gone into a side room with a table to do the coupon cutting. There was no one in the apartment excepting himself, but just as he had finished a man whom he believed to be one of the clerks entered the chamber for a second. The visitor tapped the old gentleman on the shoulder and instantly said, "Excuse me, sir, I have made a mistake," and passed out again. While the aged depositor had turned to see who it was had tapped him on the left shoulder, the supposed clerk, who was a professional sneak, picked up the bundle of bonds, which lay near the former's right hand. It happened that the lid of the tin box was down, and having no suspicion, and supposing that he had replaced the bonds, the old man returned the empty box to his compartment. Three months later, when the depositor again called at the Safe Deposit vaults to clip another set of coupons, he discovered that his bonds were missing and no one was able to account for their disappearance.

The robbery, it has been asserted, was effected in this way. In the Safe Deposit vaults was employed a clerk who was in the habit of wearing a buff-colored duster, much bedabbled with ink. On the day of the robbery the clerk was sent out on an errand and was away from his desk for nearly half an hour. During his absence a sneak thief of his build, and somewhat like him in appearance, and wearing an ink-stained duster, ran quickly down the steps, and without exciting any suspicion passed the watchman on guard at the entrance to the Safe Deposit vaults. No one paid any particular attention to the robber as he passed through the several rooms, supposing him to be the clerk. After he had captured the roll of bonds from which the coupons had been freshly cut, the man in the buff duster, unnoticed, passed out with the booty.

In robbing country banks, where the clerks are few, and generally during the dinner hour the cashier or paying teller is the only man left in the institution, sneaks have a simple and easy scheme for plundering. One first enters the bank and engages the cashier or teller in conversation, upon a subject in which the latter becomes deeply interested. While this is going on a carriage halts at the door, and the driver is sent in to tell the official inside that a gentleman who has hurt his leg and is unable to walk, desires to speak to him outside. The unsuspecting cashier or teller excuses himself to his first visitor and goes out to speak to the injured man, and in his absence the bank is ransacked.

Robberies of this kind are committed quite frequently, and gangs of sneaks travel all over the country with a circus or wild beast show. In the towns and small cities the parade of the performers creates considerable excitement, and when the cavalcade happens to pass a bank the clerks, cashiers and paying tellers seem to forget themselves and run to the windows to look out. The sneak thieves take advantage of the opportunity and quietly slip into the institution. In a twinkling their work is complete, and before the procession has passed they have escaped with whatever they could lay hands on.

If, while watching about a bank a large check is cashed and the customer turns aside to a desk to count the money, the rogues generally succeed in getting a portion of the cash. The thief will drop a bill upon the floor, and just as the man has arranged his pile of notes the criminal will politely tell him that he has dropped some of his money. When the former stoops down to pick up the greenback, the sneak will steal a portion of the cash upon the desk, and walk off unquestioned. They are not greedy in ventures of that sort, but they secure enough, with almost comparative safety, and are content. Heated arguments invariably follow thefts of this sort. After counting his money, the depositor goes back to the teller and insists that he is short. The teller is equally positive that he paid out the proper amount, and in most cases a disruption of commercial relations is the culmination of the dispute.

Bank sneak thieves are not, however, confined to these systems. They are men of adaptability, and act at all times according to circumstances. They have been known to rob messengers in the street while on their way to the bank to make a deposit. Some messengers always carry the bank book in their hand, with the bills folded between the covers. The ends of the greenbacks may extend beyond the length of the book, and these will instantly catch the quick eye of an experienced rogue. While the messenger is passing through a crowd, he will be thrown off his guard by a start of surprise, or a laughable remark. During that moment the entire amount in the book has been abstracted, and when the man reaches the bank and finds the cash gone, he cannot imagine how it was that he lost it.

JAMES BURNS, ALIAS BIG JIM, ALIAS BOSTON JIM, ALIAS BAKER, ALIAS JAMES
BOYLE, ALIAS JOHN BOWEN, ALIAS HAWKINS, ETC.
SNEAK AND BURGLAR

DESCRIPTION

Forty-six years old in 1886. Born in Boston, Mass. Single. No trade.
Height, 5 feet 8 ½ inches. Weight, about 200 pounds. Brown hair, dark
hazel eyes, dark complexion. Has fine spots of India ink between
thumb and forefinger of left hand. Generally wears a sandy-brown
mustache and whiskers.

RECORD

Jim Burns, alias Big Jim, is a celebrated bank sneak, burglar and forger.
He is a native of Boston, Mass., and is called by the fraternity "The
Prince of Thieves," on account of his great liberality with his money,
and the many charitable acts performed by him. It is a well known fact
that he has always contributed to the support of the wives and families
of his associates whenever they were in trouble.

Some years ago, after a large and successful bank sneak robbery,
Burns, and the others who were with him, returned to New York and
went to their usual rendezvous, a saloon corner of Fourth Street and
Broadway, New York, kept by one Dick Platt. The entire party
imbibed quite freely and Burns fell asleep. When he awoke he found
that he had been robbed of his portion of the plunder. On being
informed by one of his companions who had done it, Burns said, "It
was hard, that after doing a lot of work, and getting a good lump of
money, to have an associate rob me. He can't be much good, and will
die in the gutter." The fact is, that about one week after the occurrence
the party referred to was walking down Broadway and was stricken
with paralysis, fell into the gutter, and died before any assistance could
be rendered him.

Burns was connected with all of the most celebrated criminals in
this country, and took part in a large number of the most prominent
bank robberies.

Owing to his genial good-nature he never was able to save a dollar. He has served terms in prison in Sing Sing, New York, and Boston, Mass., and is well known all over America and Europe.

He was arrested in New York City on March 11, 1878, for the larceny of a carriage clock, valued at $52, from Howard, Sanger & Co., Broadway and Grand Street. He was released on $500 bail, and when his case was called for trial he failed to appear.

He was arrested again in New York City on December 17, 1878, for attempting to rescue "Red" Leary from a private detective. He was indicted, and again admitted to bail. While at large, he was arrested with George Carson for the larceny of $12,000 in money from the Government Printing Office, in Washington, D.C. No case being made out against them, they were discharged on July 1, 1879, by Commissioner Deuel, at Washington.

Burns was arrested upon his discharge on a bench warrant in the old clock case, brought to New York City, tried, convicted of grand larceny, and sentenced to three years and six months in Sing Sing prison, on July 11, 1879, by Judge Cowing.

He made his escape from Raymond Street jail in Brooklyn, N.Y., on Friday night, July 31, 1883, where he was confined for the larceny of a package containing $3,000 in money from the desk of the postmaster of Brooklyn, N.Y.

After his escape he went to London, England, and from there to Paris, where he devoted his talents to picking pockets and had to leave there to keep out of the clutches of the police. When next heard from he was in Stockholm, Sweden, with Billy Flynn, alias Connolly, and Bill Baker, alias Langford, where the party obtained about eighteen hundred kroners from a bank in that city. They were arrested for the robbery, but having no evidence against them a charge of vagrancy was preferred, and they were imprisoned for six months as vagrants. A few months after their time expired they went to Hamburg, Germany, where, on June 22, 1885, they succeeded in robbing the Vereins Bank of 200,000 marks, about $44,000. On July 15, 1885, the bank offered a reward of 10,000 marks, about $2,200, for them. They were all arrested in London, England, in the latter part of July, 1885, and returned to Paris, France, they having been tried, convicted and sentenced to one year's imprisonment each for an offense committed in that city. According to French law, any person may be tried, convicted, and sentenced for an offense during his absence. After their sentence expires they will be taken to Hamburg for trial for the larceny of the 200,000 marks.

EDWARD LYONS, ALIAS NED LYONS
BURGLAR AND SNEAK

DESCRIPTION

Forty-seven years old in 1886. Born in England. Married. Stout build. Height, about 5 feet 8 inches. Weight, about 180 pounds. Hair inclined to be sandy. Wears it long, covering the ears, one of which (the left one) has the top off. Wears a very heavy reddish mustache. Bald on front of head, forming a high forehead.

RECORD

Ned Lyons was born in Manchester, England, in 1839; came to America in 1850. His father had hard work to make both ends meet and look after his children, and in consequence young Ned had things pretty much his own way. They lived in West Nineteenth Street, New York City, a neighborhood calculated to develop whatever latent powers Ned possessed. The civil war, with its attractions in the shape of bounties, etc., proved a bonanza while it lasted, and after that Ned loomed up more prominently under the tuition of Jimmy Hope. He was afterwards a partner of Hope's, and was arrested several times, but never convicted. In 1869 Lyons, Hope, Bliss, Shinborn, and others, robbed the Ocean Bank, of New York, of money and bonds amounting to over a million dollars. The bank was situated on the corner of Fulton and Greenwich streets. A basement directly underneath was hired, ostensibly as an exchange. To this office tools were carried, and a partition erected, between which the burglars worked day and night, when opportunity served, cutting up through the stone floor of the bank, and gaining an entrance on Saturday night, after the janitor had left. To tear open the vaults was a task requiring time; but they operated so well, that on Monday morning the iron front door of the bank was found unlocked, the vault literally torn to pieces, and the floor strown with the débris of tools, mortar, stone, bricks, bonds, and gold coin—the bonds being left behind as worthless, and the gold coin as too heavy.

A few years before this robbery Lyons married a young Jewess, named Sophie Elkins, alias Levy, a *protégée* of Mrs. Mandlebaum. Her mania for stealing was so strong that when in Ned's company in public she plied her vocation unknown to him, and would surprise him with watches, etc., which she had stolen. Ned expostulated, pleaded with, and threatened her, but without avail; and after the birth of her first child, George (who, by the way, has just finished his second term for burglary in the State Reformatory at Elmira, N.Y.), Ned purchased a farm on Long Island, and furnished a house with everything a woman could wish for, thinking her maternal instinct would restrain her monomania; yet within six months she returned to New York, placed her child out to nurse, and began her operations again, finally being detected and sentenced to Blackwell's Island.

Early in the winter of 1870 Lyons, in connection with Jimmy Hope, George Bliss, Ira Kingsland, and a well known Trojan, rifled the safe of the Waterford (N.Y.) Bank, securing $150,000. Lyons, Kingsland and Bliss were arrested, and sentenced to Sing Sing prison. Hope was shortly after arrested for a bank robbery in Wyoming County, and sentenced to five years in State prison at Auburn, N.Y., on November 28, 1870. He escaped from there in January, 1873. Lyons escaped from Sing Sing, in a wagon on December 4, 1872. About two weeks after Ned's escape (December 19, 1872), he, in company of another person, drove up in the nighttime to the female prison that was then on the hill at Sing Sing. One of them, under pretense of bringing a basket of fruit to a sick prisoner, rang the bell; whereupon, by a preconcerted arrangement, Sophie, his wife, who had been sent there on October 9, 1871, for five years, rushed out, jumped into the carriage, and was driven away. They both went to Canada, where Ned robbed the safe of a pawnbroker, securing $20,000 in money and diamonds, and returned to New York, where their four children had been left—the eldest at school, the younger ones in an orphanage. About this time (September, 1874) the bank at Wellsboro, Pa., was robbed. Lyons was strongly suspected of complicity, with George Mason and others, in this robbery. Although Sophie and Ned were escaped convicts, they succeeded in evading arrest for a long time. Both of them were finally arrested at the Suffolk County (L.I.) Fair, at Riverhead, in the first week in October, 1876, detected in the act of picking pockets. Two weeks later he was tried in the Court of Sessions of Suffolk County, L.I., found guilty, and sentenced to three years and seven months in State prison, by Judge Barnard. Sophie was discharged, re-arrested on October 29, 1876, by a detective, and returned to Sing Sing prison to finish out her time. Lyons had on his person when arrested at Riverhead $13,000 of good railroad bonds. In 1869 Lyons had a street fight with the notorious Jimmy Haggerty, of Philadelphia (who was afterwards killed by Reddy the Blacksmith, in Eagan's saloon, corner Houston Street and Broadway). During the mélee Haggerty succeeded in biting off the greater portion of Lyons' left ear. On October 24, 1880, shortly after Ned's release from prison, in a drunken altercation, he was shot at the Star and Garter saloon on Sixth Avenue, New York City, by Hamilton Brock, better known as "Ham Brock," a Boston sporting man. Brock fired two shots, one striking Lyons in the jaw and the other in the body.

Lyons was arrested again on July 31, 1881, in the act of breaking into the store of J.B. Johnson, at South Windham, Conn. He pleaded guilty in the Windham County Superior Court, on September 14, 1881, and was sentenced to three years in State prison at Wethersfield, Conn. At the time of his arrest in this case he was badly shot. That he is now alive, after having a hole put through his body, besides a ball in the back, imbedded nine inches, seems almost a miracle.

Upon the expiration of Ned's sentence in Connecticut, in April, 1884, he was re-arrested, and taken to Springfield, Mass., to answer to an indictment charging him with a burglary at Palmer, Mass., on the night of July 27, 1881. Four days before he was shot at South Windham, Lyons, with two companions, entered the post office and drug store of G.L. Hitchcock, and carried away the contents of the money-drawer and a quantity of gold pens, etc. They also took a safe out of the store, carried it a short distance out of the village, broke it open, and took some things valued at $350 from it. In this case Lyons was sentenced to three years in State prison on May 29, 1884.

WILLIAM VOSBURG, ALIAS OLD BILL
SNEAK AND STALL

DESCRIPTION

Fifty-seven years old in 1886. Born in United States. Can read and write. Married. Stout build. Height, 5 feet 10 inches. Weight, 170 pounds. Hair, dark, mixed with gray. Gray eyes. Light complexion. Generally has a smooth-shaven face.

RECORD

Vosburg is one of the oldest and most expert bank sneaks and "stalls" in America, and has spent the best portion of his life in State prisons. He was formerly one of Dan Noble's gang, and was concerned with him in the Lord bond robbery in March, 1886, and the larceny of a tin box containing a large amount of bonds from the office of the Royal Insurance Company in Wall Street, New York, several years ago. Vosburg was arrested in New York City on April 2, 1877, for the Gracie King robbery, at the corner of William and Pine streets. He had just returned from serving five years in Sing Sing prison. In this case he was discharged. On April 20, 1877, he was again arrested in New York City, and sent to Boston, Mass., for the larceny of $8,000 in bonds from a man in that city. He obtained a writ in New York, but was finally sent to Boston, where they failed to convict him. On June 10, 1878, he was arrested in New York City, charged with grand larceny. On this complaint he was tried, found guilty, and sentenced to fifteen months in the penitentiary, by Recorder Hackett, on December 28, 1878. He did not serve his full time, for on May 3, 1879, he was again arrested in New York City, with one John O'Brien, alias Dempsey, for an attempt at burglary at Sixth Avenue. In this case he was admitted to bail in $1,000 by the District Attorney, on May 17, 1879. The case never was tried, for on September 23, 1879, he was again arrested, with Jimmy Brown, at Brewster's Station, New York, on the Harlem Railroad, for burglary of the post-office and bank. For this he was tried, convicted, and sentenced to four years in State prison at Sing Sing, on February 19, 1880, under the name of William Pond, by Judge Wright, at Carmel, New York. Brown never was tried.

After his release he claimed to be playing cards for a living, when in fact he was running around the country "stalling" for thieves. He was arrested in Washington, D. C., on March 4, 1885, at President Cleveland's inauguration, for picking pockets. Through the influence of some friends this case never went to trial. He then started through the country with Johnny Jourdan, Philly Phearson, and Johnny Carroll, alias The Kid. On April 1, 1885, the party tried to rob a man in a bank at Rochester, N.Y., but failed. They followed him to a hotel, and while he was in the water-closet handled him roughly and took a pocket-book from him, but not the book with the money in it. Phearson and Carroll escaped, and Vosburg and Jourdan were arrested, and sentenced to two years and six months each for assault in the second degree, by judge John S. Morgan, on June 15, 1885, at Rochester, N.Y.

HOTEL AND BOARDING-HOUSE THIEVES
The class of thieves devoting themselves to robbing rooms in hotels and in fashionable boarding-houses operate according to circumstances and always have their wits about them for any unexpected emergency. The successful ones are men of respectable appearance, good address, and cool and daring fellows. Some follow their nefarious vocation only in the morning, others in the afternoon, and still others operate at night. In their methods of procedure each of these

subdivisions has other distinguishing peculiarities. A great deal of ingenuity in getting into rooms is not infrequently shown by these men who in working run all sorts of risks and take desperate chances.

Until he has accomplished his purpose the hotel thief pursues his prey from one establishment to another with a persistency that knows no faltering. He makes it a specialty to scan the newspapers carefully, and keeps himself posted on the latest arrivals, the rooms they occupy and other data of interest. The coming and going of professionals, particularly female theatrical stars, salesmen, bankers, and bridal parties, and all persons likely to carry valuable jewelry and trinkets or a large amount of money, in this way are noted and are objects of special importance and solicitude.

When the unsuspecting prey fatigued by travel gives proof of his unconsciousness by deep, stertorous breathing, the hotel thief steals silently from his hiding-place. A slight push may let him enter the apartment, or it may be necessary to use a gimlet and a small piece of crooked wire to slide back the bolt, or a pair of nippers to turn the key left on the inside in the lock, from the corridor. Sometimes as many as a dozen rooms in the same hotel have been plundered in one night and none of the watchmen saw or heard the thief. The old style of climbing through transoms or unkeyed windows is at present not much in vogue. The hotel thief can carry his entire outfit in his vest pocket and can laugh in his sleeve at the common bolts and bars. The much boasted of chain-bolt can now be drawn back from the outside with only a piece of silk thread having a match tied to one end of it.

The shooting back of the old-fashioned slide-bolt from the outside of the apartment was for many years a bewildering mystery. As there were no marks to be found on the door in most cases when a robbery was reported, the hotel proprietor would frown and the clerk leer; both facial contortions being meant to express suspicion and incredulity. Many times the unfortunate victim has been turned away as a cheat and a fraud, who wanted to swindle the hotel out of his board bill or else to bring a suit for damages on a trumped up charge. The result has been that strangers who had also been robbed under such conditions were afraid to report the case lest they too should be regarded with suspicion and treated with insult. In all of these robberies the bolt which had been shot back so mysteriously was located either above or underneath the common key-lock. A piece of crooked wire inserted through the keyhole by the nimble rogue made the bolt worthless, and a turn of the knob was all that was required to open the door.

It does not take over a few minutes for an expert hotel thief to enter a room. After he has reached the door of the apartment in which the weary traveler is sleeping soundly, he takes from his pocket a small nippers, a bent piece of wire, and a piece of silk thread. These are the only tools some men use. Inserting the nippers in the keyhole, he catches the end of the key. Then a twist shoots back the lock bolt, and another leaves the key in a position from which it can easily be displaced. Should the slumber of the occupant of the room be disturbed by the falling of the key on the carpet or floor, time is given him to fall asleep again. By pressing on the door the thief next locates the bolt. A piece of thread is attached to the bent point of the wire, making a sort of bow; and after crooking the wire to suit, it is pushed through the keyhole and carried up or down to the bolt. The looped head throws the pin of the bolt into place; the string is moved sideways until it grapples the pin, and then the bolt is slid back out of the nosing. The door yields to a slight pressure, and the completion of the task is deftly and expeditiously performed. Some thieves always stop to lock the room door behind them.

At their leisure these thieves spend their time "fixing" rooms in hotels. This is necessary in first-class establishments, where the room doors are protected by improved locks. One of these, known as the "thumb bolt," requires to be tampered with beforehand. While the shrewd robber occupies the room which, it may not be until months afterward, he intends to rob, he prepares the lock so that it will aid him in his future operations. Removing the screws, he takes off the thumb-plate and files a slot in the spring-bar. Then he replaces the plate and screws, and marks on the outside of the door by a slight indentation in the woodwork, or by a raising made by a brad-awl from the inside, the exact point at which to strike the filed slot when the door is locked. Returning on the night of the robbery with the only tools necessary— a common brad-awl and a pair of nippers—he pierces the soft wood at the proper point, and then by pushing the awl further in strikes the slot, and is able to noiselessly turn the bolt; he then uses his nippers to unlock the door. As many as a dozen rooms in a single hotel are "fixed" in this way, and the thief, by occasionally keeping his eye upon the register, awaits his prey. If some well known character in the habit of wearing costly jewels is registered as the tenant in one of the "fixed" rooms, then the thief engages an apartment on the same floor, and during the night-time consummates the long planned crime.

Another plan, and the one that is generally adopted by rogues who prowl about hotel corridors in the daytime, is to draw the screws of the nosing of the bolt and lock. By boring the screw-holes larger and moistening the screws, the latter are replaced and maintain a sufficient grip not to be displaced by the ordinary jar. As the wood becomes dry the door at the proper time can without trouble or danger from noise be easily forced in.

The boarding-house thief, always a smooth and entertaining talker, makes acquaintances in new quarters in short order. Generally in a pleasant sort of a chat with the inquisitive landlady, before he has been many hours there, he succeeds in gleaning all the information about the other guests in the house that he desires to know. Most women have the foolish fondness of making a display of their jewels and valu-ables in the parlor or dining-room of the fashionable boarding-house. While amusing his newly-made acquaintances with his laughable sto-ries, the astute robber is at the same time making a thorough survey. His covetous eyes never miss the flash of diamonds, and should he be in doubt as to the genuineness of the sparklers, he has only to speak of them to one of the friends of the wearer, and he will be told when and where they were bought and the price paid for them.

After the cunning rogue has secured a full inventory of the jewels and valuable trinkets kept in the several rooms of the house he is ready for business. While the other guests are at breakfast or dinner the thief remains upstairs, and the thorough manner in which he rummages the several apartments in such short time is really surprising. Before his victims have finished their morning or evening chat the thief's work is complete, and with well filled valise, unnoticed he slips out of the house. Probably before the robbery is discovered, the professional criminal is aboard of a train and on his way to some other city to dispose of his plunder and resume his profitable exploits. Thieves of this class are troublesome to track, but when run down at last there is no end to the number of complainants that come forward to prosecute them.

TILLIE PHEIFFER, ALIAS MARTIN, ALIAS KATE COLLINS
HOTEL AND HOUSE SNEAK

DESCRIPTION

Thirty-six years old in 1886. Born in France. Servant. Married. Slim build. Height, 5 feet 3 inches. Weight, 128 pounds. Dark brown hair, hazel eyes, dark complexion. Mole on the right side of the nose under the eye.

RECORD

Tillie Pheiffer, or Martin, is a notorious house and hotel sneak thief. She sometimes hires out as a servant and robs her employers; but her specialty is to enter a hotel or flat, and wander up through the house until she finds a room door open, when she enters and secures whatever is handy and decamps. She is known in New York City, Brooklyn, Paterson, N.J., and Baltimore, Md., where she also served a term in prison. She is said to have kept a road-house near Paterson, N.J., some years ago.

Tillie was arrested in New York City a few years ago, endeavoring to rob the Berkeley Flats, on the corner of Ninth Street and Fifth Avenue, and sentenced to one year in the penitentiary, but subsequently released on habeas corpus proceedings in 1879.

She was arrested in Brooklyn, N.Y., disposing of a stolen watch in a pawnbroker's shop. When arrested, she drew a revolver and attempted to shoot the officer. For this she was sentenced to one year in the penitentiary there.

She was arrested again in New York City on June 15, 1881, taken to police headquarters and searched. There was found upon her person four pocket-books, which contained money and jewelry. In one of them there was $10 in money, a gold hairpin and earrings, and the address of Miss Jennie Yeamans, of East Ninth Street, New York City, who testified that her rooms had been entered by a sneak thief during her absence, and the property stolen. Two other parties appeared against her and testified that she had robbed them also. Tillie pleaded guilty in this case, and was sentenced to one year in the penitentiary on Blackwell's Island, on June 23, 1881, by Judge Cowing.

She was arrested again in New York City on June 19, 1882, for entering the apartments of Annie E. Tool, No. 151 Avenue B, and stealing a gold watch and chain and a pair of diamond earrings valued at $300. For this she was sentenced to eighteen months in the penitentiary on June 26, 1882, by Judge Gildersleeve.

WILLIAM CONNELLY, ALIAS OLD BILL, ALIAS WATSON
HOTEL THIEF

DESCRIPTION

Seventy years old in 1886. Born in Ireland. Stout build. Married. Height, 5 feet 9½ inches. Weight, about 200 pounds. Hair gray, head bald, eyes gray, complexion light. Stout, full face. Has a double chin. Mustache gray, when worn.

RECORD

Old Bill Connelly, or Watson, as he is sometimes called, is considered one of the cleverest hotel workers in America. Of late years he has worked generally in the small cities, on account of being so well known in the larger ones. He has served two terms in prison in New York State, one in Philadelphia, and several other places.

He was arrested in the Astor House, New York City, on November

24, 1876, coming out of one of the rooms with a watch and chain (one that was left for him as a decoy). He pleaded guilty, and was sentenced to four years in State prison on December 5, 1876, by Judge Gildersleeve, in the Court of General Sessions. His time expired on October 20, 1880.

Connelly was arrested again in the Continental Hotel, Philadelphia, Pa., for robbing some French naval officers, who were about visiting the Yorktown celebration. He was tried, convicted, and sentenced to three years in the county prison on October 28, 1881. He is now at large, and is liable to make his appearance anywhere.

EDW'D FAIRBROTHER, ALIAS DR. EDW'D S. WEST, ALIAS DOCTOR ST. CLAIR HOTEL AND BOARDING-HOUSE THIEF

DESCRIPTION

Fifty-five years old in 1886. Born in England. Physician. A small, nervous man. Speaks very rapidly. Has long, thin, white hair. Hollow cheeks; high, sharp cheek bones. No upper teeth. Large, long nose. Has a fine education, and speaks five languages.

RECORD

Dr. West, the name he is best known by, was arrested in New York City on July 7, 1873, for grand larceny from a boarding-house in 128th Street. The complaint was made by Charles E. Pierce. The Doctor was convicted, and sentenced to two years in State prison on July 14, 1873, by Judge Sutherland, in the Court of General Sessions, New York. West was arrested again in New York in January, 1880, charged with committing twenty-two robberies inside of seven months. He freely admitted his guilt, and confessed to all of them. The best piece of work he had done, he said, was the robbery of Major Morton's residence on Fifth Avenue, New York City, where he secured $6,000 worth of diamonds and jewelry, with which he got safely away and pawned for $450. When taken to Major Morton's residence, however, the people in the house failed to identify him, and went so far as to say that he was not the man who had called there. West told the officers how he robbed Morton's house and several others. At the time of his arrest he had $20 in his possession. Out of this he gave $13 to a poor man named Kane, from whom he had stolen a coat. A poor servant-girl also came to court. West recognized her, and offered her the last of his money, $7; but she would only take five of it. West, in speaking of himself at that time, said, "I have not always been a criminal; I have seen better days, far better days than many can boast of, and bright opportunities, too. I had no disposition for crime—in fact, no inclination that way. But time's whirligig turned me up a criminal; and I fought hard against it, too. I came to this country from England in 1855. I had just then graduated from Corpus Christi College, founded by Bishop Fox, of Winchester. I am an alumnus of Oxford. I took my degree of M.D., and came to this country, and became a practicing physician in New York City. I lived then in Clinton Place. In 1863 I was arrested for malpractice, and was sent to Sing Sing State prison for five years. While in the prison I associated with all kinds of people, and there I learned the art of robbery. After my time was up I returned to New York City, and tried to lead an honest life; but I had learned too much, and was again arrested for larceny, and sent to prison. I got out, and went back again for another term, which ended in June, 1879." West was arraigned in the Court of General Sessions in New York City on four indictments for grand larceny, and the District Attorney accepted a plea of guilty on one of them, and Judge Cowing sentenced him to five years in State prison on January 29, 1880. His sentence expired, allowing him full commutation, on August 28, 1883.

George W. Carson, alias Heywood
Hotel Thief

DESCRIPTION

Thirty-one years old in 1886. Born in United States. Clerk. Can read and write. Married. Medium build. Height, 5 feet 5½ inches. Weight,

155 pounds. Hair, brown. Eyes, hazel. Complexion, florid. Dot of India ink on right hand. Blonde color mustache.

RECORD

Carson is a very clever bank sneak, an associate of Rufe Minor, Horace Hovan, Johnny Carroll, Cruise Cummisky, and other first-class men. He was arrested at Petersburg, Va., on March 23, 1878, in company of Rufe Minor, Horace Hovan, alias Little Horace, and Charlotte Dougherty (Horace's wife), charged with the larceny of $200,000 in bonds and securities from the office of James H. Young, No. 49 Nassau Street, New York City. They were all brought to New York, and subsequently discharged.

Carson was arrested in New York City on November 15, 1880, for robbing the Middletown Bank of Connecticut, on July 27, 1880, of $8,500 in money and $56,000 in bonds. Johnny Jourdan, Horace Hovan and Rufe Minor were also arrested for this robbery. Carson was tried in Connecticut, proved an alibi, and the jury failed to agree, and he was discharged on April 26, 1881. He then traveled around the country with Charley Cummisky, alias Cruise, and was picked up in several cities, but was never convicted. He was again arrested in Brooklyn, N.Y., on August 2, 1883, with Billy Flynn (now in jail in Europe), and committed to the penitentiary for vagrancy. He was discharged on a writ by the Supreme Court on September 11, 1883, Carson and Flynn were seen in the vicinity of Raymond Street jail on the night of July 31, 1883, when Big Jim Burns, the Brooklyn Post-office robber, escaped. This celebrated criminal has been concerned in several other large robberies, and has been arrested in almost every city in the United States and Canada. He is now at liberty, but may be looked for at any moment.

SNEAK AND HOUSE THIEVES

The housebreaker and sneak are the most numerous of the thieving fraternity. It is from the slums that the lower grade are recruited, but the successful robber must combine superior qualifications to make

him an adept at the business. Still the former are not devoid of ingenuity. Locks and bolts cannot be relied upon as a rampart against these
men. There are but few dwellings in this city or country that are proof
against the assaults of the burglar and sneak thief. Some people believe
their homes secure when they have fastened the doors and windows.
The average sneak thief laughs at the flimsy barriers, and can undo
every one of them with a few simple instruments which he carries in
his vest pocket. Even the chain-bolt, which has been considered so for-
midable, is of no protection at all when pitted against the skill and sci-
ence of this class of rogues. When the massive bank vault offers no
serious obstacles that the trained and experienced burglar cannot overcome, how can it be expected that the ordinary contrivances should be
effectual? While the operations of the former class of criminals are
comparatively few and infrequent, on account of the multiplied risks
and difficulties to be encountered, the well organized army of sneak
thieves and house-breakers carry on their operations with a confidence
born of repeated success.

Some housebreakers are daring and desperate rascals. These are the
ones that enter dwellings in the night-time in search of plunder and
with masks on their faces and murder in their heart. Sometimes night
robberies are planned beforehand, but many have been committed at
haphazard. From servants or others employed in or about a residence,
confederates of these thieves collect the information they desire. The
manner of entering the premises depends upon its internal arrangements. In some cases the front basement door is entered by a false key,
in others the rogues climb up the front of the house and enter the
second-story window, and still in others an entrance is effected from
the rear. Once inside, the burglar ransacks the apartments in which he
expects to obtain the most booty. He works expeditiously, going
through an occupied chamber as carefully as he would an unoccupied
one. Often these criminals disturb the sleeper, but the latter is so fright-
ened at the presence of the robber that he lies still and offers no resis-
tance. Naturally house-breakers are not brave, and it is only when
cornered they become bold and desperate in their anxiety to evade a

long sentence. The noise made by rats has on more than one occasion scared burglars away from silverware worth hundreds and thousands of dollars, which they abandoned after collecting and packing up for removal.

Three or four of these men have been known to band themselves together, but a desperate man would rather work on his own hook. "Long John" Garvey, who was killed by falling through a house in Brooklyn, a few years since, for years before his death took no one into his confidence, but planned and executed his own robberies. He gathered all the information that he desired from the columns of the morning newspapers. He made a specialty of robbing young married couples of their jewels and wedding presents. A marriage notice or a report of a wedding was the only news that Garvey wished to read, and he gloated over the announcement that the pair had received costly presents from their friends. When the robber ascertained where the pair had taken up house, either while they were off on their wedding trip or had returned to housekeeping, Garvey, by hiring an attic room on the same block, would pay them a midnight visit. He invariably secured the prize he was in quest of, but after a long career of thievery he died as most thieves do, a violent death. Becoming reckless at his successes, he undertook to ransack a house while in a state of intoxication. He secured property worth several thousand dollars, and as he was carrying it over the roof-tops he fell through a new building into the cellar. The groans of the thief attracted attention, and Garvey was found with the stolen jewelry in his possession. He was seriously injured and was removed to an hospital, where he died next day.

Another well known housebreaker was in the habit of attending all the fashionable balls. He never went there for pleasure, but always on business. The rogue, with envious eyes, watched the ladies bedecked with expensive jewelry and wearing necklaces and pins set with brilliants. He had but little difficulty ascertaining the names and addresses of the wearers of the diamonds. When the ball was over he would, with the assistance of a companion, dog his intended victim to their homes. He would keep a constant watch upon the house or its inmates for several days, and if in the meantime the jewels had not been taken to a Safe Deposit vault, the robber would conclude that the lady was in the habit of keeping her valuables in the house. When the opportunity offered, the thief, under some pretext or other, would make his way into the premises in search of the diamonds or jewelry he had first seen in the ballroom, and he generally succeeded in getting them.

The men who make it a business ransacking flats, first watch the occupants, and learning that a certain suite of rooms is rented by two or three persons reputed to be wealthy, they ascertain and note their habits. Should several of them pass the day at business, when the lady goes out shopping and the rooms are locked up, the thieves boldly enter the house, and, with the aid of a pick-lock, make their way into the apartments, which they ransack in the absence of the tenants. "Second-story" thieves, after locating a house that they intend to rob in the early evening, watch until the tenants in a private residence are downstairs at dinner. Then a young man, with the agility of a cat, crawls up the front of the dwelling, and enters the second-story window. He rifles all the rooms in the upper part of the house in a few minutes, and with the booty noiselessly descends the stairs and leaves the house by the front door. In several cases, however, the robber has been known to drop the property out of a front window to his confederates on the street. This is only done when he has become alarmed by hearing footsteps on the stairs, and is forced to retreat in the same manner that he had entered the premises.

Other thieves, who also pillage houses during the supper hour, pick the lock of the front door and steal in without making any noise. They wear rubbers or woolen shoes, and succeed at intervals in making large hauls. Private residences are easily plundered by these rogues during the summer months, while the occupants are in the country. Then there are the several types of sneaks who, under all sorts of pretexts, manage to get inside of a dwelling for a few minutes without attracting any attention, and remain just long enough to steal whatever they can lay their hands upon. Some of these go about as peddlers, piano tuners, health and building inspectors, book canvassers, sewing machine, life and fire insurance agents, and in various other roles. They do not confine their operations to apartment houses or dwellings, but also rob business buildings in the daytime. Cash, jewelry, and valuables is the plunder most sought by the leading professional rogues of this class, but those of the lower grades seem to be satisfied with more bulky plunder. Young men make the most daring house thieves, but in the ranks may be found old criminals, who have passed the best years of their life operating in that way.

DAVID MOONEY, ALIAS LITTLE DAVE, ALIAS HILL, ALIAS FARRELL
SNEAK AND BURGLAR

DESCRIPTION

Thirty-eight years old in 1886. Born in New York. Single. Shoemaker. Medium build. Height, 5 feet 4 inches. Weight, 147 pounds. Dark wavy hair, dark eyes, dark complexion; dark brown beard, when grown. The lower lip is quite thick and projecting; high and expansive forehead. A noticeable feature is his eyes, which seem to twinkle behind eyelids almost closed, thus giving him a sharp expression. Has letters "N. E. S.," and figures "13," and two dots of India ink on left wrist.

RECORD

"Little Dave" Mooney is a well known New York thief. His specialty is private house work, entering generally by the second story window while the people are downstairs at their meals. He is well known in all the principal cities in the United States, and is considered a very clever "second-story man."

He was arrested in New York City on August 19, 1874, and delivered to the police authorities of Hunter's Point, Long Island, N.Y., where he was wanted for burglary. He was convicted and sentenced to two years in State prison at Sing Sing, in the Queens County Court of Sessions at Hunter's Point, on October 19, 1874, by Judge Pratt, under the name of John H. Smith.

He was arrested again in Albany, N. Y., on December 30, 1880, and taken to Boston, Mass., for the murder of his partner in crime, Edmond Lavoiye, alias Frenchy Lavoiye, and Charles E. Marshall, at No. 22 Florence Street, Boston, where they were rooming, on the night of February 12, 1880. He was also charged with breaking and entering the house of George Norman, in Boston, on the night of February 11, 1880, and stealing therefrom bonds and jewelry valued at $1,500. He was tried in the Supreme Judicial Court of Boston on September 16, 1881, and found guilty of murder in the second degree, and sentenced to Concord prison for life on September 19, 1881.

The following article clipped from the Boston *Herald*, of January 1, 1880, gives a detailed account of his arrest and statement concerning the murder:

MANACLED MOONEY.—PARTICULARS OF HIS ARREST IN GREENBUSH, N.Y.—HIS WHEREABOUTS SINCE HIS FLIGHT FROM BOSTON.—HE DENIES COMMITTING THE LAVOIYE MURDER.

David Mooney, alias John H. Hill, alias James P. Brady, who was arrested in Greenbush, N.Y., Thursday night, December 30, 1880, on the charge of murdering his pal, Edmund A. Lavoiye, at the house No. 22 (now No. 20) Florence Street, this city, reached here last evening in custody of Inspectors Gerraughty and Mahoney. The murder was committed on the evening of February 12, but was not discovered until several days after, when the body of the victim was found in an advanced state of decomposition by Mr. Orpen, the landlord of the house.

It appears, according to the Albany authorities, that Mooney has been residing in Greenbush, a suburb of Albany, for some time, being known to his neighbors as "David Farrell." For about four weeks Detective Riley, of Albany, has suspected him to be the fugitive, but it was not till within a few days that he became confident that Farrell was really Mooney. The detective Thursday evening went to Greenbush about nine o'clock, and, after waiting quietly in a beer saloon on Broadway, smoking a cigar, he soon had the satisfaction of seeing the man he was in search of come in with a tin pail, for the purpose of getting beer. He had no sooner set the pail on the counter than Riley approached him, and stated that he was wanted in Albany to give some information about a diamond pin that had been stolen. Detective Brennan was in company with Riley, and together they brought Mooney across the river and took him to the chief's office, where it was found that he corresponded in every particular to the description contained in the circular, thus leaving no doubt of his being the right party. He was then committed to jail by Chief Malloy.

In answer to questions put to him, Mooney stated that he had been living in Greenbush for the past three months, and had also stopped at Newburg, Hudson, and other river towns, and admitted having been in Boston quite frequently in his lifetime. On going up to the jail he said to Riley, who had previously told him what he was arrested for: "Young fellow, the parties that gave you the 'tip' gave it to you straight." The chief telegraphed to Supt. Adams, informing him of the arrest, and soon afterwards officers went to Albany. During the night Mooney maintained a sullen disposition, but early yesterday morning exhibited an inclination to be defiant. He told one detective (Dewire) that he would not be taken to Boston alive, and said it in such a way that the detective became suspicious that he might attempt to make good his threat. The officer searched him, and found, carefully concealed in his clothing, it is claimed, a piece of steel wire, some four inches long, filed down to a sharp point at one end. Mooney felt quite chagrined, but repeated his threat. He was carefully looked over, and all the marks contained in the description given of him in the Boston *Herald* at the time of the murder were found on him.

At one o'clock p.m., Detectives Gerraughty and Mahoney, of Boston, with Mr. Henry Orpen, at whose house the murder was committed, on Florence Street, arrived here. They presented their papers to Chief Malloy, who pronounced them in proper form and all right, Detectives Riley and Brennan at once proceeded to the jail, and soon after brought Mooney to police headquarters. The prisoner's appearance was in sad contrast to that which marked him while in the "Hub." He was dressed in rough and ill-fitting garments, in place of the broadcloth in which he was wont to appear while mingling in society in Boston. He wore a plush jockey cap, and, with his short and newly-grown bushy whiskers, looked more like a recently-arrived Canadian than the American he has been described. On being introduced to the Boston officers his face changed to an ashy hue, but he said nothing until placed directly before Mr. Orpen, who, without hesitation, said: "That is the man who was at my house with the murdered Lavoiye." Mr. Orpen, continuing, said: "Well, Hill, you look somewhat changed since I saw you last. Don't you know me?"

MOONEY—"Oh, yes; I know you. I don't deny that I was there. It's kind of hard. Well, I am somewhat changed, but not altogether so good-looking."

MR. ORPEN—"Well, it's many a dollar your doings at my house has cost me."

MOONEY—"Well, I am sorry for it; but I suppose you will, or ought to, get your share of the reward." Mooney soon after was questioned by Detective Gerraughty as to his threat that he would not be taken to Boston alive, whereupon the prisoner remarked he would give his word of honor that he would go to Boston peaceably and without trouble. The officers, with their man, left for Boston on the 2:30 train, and arrived here at 9:45 last evening.

During the evening a *Herald* reporter had an extended interview with Mooney. At first he declined positively to say anything bearing on the subject of the murder of Lavoiye or the robbery of Mr. George H. Norman's house, until he could have an opportunity of consulting counsel, but he finally yielded to persuasive pressure, and said:

"Why, one would think from the manner I was arrested at Greenbush that I was some sort of a wild animal. Those officers of Albany are a hard lot. After I left Boston I visited several places, but most of the time I spent at Greenbush, where I boarded and roomed nearly the whole time. It is an easy thing to try a man on circumstantial evidence, especially before he is brought before a proper jury, and I feel certain that at the proper time my claim of innocence of the crime with which I am now charged will be satisfactorily established. I can conscientiously say that I am not guilty of the murder of Lavoiye; neither do I know anything about the robbery of Mr. Norman's house. I do not, however, claim to have a fair or unblemished character, and, more than that, I do not claim to have always been honest. To make such claims would be foolish under the circumstances in which I am now placed.

"It is hardly necessary for me to go into the details of what my professional calling has been. It is enough to say that it is not altogether complimentary to myself; but yet I can truthfully say that I have never committed murder, neither have I garroted a person or broken into a house. I am now thirty years of age, and I am sorry to say that my education has been sadly neglected. I was born in New York City and during the war my father kept a hotel on the Hudson River. He died ten years ago. My mother, a brother and sister are of good character and above reproach. I am grieved at the sorrow I have caused them. I suppose I may attribute my misfortunes to the company I kept in my youth. I have for a long time been well acquainted with Boston, and was here off and on several months before the murder of Lavoiye. I never knew him by that name, however, but was always under the impression his name was Charles E. Marshall, and I called him Charley. I met him during a visit here, and went to lodge with him, but not with any desire to be connected with him in the business he followed. He was a quiet and very peaceable man, and always kept his business to himself, as I did mine. While at the house I never had any trouble with any one, and always paid my bills and treated everybody decently. I sometimes drank a glass of lager and occasionally a glass of whiskey, but never indulged in strong liquors to excess. I was seldom with my companion when he was out of the house, and never saw anything about him or the room that would indicate his calling. I did not know that he carried a revolver, and did not know anything about the robbery of Mr. Norman's house, on Beacon Street, until the day after it is said to have been committed, when I read it in the Boston *Herald*. Marshall, I suppose, also saw a report of the robbery—although he did not tell me of it—as he was in the habit of reading the daily papers.

"I remember something I read about calling on Mr. Orpen relative to the key of my room. It happened that Marshall was out, and had the key of the room with him, on the day it was said I left. Mr. Orpen said he would get a key, and I finally said, 'No matter,' and later on met Marshall and got his key. I did not leave Mr. Orpen's house on the day after the Norman robbery, but went away some days afterwards, and when I last saw Marshall he was alive and well. The day I left him I told him I was going away to be absent some time, but would return. I went to New York. While there I saw in a paper an account of Marshall's murder. I was astounded, and could hardly believe it, and read the report over and over again. I soon realized my position, felt almost bewildered, and went to get the opinion of some of my intimate friends, to see what was best for me to do. My first impulse was to surrender myself to the authorities of Boston. My friends urged me to wait, as they said a certain cop or other party was going to Boston to see if he could identify Marshall. I concluded to wait, and after the identification was established again proposed to give myself up and stand trial. On second reflection I concluded that on account of the excited state of the community, it would be best for me to wait until the heat of the people had time to cool off. I argued that if I went among strangers without money I would stand a poor chance of getting justice; so I concluded to keep out of the way, with the intention of waiting until I got together sufficient money to employ able counsel; but this wish I have never been able to realize, although I have managed to live comfortably. I soon left New York, and came up in the vicinity of Greenbush, a very retired place. I secured board and lodging in a very respectable family, which never until now suspected my calling. One night, shortly after my arrival at my new abode, I was in a saloon on South Pearl Street, Albany, when two men, representing themselves as Boston detectives, came into the place. One of these men was quite drunk, and loudly proclaimed he had come to Albany to get Mooney and the reward offered for his arrest. I stood facing him, and as he spoke he exhibited before my astonished gaze a copy of my photograph, which has been broadcast throughout the country. Although startled I tried to keep cool, and left the place without any delay, without exciting any suspicion. I went to several places from time to time, but continued to hold my residence in Greenbush. In the latter place, soon after my arrival, I learned that a woman had been attracted by a certain resemblance between me and a cut of myself in the *Police Gazette*. She made allusion to it, but hearing nothing further from her, I came to the conclusion that she had forgotten all about the matter. During last summer I went once or twice to Springfield, where I had friends interested in horses, and was not discovered, or 'given away.' I felt at times that I would not be discovered, because my brother, since Marshall's death, has twice been mistaken for me by officers. I felt, however, that at some time or another I must surely stand my trial. For weeks I have anticipated arrest. Several times I again thought of surrendering myself, but the old fear—lack of money to supply desirable counsel—would always come up, and I would give up the idea. I am now glad, however, that I am arrested, and that I will be tried, as the agony I have suffered has been terrible; not because of any crime I have committed, but simply because the charge of murder was constantly hanging over my head. All I ask now is a fair trial, and I am willing to abide by whatever may be the result. I understand one suspicious circumstance counted against me is the fact that I stood with the door of my room ajar while the little girl of Mr. Orpen came up to deliver towels on the day the murder was committed. The inference I draw is that I was supposed to have kept the little girl out so that she could not see anything that had occurred within. This is a very funny circumstance if it is to be considered as evidence, considering that both Marshall and myself commonly stood in the doorway in the same way when either of us was lying on the bed and did not want to be seen. Then it is hinted that I wrote the slip which was found in the room with the body, and signed 'Charles E. Marshall.' I can hardly read, let alone writing. The letter which was sent to Miss Annie Sullivan, the young girl who worked in a restaurant on Harrison Avenue, and who resided in South Boston, was written by Marshall for me. He signed the name 'John H. Hill,' and the letter was purely in fun. That is how, I suppose, I have got the alias of 'Hill.' I never heard myself called James H. Brady until the police of Boston sent out their circulars for the purpose of effecting my arrest. I suppose I will find myself possessed of other aliases before I get through with Boston. Now, in relation to the Sullivan girl, I always considered her a good young lady. I never courted her, or proposed marriage to her. My relations to her were like those of a person charitably inclined. I have never been troubled about women, and I never have intrusted any of my secrets with them. I do suspect, however, that the woman who thought she saw a similarity between my face and the police photograph was the woman who finally caused my arrest by apprising Detective Riley of her suspicions. When the detectives appeared in the beer saloon in Greenbush I supposed they were a crowd of railroad men who had dropped in to pass away a few hours. The first I knew, I was pounced upon by five of them, and although I called for an explanation, they hustled me off in a hurry towards Albany. They carried me to the ferry, and then only did they condescend to tell me a falsehood when they said I was wanted in the city for the larceny of a diamond pin. When I reached headquarters I was shown my photograph, and of course at once surmised the real object of my arrest. In regard to my friend Marshall, I wish to say that while I was with him in Boston he frequently had other men call at the house, 22 Florence Street, to see him. I knew them by sight, and probably could recall some of the places they were in the habit of visiting. I knew them by their given names simply; they came frequently, at all hours, and it is possible that some one of them might have murdered Marshall. I know of one instance, when I came home from the 'road' one morning, that I found a man asleep with Marshall. Another circumstance which has been held up to sustain the supposition that I committed murder is that the gold watch owned by the murdered man was missing when the body was found. Now I know that in January, prior to the murder, Marshall pawned his watch in Providence, because he told me he did. I asked him why he did not borrow from me, but he said he had rather pawn the watch. I had plenty of ready money at the time. I also know that Marshall had a large account in some bank in one of the Eastern cities, but he never told me which city. I am willing to bet that bank account is still standing, but I suppose it will be hard to find it, as it cannot be ascertained under what name he made the deposits. I think Marshall had considerable money, but cannot say how much. While living on Florence Street he frequently made trips to New York, but for what purpose I cannot say. I was acquainted with a man named Glover in New York, and I suppose Marshall also knew him. I never had any dealings with the man. I never saw anything about Marshall to indicate that he was mixed up with the Norman robbery, and I do not know anything about the bonds said to have been stolen at the time. I never saw any crucibles about the room for melting jewelry; neither did I, to my recollection, hire a hack on Kneeland Street, in which I was said to have dropped a diamond ring which was claimed to have been stolen from the house of Mr. Norman. I did not get shaved on the day I left Boston; I had nothing I wished to shave off. It is very funny how stories get started. Time will show my innocence of the charges against me, and all I ask is that the press and the people will give me a fair chance."

After arriving at the central office in Boston, Mooney was, after a short delay, placed in a cell in the basement of the City Hall, in charge of an officer. He appeared quite fatigued, and soon after reaching his cell fell into a sound slumber. He will be committed to jail today, to await trial.

The following article also appeared in one of the New York papers:

A MURDERER'S CONFESSION.—WHY ONE BURGLAR KILLED
ANOTHER.—A WOMAN AND DIAMONDS THE CAUSE.

(Special Dispatch to the New York Evening Telegram.)

BOSTON, September 27, 1881.—Mooney, the New York burglar, recently sentenced to imprisonment for life for killing
his confederate, Lavoiye, has confessed his guilt. A quarrel
arose, it appears, about a pair of diamond earrings. Mooney
discovered that Lavoiye had given them to a woman, and
Lavoiye denied the fact. Mooney, who had obtained them
from the woman, then drew them from his pocket. Lavoiye
became angered, and attempted to draw his pistol, when
Mooney shot him. The earrings were stolen property, and
Mooney feared they might serve as a clue.

The Annals of Manhattan Crime
by Patrick M. Wall

Patrick M. Wall is a criminal attorney in New York. He wrote this description of Manhattan's most famous crimes for New York *magazine in 1988.*

The ghosts of criminals and victims are all around us. Rioters, poisoners, gang bosses killed by other gang bosses, lovers who killed in passion, robbers who murdered for greed, assassins, bystanders, snipers—all have left their mark on Manhattan. The Strong Arm Squad was born here. A baby-faced cop killer inspired a famous Cagney role. *Looking for Mr. Goodbar* became a parable of the lonely singles life.

I often pass by 149 West 43rd Street, a rather dreary building near Broadway. Years ago, I learned what had happened there one night in July 1912, when it was the Hotel Metropole. Now I cannot walk by the spot without imagining the gambler Herman Rosenthal as he left the hotel early one morning and wandered into a fatal ambush. And when I pass Sparks Steak House, on 46th Street near Third Avenue, I see not only the body of crime boss Paul Castellano but also the mob of thousands that sacked the nearby Provost Marshal's office in 1863, setting off the biggest riot in the nation's history.

I practice criminal law, and my fascination with crime is professional rather than morbid. At least, I can make a good argument to that effect. I am also a native New Yorker; I love this city and try to learn all I can about its past. The combination of my vocation and avocation has produced this article. I've selected these particular crimes because of their notoriety and historical importance—but also to illustrate that human nature (and the crimes it produces) remains remarkably consistent through the ages. Someone else would come up with a different list, certainly, but most of these crimes belong in any accounting of the dark side of the island's heritage.

1. The "Alehouse Plot"
1741

By the 1740s, the colony of New York, at Manhattan's southern tip, had 12,000 people, including 2,000 slaves. On February 28, 1741, Robert Hogg's tobacco shop on Broad and South William Streets was burglarized. The investigation led to two slaves, Caesar and Prince, and to Hughson's Alehouse, at 10 West Street, where the money was found buried. Mary Burton, a teenage alehouse servant, soon claimed that slaves at the alehouse had hatched a plot to seize control of Manhattan, kill the white men, and divide the women among themselves. Panic followed. By the time sanity returned some months later, 4 whites and 25 blacks—all probably innocent—had been either hanged or burned at the stake.

2. The Doctors' Riot
1788

On April 13, a student at New York Hospital joked to a boy that students were dissecting the body of the boy's mother. By an unhappy coincidence, she had recently died; when her grave was checked later that day, her body was missing. Word of the body snatching and of the student's remark spread quickly. A mob entered the hospital and found evidence of recently unearthed bodies. The next day, an angry crowd marched toward Columbia College, between Barclay and Murray Streets, west of Church Street. The mob pushed past a protesting Alexander Hamilton and searched the building. Finding nothing, the rioters headed toward The Fields (now City Hall Park), storming the city jail, where some doctors and students had been sheltered since the day before. The mob demanded the doctors. Governor George Clinton finally ordered troops to open fire on the advancing rioters. Eight were killed and many injured.

3. The Hanging of John Johnson
1824

A man named John Johnson learned that a tourist named James Murray was carrying a lot of money. Johnson invited Murray to his home at 65 Front Street, killed him, and abandoned the body nearby. The unidentified body was placed on display in City Hall Park. One of the thousands who passed identified it as Murray's. Johnson, known to have been Murray's host, was soon arrested. His confession and conviction followed. On April 2, about 50,000 people gathered at Second Avenue and 13th Street to witness his hanging.

4. The Murder of Helen Jewett
1836

In the mid-1830s, Helen Jewett was Manhattan's most famous prostitute. Called "The Girl in Green" because of the color of her wardrobe, she was in her early twenties. Her many lovers included Richard P. Robinson. Early on Sunday, April 10, Robinson visited Helen at a brothel at 41 Thomas Street, a hatchet hidden under his coat. After he left, Helen's body was found, her head caved in from ax wounds. Robinson was arrested, but the citizenry did not favor his prosecution.

Most newspapers argued that he had rid Manhattan of a notorious sinner. The common cry was that "no man should hang for the murder of a whore." Robinson was acquitted by a jury, some of whose members had been bribed and none of whom had heard from a key witness who died of a suspicious poisoning shortly before the trial. Helen Jewett's murder went unpunished.

5. The Flour Riot
1837

The price of flour had risen to $12 a barrel; bread was scarce, and some of Manhattan's poor were starving. On February 10, a crowd at a meeting in City Hall Park marched on Eli Hart & Company, a wheat-and-flour store on Washington Street. The resulting riot led to several deaths and injuries and to the destruction of much of the store's grain. Virtually nothing was stolen. The price of flour soon increased again.

6. The Murder of Mary Rogers
1841

Mary Cecilia Rogers, 21, worked at a cigar stand at 319 Broadway and was known as "The Beautiful Cigar Girl." She lived in her mother's boardinghouse at 126 Nassau Street and was engaged to Daniel Payne. On Sunday afternoon, July 25, she told Payne that she was going to visit a relative and asked him to pick her up at six on Jane Street. When he arrived, she was not there. Three days later, her body was found in the Hudson River and some of her clothing nearby on the shore. She had been strangled with a piece of her own petticoat. Some months later, Payne was found dead at the place where Mary's clothing had been found, an empty bottle of laudanum nearby and a note in his pocket reading, "Here I am on the very spot. God forgive me for my misspent life." Her murder was never solved. A year later, Edgar Allan Poe, who had patronized her cigar stand, published a story based on her case though set in Paris: "The Mystery of Marie Roget."

7. The Suicide or Escape of a Condemned Millionaire
1842

John C. Colt, the brother of Samuel Colt, the inventor of the revolver, had been sentenced to death for murder and was awaiting execution in the Tombs Prison, bounded by Lafayette, Leonard, Mulberry, and White Streets. Skeptics predicted that no rope would ever stretch such a rich and well-connected neck. On November 18—the date set for his hanging—he was allowed to marry his fiancée, Caroline Henshaw. Later, just before he was to walk to the gallows, a fire broke out, and smoke filled the prison. Several prisoners escaped. When the commotion died down, a body was found in Colt's cell, a knife in its heart. That same day—apparently without a proper identification of the body—officials announced Colt's suicide. The body was buried later that night. It was widely assumed, though never proved, that the body so quickly buried was that of a ringer and that Colt had fled during the planned fire. Years later, rumors held that Colt was living in California with Henshaw, who had disappeared soon after his "suicide."

8. The Astor Place Riots
1849

A feud between English actor William Charles Macready and American actor Edwin Forrest ended tragically after the Englishman beat out the American for the role of Macbeth at the Opera House on Astor Place. Macready's first appearance was thwarted by demonstrators who threw things onto the stage. On May 10, Macready tried again, but a crowd of more than 10,000 protesters gathered outside. A few entered the building, bent upon kidnapping him, but were arrested by the police, who escorted Macready, in disguise, to safety. The crowd rioted and troops were called in. When the mob attacked the troops, gunfire broke out. More than 20 rioters died and more than 100 were injured. Peace was not restored for several days. Macready escaped by train to Boston and by boat to England, never to return.

9. The End of the Old Brewery
1852

By the middle of the nineteenth century, Manhattan's major hotbed of crime was the Old Brewery, a 50-year-old building located at 59 Cross Street (now Park Street) in the middle of the notorious Five Points area. About 1,000 people lived there in unspeakable squalor. The police estimated that an average of a murder a day was committed in the building. The New York Missionary Society finally bought it and planned to raze it to make room for a mission house. The inhabitants refused to leave. On December 2, police invaded the building and evicted its occupants, including many criminals. The Old Brewery was then demolished. In the process, workers uncovered the bones of many victims of the violence that had ruled the place for more than a decade.

10. The Honeymoon Gang's Fall
1853

A group called the Honeymoon Gang began a reign of terror in the mid-nineteenth century, regularly standing near the intersection of Madison Avenue and 29th Street and robbing passing pedestrians. In 1853, George W. Walling became captain of the police precinct covering the area. He armed his strongest cops with clubs and ordered them to beat Honeymooners on sight without mercy. The Strong Arm Squad was born. The infamous Honeymooners were quickly gone, at least from Walling's precinct.

11. Good-Bye to "The Butcher"
1855

A bar owner named Bill "The Butcher" Poole was one of the Manhattan leaders of the disreputable Know-Nothing Party. On February 24, he entered Stanwix Hall, at Broadway near Prince Street, and confronted a political opponent named John Morrissey and some of

Morrissey's friends. A fight erupted, and Poole was fatally shot by a man named Lewis Baker, who fled by boat to the Canary Islands and was captured there by law officers. The Know-Nothings, capitalizing on the killing, arranged an enormous funeral. The procession included an estimated 200,000 people, and Broadway was crowded with "mourners" from Bleecker Street to the ferry landing at the southern tip of Manhattan. Baker was tried three times for the murder; all three trials resulted in hung juries. The prosecution against him was ultimately abandoned.

12. The Bond Street Murder
1857

Late on January 29, bachelor Harvey Burdell, 46, returned to his home at 31 Bond Street. Neighbors saw him enter and heard him shriek the word "murder." Next morning, police found his brutally stabbed and strangled body. Nothing was missing from his room. A boarder in his house, Emma Cunningham, then claimed that she was entitled to Burdell's estate because she had recently married him (he wore a false set of whiskers at the ceremony, she said). She produced a marriage certificate and witnesses who had seen her wed the oddly bearded man. Cynics suspected that under that false beard was the face of John Eckel, who also lived at 31 Bond and was thought to be Emma's lover. She was arrested for murder, but a jury found insufficient evidence and acquitted her. She later served time for fraud after she had passed off another woman's newborn as her own child by Burdell and once again sought Burdell's money.

13. The Police Riot
1857

In the mid-1850s, the corrupt Fernando Wood was mayor and depended for much of his graft on the equally corrupt Municipal Police. In 1857, the legislature abolished the Municipal Police and created the Metropolitan Police. Wood refused to go along. Captain Walling, originator of the Strong Arm Squad, agreed to join the Metropolitans, and on June 16, he led 50 of them to City Hall to arrest Wood. A battle broke out in City Hall and on its nearby grounds. Walling's small force was overwhelmed by 800 Municipals loyal to Wood. More than 50 people were injured. The Seventh Regiment, marching (by chance) nearby, was called into action on behalf of the Metropolitans and surrounded City Hall. Wood surrendered and was arrested. A legal battle over which force had jurisdiction in the city was decided in favor of the Metropolitans.

14. The Great Gang Fight
1857

Rivalry among such gangs as the Dead Rabbits, the Plug Uglies, and the Bowery Boys resulted in a gang fight on July 4. Nearly 1,000 gang members joined in a mélée that began on Bayard Street and spilled over to the Bowery and to nearby Mulberry, Baxter, and Elizabeth Streets. Federal troops finally ended the brawl. Eight gang members died in the fight, and more than 100 were injured.

15. The Burning of the Crystal Palace
1858

Built in 1852, the Crystal Palace was one of America's greatest museums. It stood where Bryant Park is now, just west of Manhattan's reservoir. On October 5, an unidentified arsonist put the torch to it, and the palace burned to the ground. More than $2 million in art was lost.

16. The Draft Riot
1863

Manhattan's poor bitterly opposed the Conscription Act of 1863, which provided for a draft but also permitted a man to avoid service by paying $300. On the morning of July 13, names of draftees were to be drawn at the United States Provost Marshal's office at Third Avenue and 46th Street. A mob gathered outside and set fire to the building. Thus began a four-day riot unmatched in this country before or since. More than 50,000 rioters fought fewer than 1,000 policemen. When the riot ended on July 16—with troops from the battle of Gettysburg on the way—more than 100 buildings had been burned, estimates of the dead ranged from the hundreds to 2,000, and thousands had been injured. The rioters deemed blacks to be the cause of the Civil War and thus of the hated draft; more than 70 blacks were lynched or otherwise murdered.

17. The Parade Killings
1869

On July 12, the Orange Society held a parade on Eighth Avenue to celebrate the Protestant Irish victory over the Catholic Irish at the Battle of the Boyne. At Eighth Avenue and 24th Street, a sniper fired into the procession from a window. Various regiments at the parade opened fire, and a furious battle erupted. By the time the smell of gun smoke left the air, up to 50 people (including three police officers) lay dead or dying, and hundreds had been wounded.

18. The Killing of "Big Jim" Fisk
1872

James "Big Jim" Fisk, 37, had become rich through financial manipulations and famous for his flamboyance. He had a mistress named Helen Josephine "Josie" Mansfield. Neither was faithful to the other, and she became the lover of Edward S. Stokes, who then tried to use her relationship with Fisk to blackmail the tycoon. Stokes eventually sued Fisk for libel after Fisk said that Stokes and Josie were living together. On January 6, Fisk won the case, and Stokes learned that he would be arrested for blackmail. That evening, Fisk went to the Broadway Central Hotel, on Broadway between Bleecker and West 3rd Streets. While Fisk was walking up a staircase, Stokes shot him fatally in the stomach. One trial ended in a hung jury, and a murder conviction in a second was reversed; Stokes was finally found guilty of manslaughter and sentenced to prison for four years.

19. The Escape of Boss Tweed
1875

Justice finally caught up with Tammany Hall boss William Marcy Tweed in 1873, when he got a year in prison for various crimes. Released in January 1875, he was soon jailed again for failing to post $3 million bail in a civil case. His guards often took him out for a meal—shared by all—at the Tweed home at 647 Madison Avenue, between 59th and 60th Streets. During one of these friendly dinners, at 6:30 on December 4, Tweed escaped. He hid in New Jersey, Florida, and Cuba and then sailed for Spain under an assumed name. Spotted en route, he was captured in Spain and returned to the Ludlow Street jail, where he died on April 12, 1878.

20. The Death of an Abortionist
1878

Ann Trow Lohman (alias "Madame Restell") was indicted for abortion-related crimes early in 1878, after almost 40 years as Manhattan's most famous and despised abortionist. On the morning of April 1—the day her trial was to begin—she lay in the bathtub in her mansion on the corner of Fifth Avenue and 52nd Street and slit her throat with a carving knife. She left an estate worth more than $1 million. The next day's New York *Times* stated that she had "made an attractive part of the finest avenue in the City odious by her constant presence."

21. The Great Burglary
1878

The Manhattan Savings Institution at Broadway and Bleecker Street was the scene of the nineteenth century's greatest bank theft. Its mastermind was George Leonidas Leslie, a society figure who was also a major thief. On October 27, while the local cop on the beat acted as a lookout, Leslie and his accomplices cracked the safe and walked off with $2,747,000. Many of the thieves were convicted and received long prison terms. Leslie was not among them. It was rumored that he had made a deal and turned in his accomplices.

22. Death on the Bridge
1883

On May 30, within days of the celebrated opening of the Brooklyn Bridge, pickpockets were working the crowd strolling across the city's newest marvel. When some victims shouted, the crowd panicked and ran. Twelve people died in the crush, and many were injured.

23. A Morphine Murder
1891

In 1890, nineteen-year-old Helen Potts secretly married medical student Carlyle W. Harris, unaware that Harris was secretly wed to another. Harris soon tired of Helen. He got some quinine pills from a pharmacist and gave them to Helen, who had complained of headaches. In one pill, he had placed a lethal dose of morphine. Helen took the deadly pill on the night of January 31, 1891, in her room at Miss Comstock's Boarding School for Girls, at 32 West 40th Street. She died the next morning. The pupils of her eyes were contracted—a primary symptom of morphine poisoning—but the attending physician granted her family's request that publicity be avoided (she'd had a recent abortion) and said nothing. New York *World* reporter Isaac

"Ike" White, however, became interested in the case and soon learned of the secret marriage, the pills, and the contracted pupils. His exposé led to the exhumation of Helen's body; the autopsy showed morphine poisoning. Harris was convicted of her murder and was executed.

24. The Murder of "Old Shakespeare"
1891

Late in the nineteenth century, an alcoholic prostitute who haunted the Bowery had earned the nickname "Old Shakespeare," because she often quoted at length from the Bard. On April 23, she took a client to Room 31 of the East River Hotel, on the corner of Catherine and Water Streets. Her body was found there the next morning, so badly mutilated that rumors spread that Jack the Ripper—then at large in London—had come to Manhattan. The resulting publicity pressured the police to find the killer. Ameer Ben Ali, an Algerian who lived across the hall from her, was arrested on the scantiest of circumstantial evidence and was convicted. The unfortunate Ben Ali served eleven years in prison before some concerned citizens proved him innocent. The murder was never solved.

25. Ike White Solves Another Morphine Murder
1892

When prosperous Dr. Robert Buchanan, 32, divorced his attractive wife, Helen, in 1890 and married a 50-year-old brothel keeper named Anna Sutherland, people took notice. The couple made a home at 267 West 11th Street. Within a year or so, Buchanan began talking about "dumping the old hag" around the same time as she was talking about writing him out of her will. In February 1892, after Carlyle Harris had been convicted of the murder of Helen Potts, Buchanan told his drinking companions that Harris had "not understood his business," adding—mysteriously—"Every agent has its reagent." Although she had been in good health, Anna took gravely ill after breakfast on April

21. She died the next day, and attending physicians attributed her death to a cerebral hemorrhage. But *World* reporter Ike White doubted the diagnosis and began his own investigation. He was soon able to persuade the authorities to exhume Anna's body and perform an autopsy. Her body contained a lethal dose of morphine and traces of atropine, a derivative of belladonna. The pupils of Anna's eyes had not been contracted like those of Helen Potts, because belladonna dilates the pupils; the two drugs had canceled each other out. "Every agent has its reagent," Buchanan had said. He was soon convicted of murder and executed.

26. The Nan Patterson Case
1904

On the morning of June 4, former Floradora Girl Nan Patterson rode downtown in a hansom cab with her lover, Francis Thomas "Caesar" Young, a well-known gambler. They were heading for a pier from which Young was to embark on a second-honeymoon cruise with his wife, with whom he had recently reconciled over Nan's strong objections. At West Broadway and Franklin Street, a shot rang out from inside the cab, and the driver heard Nan yell, "Why did you do it?" Young was found with a bullet in his chest. Nan claimed he had shot himself, unhappy that their affair was ending. The police were skeptical, since the angle of the bullet's entry was inconsistent with a self-inflicted wound and the gun had been found in Young's pocket. Nan was arrested for murder, but the question of her guilt resulted in two hung juries. The prosecutor concluded that no jury would unanimously believe that such a sweet young thing could commit so brutal a crime. When Nan was released from the Tombs, a crowd of thousands cheered her. She resumed her show-business career but soon faded into obscurity.

27. The Stanford White Murder
1906

On June 25, Stanford White, the nation's most famous architect, sat at the opening-night performance of *Mam'zelle Champagne*, playing at the roof garden of Madison Square Garden—a building he had designed for the block between Madison and Fourth Avenues and 26th and 27th Streets. Millionaire Harry K. Thaw approached White's table and shot him three times in the face, killing him instantly. After saying, "He deserved it. He ruined my wife," Thaw meekly surrendered. His wife was Evelyn Nesbit, 20, an ex-Floradora Girl who had been White's mistress. Thaw had brought her to the Garden that night so she'd see the killing. He was acquitted of murder by reason of insanity and committed to an asylum.

28. A Chinatown Murder
1909

Early in [the 20th] century, the undisputed leader of Chinatown was Mock Duck, head of the Hip Sing Tong. In April 1909, during a war between the Hip Sings and the On Leong Tong, a comedian named Ah Hoon began publicly poking fun at Mock Duck. The tong leader's sense of humor quickly ran out, and later in the year, he announced that Ah Hoon would die on December 30. That day, the comedian was well guarded during his stage show and was then taken to his room in a building on Chatham Square. He seemed invulnerable. His only window faced the wall of the building next door. On Leongs guarded his door. But the next morning, he was found dead. Before midnight, a man with a silencer-equipped gun had been lowered down from the roof by rope. Ali Hoon had been shot to death through the window.

29. Behind the "Sullivan Law"
1911

At 1:45 p.m. on January 23, Fitzhugh Coyle Goldsborough, a mentally unbalanced Harvard graduate, lay in wait for someone—anyone—a few doors from the Princeton Club, at 119 East 21st Street. As author David Graham Phillips was about to enter the club, Goldsborough shot him fatally, then took his own life. Public outrage caused Tammany

Hall boss Timothy "Big Tim" Sullivan to obtain passage of strict gun-control legislation, thereafter known as the Sullivan Law.

30. A Deadly Fire
1911

On March 25, a fire at the Triangle Shirt Waist Company, at 23 Washington Place, killed 147 employees, most of them young women, Thirteen engagement rings were found in the ruins. Some would-be victims were rescued from the roof by NYU law students who stretched a ladder from the roof of the law school next door. The building's owners, who had permitted exit doors to be locked, were tried for criminally negligent homicide and acquitted. The outcry over the tragedy caused the legislature to pass unprecedented fire-safety laws.

31. A Life Behind Bars
1911

Shortly after midnight on July 27 in the Hotel Iroquois, at 49 West 44th Street, former bellboy Paul Geidel, 17, robbed and killed William Henry Jackson, 73, a wealthy stockbroker. Geidel confessed, was convicted, and was sentenced to life. An unfortunately commonplace story, perhaps, but Geidel was not released until May 1980. His imprisonment for more than 68 years is believed the longest in U.S. history for a single crime.

32. Owney Madden Strikes
1912

By the twenties, Owney "The Killer" Madden had become one of the city's most prominent gangsters. But "success" has to start somewhere. On February 3, Madden, then 20, tracked William Henshaw—with whom he was angry for some reason—to a trolley car at Ninth Avenue and 16th Street and shot him dead. Madden was arrested, but no one seemed willing to testify against him. He was never prosecuted.

33. Death of a Gambler
1912

At 2 a.m. on July 16, gambler Herman Rosenthal was shot dead outside the Hotel Metropole, at 149 West 43rd Street. The killers included thugs like Whitey Lewis, Dago Frank, Leftie Louie, and Gyp the Blood. Lieutenant Charles Becker, a cop whom Rosenthal had identified as a "graftee," was suspected of being behind the murder. Three men who claimed to have plotted the killing with Becker were granted immunity from prosecution, and Becker was indicted for murder. After his first conviction was reversed on appeal, a second trial—prosecuted by district attorney Charles S. Whitman—resulted in a conviction that stood up. Whitman was later elected governor and, in that role, denied Becker's clemency application. After Becker was executed at Sing Sing on July 30, 1915, his widow attached a plaque to his coffin reading, CHARLES BECKER, MURDERED JULY 30, 1915 BY GOVERNOR WHITMAN. The plaque was removed by the police under orders from the Bronx County district attorney.

34. The Wall Street Bombing
1920

At noon on September 16, a bomb concealed in a horse-drawn wagon exploded just opposite the J.P. Morgan Building, at Wall and Broad Streets. Thirty-eight people died and more than 400 were injured. Anarchists were suspected and a massive investigation followed, but no charges were ever brought.

35. The End of Monk Eastman
1920

At the turn of the century, Monk Eastman had been the city's most feared gang leader. But a prison term had cost him his power, and service in the Army in World War I may have cost him his killer instinct. In 1920, he was engaged in a bitter quarrel with competitors (or possibly allies) over the proceeds from illegal liquor sales. Sometime between four and five in the morning of December 26, one of his enemies put five slugs into him just outside the subway entrance on the south side of 14th Street west of Fourth Avenue. He quickly bled to death.

36. A Hit on "Legs" I
1924

Jack "Legs" Diamond was a vicious but strangely popular gangster of the twenties. Allied with "Little Augie" Orgen, Diamond began hijacking bootleg-liquor trucks owned by "Big Bill" Dwyer, a partner of Frank Costello's. In October 1924, Legs was driving alone on Fifth Avenue when some of Dwyer's men pulled alongside near 110th Street and opened fire with shotguns. Diamond was seriously wounded, but he drove to nearby Mount Sinai Hospital, where he was treated and recovered.

37. A Theater "Orgy"
1926

On February 22, Earl Carroll, one of Broadway's most famous producers, threw a party at his theater, at Seventh Avenue near 50th Street, after a performance of *Vanities*. An attractive young lady brightened the festivities early the next morning by bathing nude in a tub of champagne. Prohibition was in effect, and federal authorities subpoenaed Carroll to explain the source of the alcohol. He foolishly swore before a grand jury that no lady had bathed in a tub. He was convicted of perjury. Sentenced to a year in prison, he was released within four months after suffering a breakdown.

38. A Hit on "Legs" II
1927

On the night of October 15, Louis "Lepke" Buchalter and Jacob

"Gurrah" Shapiro found their rival Little Augie Orgen standing with his bodyguard, Legs Diamond, on the corner of Norfolk and Delancey Streets. They killed Little Augie and left Legs for dead with two bullets in his chest, just under his heart. Taken to Bellevue Hospital, Diamond was reported by the *Times* to be dying. He recovered again.

39. Death of a Crime Kingpin
1928

On November 4, at about 10:45 p.m., Arnold Rothstein, America's richest and most powerful criminal for more than a decade, was shot in Room 349 of the Park Central (now the Omni Park Central), at Seventh Avenue and 55th Street. He managed to stagger down to the 56th Street service entrance before collapsing. He died after refusing to say who shot him. There were rumors, never confirmed, that he was killed because he had reneged on card-game losses of $300,000. An overcoat belonging to one George A. McManus was found in the room. McManus was tried for murder, but the evidence was too weak, and the judge directed an acquittal.

40. The "Hotsy-Totsy" Killings
1929

Legs Diamond owned the Hotsy-Totsy Club, a speakeasy on the second floor of 1721 Broadway (between 54th and 55th Streets). At about 3:45 a.m. on July 13, two rough-and-tumble brothers, Peter and William "Red" Cassidy, entered the club and picked a fight (for reasons unknown) with Diamond and one of his henchmen, Charles Entratta. The Cassidys were unarmed, but Diamond and Entratta did not hold out for a fair fight. Red died with five bullets in him, and an "innocent bystander"—an ex-con armed with two loaded guns—was killed by gunfire. Word of the killings soon spread, and thousands gathered outside the club, blocking traffic. Diamond and Entratta fled but were soon indicted for the double killing. They eventually returned, but not until virtually all the known witnesses had either disappeared or been murdered. Neither Diamond nor Entratta was ever convicted of the killings.

41. The Great Vanishing Act
1930

On August 6, at 9:15 p.m., New York State Supreme Court Justice Joseph Force Crater, 41, said good-bye to friends in front of Billy Haas's Restaurant, at 332 West 45th Street, entered a cab, and headed for oblivion. His disappearance became the most famous in the nation's history. Over the years, there were many supposed sightings of the judge or his body, but his fate remains unknown.

42. A Hit on "Legs" III
1930

Just before noon on October 12, Diamond had been relaxing with his lady friend Marion "Kiki" Roberts in Room 829 of the Hotel Monticello, at 35 West 64th Street. Two gunmen entered his room and pumped five bullets into him, including two in his chest and one in his forehead. He was rushed to Polyclinic Hospital, where, as the *Times* reported, he was "expected to die." The district attorney and police commissioner rushed to his bedside, but Diamond said he did not recognize the gunmen and had no idea why anyone would wish him harm. "He's lying about that, of course," said the commissioner. Diamond said he'd survived by taking "two good shots of whiskey." This was the last Manhattan attempt on his life. He was finally killed by two thugs in a boardinghouse at 67 Dove Street in Albany on December 18, 1931.

43. The Capture of "Two-Gun" Crowley
1931

On May 7, two days after killing a police officer, Francis "Two-Gun"

Crowley was tracked to a small apartment on the top floor of a five-story building at 303 West 90th Street. Crowley was hiding with his girl-friend and another killer. Around 300 police surrounded the building, and 10,000 people watched the greatest siege in Manhattan's history. The cops fired more than 700 rounds. Crowley, who was wounded, fired almost 200 himself before being captured. Crowley was convicted of murder and executed at 20. A 1937 movie, *Angels With Dirty Faces*, starring James Cagney, was based upon his life and death.

44. The Murder of a Little Boy
1931

As part of a bloody feud with Arthur "Dutch Schultz" Flegenheimer, Vincent Coll set out on July 28 to kill Joey Rao, Schultz's policy boss. The attempt failed, and machine-gun fire from a car in front of Rao's Helmar Social Club, at 208 East 107th Street, struck a group of young children, killing five-year-old Michael Vengalli. One of Manhattan's biggest manhunts followed. Coll was caught and hired famed criminal lawyer Samuel S. Leibowitz with ransom money obtained by kidnapping one of Owney Madden's henchmen. Leibowitz won an acquittal, and Coll returned to the streets with the new nickname "Mad Dog" and with bitter enemies—the public, the police, and most of Manhattan's gang leaders.

45. Death of a Mafia Boss
1931

On September 10, crime boss Salvatore Maranzano was in his office at the Grand Central (now the Helmsley) Building, at 230 Park Avenue, awaiting a visit from Lucky Luciano and Vito Genovese. Maranzano had arranged for Mad Dog Coll to kill them there for $50,000, half of which had been paid in advance. The intended victims learned of the plot and hired four men to turn the tables on Maranzano. The four, posing as federal agents, entered the office and murdered Maranzano.

On their way out, they passed Coll, who wisely thought it best not to pursue the contract. Luciano was quickly recognized as organized crime's new leader.

46. The End of "Mad Dog" Coll
1932

On February 8, the war between Mad Dog Coll and Dutch Schultz ended at the Lincoln Chemist's Drugstore, at 314 West 23rd Street. Coll was in a phone booth there trying to extort money from Owney Madden. Madden kept Coll on the phone while the call was traced. Within minutes, three assassins arrived and Coll was machine-gunned to death. He was 23.

47. A Lindbergh Clue
1934

On September 15, Walter Lyle was working at a Warner-Quinlan gas station at 2115 Lexington Avenue, at 127th Street. A man drove in and asked for five gallons of gas, paying with a five-dollar bill. As the man drove off, Lyle noticed that the bill was a gold certificate. Since such currency had been removed from circulation in 1933, Lyle thought the bank might reject it. He wrote on the bill the car's license-plate number—4U13-14. Someone at his bank noticed that the bill's serial number checked out as a number on ransom money paid for the kidnapped baby of Charles Lindbergh. Bruno Richard Hauptmann, the driver of the car, was arrested on September 19. After one of the nation's most sensational trials, Hauptmann was convicted of murder—a verdict still in doubt by some—and was executed.

48. A Harlem Riot
1935

At 4 p.m. on March 18, a young black boy was caught stealing a small item from the S.H. Kress Five and Ten Cent Store at 356 West 125th Street. The boy was scolded by store personnel and allowed to leave. Rumors soon spread, however, that he had been brutally beaten and that a black woman who had protested his treatment had had both her arms broken and had been arrested. A crowd gathered near the store. When a hearse chanced to stop nearby, the crowd assumed the boy had been killed. The crowd—now a mob—destroyed the store. A riot began. Passersby were beaten, police were attacked, stores were looted, and cars were burned. The mayhem lasted into the night. When morning came, the accounting read 1 dead, 11 shot, more than 100 hospitalized, and almost 100 under arrest.

49. A Night of Mob Violence
1933

Shortly after midnight on October 23, Marty Krompier, one of Dutch Schultz's lieutenants in the policy racket, was in the Hollywood Barber Shop, in the subway arcade at Broadway and 47th Street. A gunman entered and shot him four times—the culmination of a night of violence that included the shootings in Newark of Schultz and three of his bodyguards. The killings had been ordered by Lucky Luciano and other organized-crime leaders to prevent Schultz from pursuing his plan to kill special prosecutor Thomas E. Dewey. Krompier actually survived; Schultz and his bodyguards were not so fortunate. Luciano had saved Dewey's life, for there was little doubt that Schultz was serious about murdering him.

50. A Beekman Tower Killing
1935

At 2 a.m. on November 12, Greta Peitz, 31, shot and killed her lover, Fritz Gebhardt, in his apartment on the twenty-first floor of Beekman Tower, at First Avenue and 49th Street, near Mitchell Place. They'd met the year before on a cruise; she was a divorcée, he a German whose

Jewish wife was still in Germany. He rented Greta her own apartment in the Beekman Tower and promised he was about to divorce his wife because of her religion. Later, he reneged. Greta was defended by Samuel S. Leibowitz. Near the end of one of Manhattan's most sensational trials of the thirties, she claimed she had acted in self-defense after Gebhardt tried to force her into an unnatural sex act. Nothing supported this defense except her own word. But Gebhardt (who had been painted by Leibowitz as a pro-Nazi supporter of the master-race theory) was not around to refute it. She was acquitted.

51. "Lepke" Surrenders
1939

Louis "Lepke" Buchalter, head of Murder, Inc., organized crime's enforcement arm, had been the object of a nationwide manhunt since he jumped bail on federal narcotics charges. His fugitive status was causing the Mob severe problems through increased law-enforcement pressure, so the Mob bosses deceived Lepke into giving himself up. He was told that if he surrendered personally to J. Edgar Hoover, he would be prosecuted solely by federal authorities and not turned over to Manhattan district attorney Thomas E. Dewey, who had far more serious charges to bring. At about 10 p.m. on August 24, Lepke got into a car parked at Fifth Avenue and 28th Street. Seated inside were Hoover and columnist Walter Winchell, present at Lepke's request as a safety measure. His federal conviction later that year was followed by another at Dewey's hand, and new evidence resulted in his conviction for a 1936 Brooklyn murder. He was executed in March 1944.

52. The "Mad Bomber" Strikes
1940

On November 18, a bomb was found in a Con Edison building at 170 West 64th Street. It was removed and disarmed. No one was hurt. And no one knew that it had been planted there by a man who would later become known as the "Mad Bomber" and would terrorize the city for years.

53. The *S.S. Normandie* Burns
1942

On the afternoon of February 11, Mafia soldiers set fire to the *S.S. Normandie,* a French luxury liner being converted to a troop transport, at Pier 88 on the Hudson River at West 48th Street. One man was killed and at least 128 were injured. The arson had been ordered by the imprisoned Lucky Luciano, who reasoned that the government would think foreign agents were responsible and would seek the Mafia's help in protecting the waterfront. Luciano was correct. The government worked out a deal. Luciano was transferred from Dannemora (near the Canadian border) to a more comfortable prison and was eventually deported to Italy after serving 10 years of a 50-year sentence.

54. A Visit by Saboteurs
1942

On the afternoon of June 13, Georg Dasch and Ernest Burger checked into the Governor Clinton Hotel, at Seventh Avenue and 31st Street, across the street from Penn Station. They had been put ashore on a Long Island beach by a German U-boat shortly after midnight and had traveled to Manhattan with plans to sabotage plants and bridges. Within a day, they lost heart for their venture and made arrangements to turn themselves in and aid in the capture of two colleagues in New York and four who had landed in Florida. All eight were quickly captured. A secret trial was held in Washington, and all were convicted and sentenced to death. President Roosevelt reduced the sentence of the two informants, but the other six were electrocuted on August 8. In 1948, Dasch and Burger were freed and deported to Germany.

55. The "Green Parrot" Murder
1942

On July 12, a gunman entered the Green Parrot Restaurant, at 1806 Third Avenue, near 100th Street, and shot owner Max Geller to death while the bird for which the restaurant was named seemed to screech, "Robber, robber, robber." None of the restaurant's patrons could (or would) identify the killer, and the police had no clues. When one of the detectives learned, however, that the parrot had been trained to recognize regular patrons and call them by name, he had a hunch that the parrot had actually screeched "Robert, Robert, Robert." Suspicion focused on a man named Robert Butler, 28, who had left Manhattan shortly after the shooting. He was traced to Maryland and arrested. He confessed, admitting he had shot Geller in a drunken rage after being refused a drink. He was sentenced to fifteen years.

56. Death of an Anti-Fascist
1943

Il Martello was a strongly anti-Fascist and anti-Communist New York–based Italian newspaper, and its editor, Carlo Tresca, was a longtime enemy of Benito Mussolini. Vito Genovese—an American mobster living in Italy to avoid American justice—became friendly with *Il Duce* and offered to have Tresca killed. Mussolini accepted. Genovese put out a long-distance contract on Tresca, and it was assigned to a young Brooklyn thug named Carmine Galante (later to become a Mob leader in his own right). On January 11, at about 9:40 p.m., Tresca left *Il Martello*'s office at 96 Fifth Avenue, at 15th Street, walked across the street, and was shot dead by Galante. Witnesses did not see the killer's face but noted his car's license number—IC 9272. A few hours before, Galante's parole officer had noted that same number on a car Galante drove off in after a visit. Galante denied everything, and there was nothing else at the time to connect him with the murder.

57. Another Harlem Riot
1943

At about 7:30 p.m. on August 1, a white policeman arrested a black woman in the Hotel Braddock, at 272 West 126th Street. A black soldier intervened, and the officer shot him. Although the soldier's wound was minor, rumors spread that he had been seriously hurt in the presence of his mother. A riot broke out, and before it was quelled, 5 blacks had been killed, 500 injured, and 500 arrested. For a time, sales of liquor were banned from river to river from 100th to 170th Street.

58. A "Secret" Disclosed
1944

In December, at 226 Stanton Street, David Greenglass gave his brother-in-law Julius Rosenberg what was later described as the "sketch of the lens mold" for the atomic bomb. Rosenberg and his wife, Ethel, were convicted of espionage in 1951 and executed in 1953.

59. Death at the Polo Grounds
1950

On July 4, Bernard Lawrence Doyle of Fairview, New Jersey, was in his seat in Section 42 of the Polo Grounds, waiting for the start of a Giants-Dodgers doubleheader. From a nearby Edgecomb Avenue rooftop, a fourteen-year-old boy with a .45-caliber pistol fired a shot in the direction of the ballfield. The bullet killed Doyle.

60. The Murder of a Poet
1954

Poet Maxwell Bodenheim, 64, was a famous Greenwich Village character. By the early fifties, he was spending his hours in Washington Square Park or in his favorite booth at the San Remo Cafe, on MacDougal Street, and writing a few lines of verse in exchange for enough money to buy drinks of gin. On the evening of February 6, 1954, Bodenheim and his third wife, Ruth, 33, were invited by an acquaintance, Harold Weinberg, to have some drinks in Weinberg's squalid room at a boarding-house at 97 Third Avenue, just off 13th Street. Early the next morning, February 7, Weinberg stabbed them both to death. Weinberg claimed that he and Bodenheim had fought after the poet awoke from a drunken stupor and found Weinberg and Ruth making love. Ruth, a witness to the killing, was then slain to seal her lips. Weinberg was committed to an asylum.

61. Death of a Playboy
1955

Serge Rubinstein, 46, was a multimillionaire financial genius and playboy who had served time during World War II for draft evasion. His ruthless financial dealings had led to a charge of stock fraud (of which he was acquitted) and created many enemies. In the early morning of January 27, in his five-story mansion at 814 Fifth Avenue, between 62nd and 63rd Streets, someone bound him hand and foot, gagged him with adhesive tape, and strangled him. The clues were few; his enemies were many. Numerous women had keys to his apartment. Who knew how many copies had been made? Hundreds of people were questioned; none was charged. His murder remains unsolved.

62. A Great Manhunt
1955

The city's greatest manhunt and siege in almost a quarter-century ended on the afternoon of February 20 in apartment 14 on the fourth floor of 67–69 East 112th Street. Two days before, August Robles, 44, a suspect in a recent contract killing, had disarmed and fled from three detectives and, an hour later, had shot it out with four other detectives.

Virtually every cop in the city had been given Robles's photograph. A tip led police to the 112th Street address, and six officers entered the building while ten others stayed outside to guard against another escape. The six broke in the door of the apartment and were met by a fusillade of shots. The officers retreated, reinforcements were called, and the siege began. Over the next hour or so, thousands of curious onlookers (including commuters in passing trains on the nearby Park Avenue railroad tracks) saw hundreds of policemen fire almost 300 shots into the apartment. A tear-gas bomb set the apartment ablaze, and Fire Department hoses flooded it. At about 5 p.m., Robles—who had vowed never to be taken alive—was found dead in the apartment with five bullet wounds.

63. An Acid Attack
1956

Around 3 a.m. on April 5, 1956, Victor Riesel, a famous labor columnist, left Lindy's Restaurant, at Broadway and 51st Street. Earlier that night, he'd given a radio broadcast attacking corruption in the International Union of Operating Engineers. Now he walked to his car, parked a few yards west of Broadway on the north side of 51st Street. As he was about to open the car door, a young man stepped from the shadows of the Mark Hellinger Theatre. Thinking the stranger was a panhandler, Riesel reached into his pocket for some money. The man threw acid into Riesel's face, permanently blinding him. Law-enforcement officials theorized that John "Johnny Dio" Dio Guardi had ordered the attack to stop Riesel's investigative reporting on corrupt unions, but the evidence against him was insufficient. It was also believed that a man named Abe Telvi had thrown the acid, but he was slain gangland-style before he could be tried. Telvi's brother Leo and two friends were indicted for conspiracy in connection with the attack on Riesel, and all three were convicted in federal court later that year and sentenced to long prison terms.

64. A Muffed Mob Hit
1957

By the mid-fifties, Vito Genovese was making a grab for leadership of the Mafia. Frank Costello, still a prestigious underworld figure, was getting in his way. Genovese put a contract out on Costello, and Vincent "The Chin" Gigante got the job. Just before 11 p.m. on May 2, 1957, Costello entered the lobby of his apartment house—the Majestic, at 115 Central Park West and 72nd Street. Gigante approached him from behind and said, "This is for you, Frank." A single bullet grazed Costello's head. Costello agreed to retire on Genovese's promise not to try again to kill him. Gigante was indicted on rather thin evidence and was acquitted when Costello said he couldn't identify his assailant. Despite the "truce" between them, Costello got his revenge. He and some friends set up Genovese on a drug charge. He was convicted and sentenced to fifteen years in prison and died there.

65. The Mad Bomber's Last Bomb
1957

After planting more than 30 bombs in sixteen years, causing a number of injuries (one serious), the Mad Bomber was finally identified in January 1957 as George Metesky, a Connecticut resident with a grudge against Con Edison, his former employer. On September 9—almost eight months after Metesky's arrest—a bomb he had planted in 1953 was found inside a seat in the Loew's Lexington Theatre, at Lexington Avenue and 51st Street—the site of a 1952 Metesky bombing. With the discovery of this well-concealed device (a prior search had failed to uncover it), the police closed the case.

66. "The Executioner's" Last Haircut
1957

Believing he had made peace with Frank Costello, Vito Genovese set out to dispose of another Mob leader. His target was Albert Anastasia, 54, called "The Executioner" because he was believed to have killed more than 30 men. A contract was put out on Anastasia with the Profaci family and was assigned to "Crazy Joey" Gallo and his brothers. At 10:20 a.m. on October 25, Anastasia sat in a barber's chair at the Park Sheraton Hotel barbershop. Two men, their faces covered with scarves, came up behind him and shot him five times, once in the back of the head. Anastasia died instantly. The gunmen fled. Not long afterward, while Crazy Joey was sitting around with four friends, he was heard to joke that the five should be called the "Barbershop Quintet." No one was ever prosecuted for the murder.

67. The "Cape Man" Murders
1959

At 12:15 a.m. on August 30, six teenagers sat on a bench in a playground between Ninth and Tenth Avenues and 45th and 46th Streets. A group of youths approached, including Salvador Agron, 16, who was wearing a red-lined cape. The "Cape Man," as he was later called, stabbed two of the teenagers to death and critically wounded a third. He was convicted of murder and sentenced to death. His sentence was later commuted to life by Governor Rockefeller at the request of district attorney Frank Hogan. The Cape Man was paroled in 1979 and died of pneumonia in 1986.

68. Death of a Cop Killer
1963

In the early morning hours of August 28, police gathered outside a room on the twenty-third floor of the Manhattan Hotel, at Eighth Avenue and 44th Street. A man named Frank Falco lay sleeping inside. Two days before, Falco and his buddy Thomas Trantino had brutally murdered two cops in Lodi, New Jersey, after a night of carousing. An anonymous tip had led the police to Falco's room, which they silently entered with a passkey. Although he awoke with a gun pressed to his neck, the police reported that Falco chose to fight. He died with seven bullets in him. Trantino surrendered to the police with a lawyer later that day. He remains a prisoner in New Jersey, now seeking parole.

69. The "Career Girl" Murders
1963

On August 28, in mid-morning, an intruder sadistically murdered Janice Wylie and Emily Hoffert in their third-floor apartment at 57 East 88th Street, between Madison and Park Avenues. Eight months later, police in Brooklyn induced a young drifter named George Whitmore Jr. to confess to the killings. After a thorough investigation, however, prosecutors came to doubt Whitmore's guilt. In January 1965, Whitmore was exonerated, and Richard Robles, a drug addict, was charged with the crime and was eventually convicted. One of the prosecutors who cleared Whitmore later claimed that if the case had been a run-of-the-mill murder, without publicity, Whitmore might well have been executed. Robles is now seeking parole.

70. The Murder of a Bookie
1963

Mark Fein, 32, bet heavily on the Yankees in the World Series. After the Dodgers swept the series, Fein's bookie, Reuben Markowitz, sought payment. Fein invited Markowitz to an apartment at 406 East 63rd Street on the night of October 10. When Markowitz arrived, Fein killed him, hid his body in a trunk, and arranged for a lady friend to have the trunk thrown into the Harlem River. The body surfaced, and an investigation led to Fein's indictment. He was convicted and sentenced to life.

71. A Mob Boss Is "Kidnapped"
1964

A federal grand jury investigating organized crime had issued sub-
poenas to a number of crime bosses, including Joseph "Joe Bananas"
Bonanno. Shortly after midnight on October 21—the day Bonanno
was to testify—he and his lawyer were about to enter the lawyer's
apartment building at 35 Park Avenue, near 36th Street. Two men
approached and dragged Bonanno into a waiting car; a wild shot was
fired toward the protesting lawyer. Bonanno was missing for nineteen
months; when he reappeared, he claimed he'd been kidnapped by
Mob enemies. Few believed him.

72. Stealing the Star of India
1964

Sometime after 9 p.m. on October 29, three Florida beach bums
(including Jack Rolland "Murph the Surf" Murphy), who had perfected
their plan by viewing *Topkapi*, broke into the Museum of Natural History, at Central Park West and 81st Street, and stole various gems,
including the Star of India—the world's largest star sapphire. They
were arrested within two days. Eventually, the jewels were returned and
the burglars served short prison sentences.

73. The Murder of Malcolm X
1965

On February 21, Malcolm X, a charismatic black leader who had broken
away from the Black Muslims, began to speak to a crowd in the Audubon
Ballroom, at Broadway and 166th Street. Three men approached the
stage and shot him dead. The three fled, but one was captured by people
in the crowd and had to be rescued by the police. Three men were convicted and received life terms; one admitted guilt and exonerated the
others, who have maintained their innocence to this day.

74. A Brothel Murder
1968

On December 24, shortly after 8:30 p.m., a corrupt cop named William Phillips visited a brothel on the eleventh floor of 157 East 57th Street. He shot and killed a hooker named Sharon Stango along with her pimp, "Jimmy Smith," from whom he had been extorting money. One of Sharon's customers, Charles Gonzales, was there at the time. Phillips shot him, too, but Gonzales survived and gave the police a description of the killer. When Phillips later became a star witness at the Knapp Commission hearings, the detective assigned to the case saw him and made the connection. Phillips was convicted and sentenced to life imprisonment.

75. A Double Cop Murder
1971

Shortly after 10 p.m. on May 21, two young policemen, Waverly Jones and Joseph A. Piagentini, were on patrol at the Colonial Park Houses, at 159th Street and the Harlem River Drive. They had just responded to a call and were returning to their patrol car when they were approached from behind and shot dead. Three men were eventually convicted in the killings and sentenced to life in prison.

76. The Murder of Joe Colombo
1971

On June 28, around 11:45 p.m., crime boss Joseph Colombo was about to lead an Italian-American civil-rights rally at Columbus Circle. Among thousands of spectators and a heavy police guard, Jerome A. Johnson, 25, wearing a press pass, approached Colombo and shot him in the head. Johnson, who had been hired by Crazy Joey Gallo, was immediately killed by one of Colombo's bodyguards. Colombo lingered, virtually senseless, for seven years before dying. Gallo was not charged but did not escape unpunished.

77. The Ambush of Two Cops
1972

Two rookie policemen, Gregory Foster and Rocco Laurie, were on foot patrol at the southeast corner of East 11th Street and Avenue B at 10:50 p.m. on January 27. They were ambushed and shot to death by two or three men, who escaped in a waiting car. A supposed member of the Black Liberation Army was tried in 1974 for the killings but was acquitted.

78. The Killing of "Crazy Joey"
1972

At 5:30 in the morning on April 7, Crazy Joey Gallo was celebrating his forty-third birthday at Umbertos Clam House, at the corner of Mulberry and Hester Streets. His bride, his stepdaughter, his bodyguard, and the bodyguard's date were gathered around. A group of assassins entered the restaurant and shot Gallo three times. The bodyguard and an unknown man returned the fire. The assassins escaped. Gallo staggered outside and died on Hester Street. Within a month, an informant from the Colombo family told police that he and four other family members had done the job, though no one was ever convicted of the killings.

79. The "Wrong Men" Murder
1972

On August 11, at about 9:30 p.m., four members of the Colombo crime family stood at the bar of the Neopolitan Noodle, at 320 East 79th Street. Outside, a killer hired by the Gallo forces—in retaliation for the assassination of Crazy Joey earlier in the year—stalked them. Before the killer could strike, however, the four Colombo associates left the bar, and their places were taken by four businessmen. The killer opened fire, killing two of the innocent men and wounding two. He was never caught—at least not by law-enforcement

80. The "Mr. Goodbar" Slaying
1973

Roseann Quinn, a 28-year-old teacher at St. Joseph's School for the Deaf, lived alone in an apartment at 253 West 72nd Street. From time to time, she would drink at a nearby bar, meet a man, and bring him home. Her friends advised her of the danger involved in such casual relationships, but she paid them little mind. Early in the morning of January 2, she asked John Wayne Wilson, whom she had brought home a few hours before, to leave. He refused. They fought and he stabbed her fourteen times, killing her. Wilson was indicted but hanged himself in the Tombs before his trial. The killing became the basis for the novel and movie *Looking for Mr. Goodbar*.

81. Murder over a Model
1978

Wealthy horse trainer and playboy Howard "Buddy" Jacobson, 48, lived in and owned a small apartment building at 155 East 84th Street. His girlfriend, Melanie Cain, 23, a beautiful model, also lived in the building. She took a romantic interest in another tenant, John Tupper, 34, and moved in with him. Jacobson got jealous. On the morning of August 6, he killed Tupper in Tupper's apartment and then botched the job of disposing of the body in the Bronx. He was convicted after a sensational trial and was sentenced to life in prison.

82. Murder at the Met
1980

On July 23, Helen Hagnes, a talented violinist, was playing in the

Metropolitan Opera House orchestra at a performance of the Berlin Ballet. During an intermission, she was accosted by stagehand Craig Steven Crimmins, 21, who forced her to the roof of the opera house, raped her, bound her, and then threw her, still alive, down an air shaft, killing her. He was convicted and received a life term.

83. Death of a Beatle
1980

Ex-Beatle John Lennon and his wife, Yoko Ono, having completed a recording session, headed home to the Dakota Apartments, at 1 West 72nd Street, on the night of December 8. As they passed through the entrance, at about 10:45, Mark David Chapman, 25, stepped out of the shadows and shot Lennon four times, killing him. Then he sat and, while waiting for the police to arrive, calmly read J.D. Salinger's *The Catcher in the Rye.* Chapman pleaded guilty and received a life sentence.

84. A Writer Kills
1981

Jack Henry Abbott was the best-selling author of *In the Belly of the Beast,* a book about his prison life. His release on parole was encouraged by Norman Mailer and others who were impressed by Abbott's literary talent. In the early morning of July 18, after two months in a halfway house, prior to parole, Abbott was eating with friends at the Binibon, a restaurant at Second Avenue and 5th Street, when he took offense at a remark by a waiter, Richard Adan, 22. After a confrontation, Abbott stabbed Adan to death. He fled but was captured and returned for trial. Convicted of manslaughter, he was sentenced to life in prison.

85. Death of a Crime Boss
1985

At 5:26 p.m. on December 16, Mob boss Paul Castellano and his chauffeur/bodyguard Thomas Bilotti got out of the car that Bilotti had just parked on the south side of 46th Street, east of Third Avenue. They were headed for Sparks Steak House, at 210 East 46th. Three men approached, drew guns, and put six bullets in each mobster. The killers ran to Second Avenue, where a waiting car picked them up. Though the killing has been attributed to John Gotti, the crime is officially unsolved.

86. Attack on a Model
1986

On the night of June 5, model Marla Hanson had a drink with Steven Roth at Shutters, a bar on the ground floor of the building in which she lived, at 433 West 34th Street, between Ninth and Tenth Avenues. Roth was her former landlord and had vainly hoped to be her lover. They discussed his refusal to return her $850 rent deposit. She agreed to his suggestion that they take a walk outside the bar, where she was grabbed by two men, one of whom slashed her face with a knife. Roth had hired them to attack her. All three were convicted and received maximum prison sentences.

87. The "Preppy Murder"
1986

Early in the morning of August 26, Robert Chambers and Jennifer Levin left Dorian's Red Hand bar, at 300 East 84th Street, at Second Avenue, and strolled toward Central Park. Several hours later, her body was found by passersby near Park Drive East at 81st Street, behind the Metropolitan Museum of Art. While the police examined the body, Chambers was nearby, watching. He claimed self-defense throughout his murder trial. While the jury deliberated, however, he pleaded guilty to manslaughter and was sentenced to fifteen years. He's at the Great Meadow Correctional Facility.

Jeeves and the Unbidden Guest
by P. G. Wodehouse

P.G. Wodehouse's (1881–1975) guileless and incompetent Englishman Bertie Wooster occasionally spent time in New York. Fortunately, Wooster brought with him his butler Jeeves.

'm not absolutely certain of my facts, but I rather fancy it's Shakespeare who says that it's always just when a fellow is feeling particularly braced with things in general that Fate sneaks up behind him with the bit of lead piping. And what I'm driving at is that the man is perfectly right. Take, for instance, the business of Lady Malvern and her son Wilmot. That was one of the scaliest affairs I was ever mixed up with, and a moment before they came into my life I was just thinking how thoroughly all right everything was.

I was still in New York when the thing started, and it was about the time of year when New York is at its best. It was one of those topping mornings, and I had just climbed out from under the cold shower, feeling like a million dollars. As a matter of fact, what was bucking me up more than anything was the fact that the day before I had asserted myself with Jeeves—absolutely asserted myself, don't you know. You see, the way things had been going on I was rapidly becoming a dashed serf. The man had jolly well oppressed me. I didn't so much mind when he made me give up one of my new suits, because Jeeves's judgment about suits is sound and can generally be relied upon.

But I as near as a toucher rebelled when he wouldn't let me wear a pair of cloth-topped boots which I loved like a couple of brothers. And, finally, when he tried to tread on me like a worm in the matter of a hat, I put the Wooster foot down and showed him in no uncertain manner who was who.

It's a long story, and I haven't time to tell you now, but the nub of the thing was that he wanted me to wear the White House Wonder— as worn by President Coolidge—when I had set my heart on the Broadway Special, much patronised by the Younger Set; and the end of the matter was that, after a rather painful scene, I bought the Broadway Special. So that's how things were on this particular morning, and I was feeling pretty manly and independent.

Well, I was in the bathroom, wondering what there was going to be for breakfast while I massaged the spine with a rough towel and sang slightly, when there was a tap at the door. I stopped singing and opened the door an inch.

"What ho, without there!" I said.

"Lady Malvern has called, sir."

"Eh?"

"Lady Malvern, sir. She is waiting in the sitting-room."

"Pull yourself together, Jeeves, my man," I said rather severely, for I bar practical jokes before breakfast. "You know perfectly well there's no one waiting for me in the sitting-room. How could there be when it's barely ten o'clock yet?"

"I gathered from her ladyship, sir, that she had landed from an ocean liner at an early hour this morning."

This made the thing a bit more plausible. I remembered that when I had arrived in America about a year before, the proceedings had begun at some ghastly hour like six, and that I had been shot out on to a foreign shore considerably before eight.

"Who the deuce is Lady Malvern, Jeeves?"

"Her ladyship did not confide in me, sir."

"Is she alone?"

"Her ladyship is accompanied by a Lord Pershore, sir. I fancy that his lordship would be her ladyship's son."

"Oh, well, put out rich raiment of sorts, and I'll be dressing."

"The heather-mixture lounge is in readiness, sir."

"Then lead me to it."

While I was dressing I kept trying to think who on earth Lady Malvern could be. It wasn't till I had climbed through the top of my shirt and was reaching out for the studs that I remembered.

"I've placed her, Jeeves. She's a pal of my Aunt Agatha."

"Indeed, sir?"

"Yes. I met her at lunch one Sunday before I left London. A very vicious specimen. Writes books. She wrote a book on social conditions in India when she came back from the Durbar."

"Yes, sir? Pardon me, sir, but not that tie."

"Eh?"

"Not that tie with the heather-mixture lounge, sir."

It was a shock to me. I thought I had quelled the fellow. It was rather a solemn moment. What I mean is, if I weakened now, all my good work the night before would be thrown away. I braced myself.

"What's wrong with this tie? I've seen you give it a nasty look before. Speak out like a man! What's the matter with it?"

"Too ornate, sir."

"Nonsense! A cheerful pink. Nothing more."

"Unsuitable, sir."

"Jeeves, this is the tie I wear!"

"Very good, sir."

Dashed unpleasant. I could see that the man was wounded. But I was firm. I tied the tie, got into the coat and waistcoat, and went into the sitting-room.

"Hullo-ullo-ullo!" I said. "What?"

"Ah! How do you do, Mr. Wooster? You have never met my son Wilmot, I think? Motty, darling, this is Mr. Wooster."

Lady Malvern was a hearty, happy, healthy, overpowering sort of dashed female, not so very tall but making up for it by measuring about six feet from the O.P. to the Prompt Side. She fitted into my biggest arm-chair as if it had been built round her by someone who knew they were wearing arm-chairs tight about the hips that season. She had bright, bulging eyes and a lot of yellow hair, and when she spoke she showed about fifty-seven front teeth. She was one of those women who kind of numb a fellow's faculties. She made me feel as if I were ten years old and had been brought into the drawing-room in my Sunday clothes to say how-d'you-do. Altogether by no means the sort of thing a chappie would wish to find in his sitting-room before breakfast.

Motty, the son, was about twenty-three, tall and thin and meek-looking. He had the same yellow hair as his mother, but he wore it plastered down and parted in the middle. His eyes bulged, too, but they weren't bright. They were a dull grey with pink rims. His chin gave up the struggle about half-way down, and he didn't appear to have any eyelashes. A mild, furtive, sheepish sort of blighter, in short.

"Awfully glad to see you," I said, though this was far from the case, for already I was beginning to have a sort of feeling that dirty work was threatening in the offing. "So you've popped over, eh? Making a long stay in America?"

"About a month. Your aunt gave me your address and told me to be sure to call on you."

I was glad to hear this, for it seemed to indicate that Aunt Agatha was beginning to come round a bit. As I believe I told you before, there had been some slight unpleasantness between us, arising from the occasion when she had sent me over to New York to disentangle my cousin Gussie from the clutches of a girl on the music-hall stage. When I tell you that by the time I had finished my operations Gussie had not only married the girl but had gone on the Halls himself and was doing well, you'll understand that relations were a trifle strained between aunt and nephew.

I simply hadn't dared go back and face her, and it was a relief to find that time had healed the wound enough to make her tell her pals to call on me. What I mean is, much as I liked America, I didn't want to have England barred to me for the rest of my natural life; and, believe me, England is a jolly sight too small for anyone to live in with Aunt Agatha, if she's really on the warpath. So I was braced at hearing these words and smiled genially on the assemblage.

"Your aunt said that you would do anything that was in your power to be of assistance to us."

"Rather! Oh, rather. Absolutely."

"Thank you so much. I want you to put dear Motty up for a little while."

I didn't get this for a moment.

"Put him up? For my clubs?"

"No, no! Darling Motty is essentially a home bird. Aren't you, Motty, darling?"

Motty, who was sucking the knob of his stick, uncorked himself.

"Yes, Mother," he said, and corked himself up again.

"I should not like him to belong to clubs. I mean put him up here. Have him to live with you while I am away."

These frightful words trickled out of her like honey. The woman simply didn't seem to understand the ghastly nature of her proposal. I gave Motty the swift east-to-west. He was sitting with his mouth nuzzling the stick, blinking at the wall. The thought of having this planted on me for an indefinite period appalled me. Absolutely appalled me, don't you know. I was just starting to say that the shot wasn't on the board at any price, and that the first sign Motty gave of trying to nestle into my little home I would yell for the police, when she went on, rolling placidly over me, as it were.

There was something about this woman that sapped one's willpower.

"I am leaving New York by the midday train, as I have to pay a visit to Sing-Sing prison. I am extremely interested in prison conditions in America. After that I work my way gradually across to the coast, visiting the points of interest on the journey. You see, Mr. Wooster, I am in America principally on business. No doubt you read my book, *India and the Indians?* My publishers are anxious for me to write a companion volume on the United States. I shall not be able to spend more than a month in the country, as I have to get back for the season, but a month should be ample. I was less than a month in India, and my dear friend Sir Roger Cremorne wrote his *America from Within* after a stay of only two weeks. I should love to take dear Motty with me, but the poor boy gets so sick when he travels by train. I shall have to pick him up on my return."

From where I sat I could see Jeeves in the dining-room, laying the breakfast table. I wished I could have had a minute with him alone. I felt certain that he would have been able to think of some way of putting a stop to this woman.

"It will be such a relief to know that Motty is safe with you, Mr. Wooster. I know what the temptations of a great city are. Hitherto dear Motty has been sheltered from them. He has lived quietly with me in the country. I know that you will look after him carefully, Mr. Wooster. He will give very little trouble." She talked about the poor blighter as if he wasn't there. Not that Motty seemed to mind. He had stopped chewing his walkingstick and was sitting there with his mouth open. "He is a vegetarian and a teetotaller and is devoted to reading. Give him a nice book and he will be quite contented." She got up. "Thank you so much, Mr. Wooster. I don't know what I should have done without your help. Come, Motty. We have just time to see a few of the sights before my train goes. But I shall have to rely on you for most of my information about New York, darling. Be sure to keep your eyes open and take notes of your impressions. It will be such a help. Good-bye, Mr. Wooster. I will send Motty back early in the afternoon."

They went out, and I howled for Jeeves.

"Jeeves!"

"Sir?"

"What's to be done? You heard it all, didn't you? You were in the dining-room most of the time. That pill is coming to stay here."

"Pill, sir?"

"The excrescence."

"I beg your pardon, sir?"

I looked at Jeeves sharply. This sort of thing wasn't like him. Then I understood.

"Lord Pershore will be staying here for tonight, Jeeves," I said coldly.

"Very good, sir. Breakfast is ready, sir."

I could have sobbed into the bacon and eggs. That there wasn't any sympathy to be got out of Jeeves was what put the lid on it. For a moment I almost weakened and told him to destroy the hat and tie if he didn't like them, but I pulled myself together again. I was dashed if I was going to let Jeeves treat me like a bally one-man chain-gang.

But, what with brooding on Jeeves and brooding on Motty, I was in a pretty reduced sort of state. The more I examined the situation, the more blighted it became. There was nothing I could do. If I slung Motty out, he would report to his mother, and she would pass it on to Aunt Agatha, and I didn't like to think what would happen then. Sooner or later I should be wanting to go back to England, and I didn't want to get there and find Aunt Agatha waiting on the quay for me with a sandbag. There was absolutely nothing for it but to put the fellow up and make the best of it.

About midday Motty's luggage arrived, and soon afterward a large parcel of what I took to be nice books. I brightened up a little when I saw it. It was one of those massive parcels and looked as if it had enough in it to keep him busy for a year. I felt a trifle more cheerful, and I got my Broadway Special and stuck it on my head, and gave the pink tie a twist, and reeled out to take a bite of lunch with one or two of the lads at a neighbouring hostelry; and what with excellent browsing and sluicing and cheery conversation and what-not, the afternoon passed quite happily. By dinner-time I had almost forgotten Motty's existence.

I dined at the club and looked in at a show afterward, and it wasn't till fairly late that I got back to the flat. There were no signs of Motty, and I took it that he had gone to bed.

It seemed rummy to me, though, that the parcel of nice books was still there with the string and paper on it. It looked as if Motty, after seeing mother off at the station, had decided to call it a day.

Jeeves came in with the nightly whiskey-and-soda.

"Lord Pershore gone to bed, Jeeves?" I asked, with reserved hauteur and what-not.

"No, sir. His lordship has not yet returned."

"Not returned? What do you mean?"

"His lordship came in shortly after six-thirty, and, having dressed, went out again."

At this moment there was a noise outside the front door, a sort of scrabbling noise, as if somebody were trying to paw his way through the woodwork. Then a sort of thud.

"Better go and see what that is, Jeeves."

"Very good, sir."

He went out and came back again.

"If you would not mind stepping this way, sir, I think we might be able to carry him in."

"Carry him in?"

"His lordship is lying on the mat, sir."

I went to the front door. The man was right. There was Motty huddled up outside on the floor. He was moaning a bit.

"He's had some sort of dashed fit," I said. I took another look. "Jeeves! Someone's been feeding him meat!"

"Sir?"

"He's a vegetarian, you know. He must have been digging into a steak or something. Call up a doctor!"

"I hardly think it will be necessary, sir. If you would take his lordship's legs, while I—"

"Great Scott, Jeeves! You don't think—he can't be—"

"I am inclined to think so, sir."

And, by Jove, he was right! Once on the right track, you couldn't mistake it. Motty was under the surface. Completely sozzled.

It was the deuce of a shock.

"You never can tell, Jeeves!"

"Very seldom, sir."

"Remove the eye of authority and where are you?"

"Precisely, sir."

"Where is my wandering boy tonight and all that sort of thing, what?"

"It would seem so, sir."

"Well, we had better bring him in, eh?"

"Yes, sir."

So we lugged him in, and Jeeves put him to bed, and I lit a cigarette and sat down to think the thing over. I had a kind of foreboding. It seemed to me that I had let myself in for something pretty rocky.

Next morning, after I had sucked down a thoughtful cup of tea, I went into Motty's room to investigate. I expected to find the fellow a wreck, but there he was, sitting up in bed, quite chirpy, reading *Gingery Stories*.

"What ho!" I said.

"What ho!" said Motty.

"What ho! What ho!"

"What ho! What ho! What ho!"

After that it seemed rather difficult to go on with the conversation.

"How are you feeling this morning?" I asked.

"Topping!" replied Motty, blithely and with abandon. "I say, you know, that fellow of yours—Jeeves, you know—is a corker. I had a most frightful headache when I woke up, and he brought me a sort of rummy dark drink, and it put me right again at once. Said it was his own invention. I must see more of that lad. He seems to me distinctly one of the ones."

I couldn't believe that this was the same blighter who had sat and sucked his stick the day before.

"You ate something that disagreed with you last night, didn't you?" I said, by way of giving him a chance to slide out of it if he wanted to. But he wouldn't have it at any price.

"No!" he replied firmly. "I didn't do anything of the kind. I drank too much. Much too much. Lots and lots too much. And, what's more, I'm going to do it again. I'm going to do it every night. If ever you see me sober, old top," he said, with a kind of holy exaltation, "tap me on the shoulder and say, 'Tut! Tut!' and I'll apologise and remedy the defect."

"But I say, you know, what about me?"

"What about you?"

"Well, I'm, so to speak, as it were, kind of responsible for you. What I mean to say is, if you go doing this sort of thing I'm apt to get in the soup somewhat."

"I can't help your troubles," said Motty firmly. "Listen to me, old thing: this is the first time in my life that I've had a real chance to yield to the temptations of a great city. What's the use of a great city having temptations if fellows don't yield to them? Makes it so bally discouraging for the great city. Besides, mother told me to keep my eyes open and collect impressions."

I sat on the edge of the bed. I felt dizzy.

"I know just how you feel, old dear," said Motty consolingly. "And, if my principles would permit it, I would simmer down for your sake. But duty first! This is the first time I've been let out alone, and I mean to make the most of it. We're only young once. Why interfere with life's morning? Young man, rejoice in thy youth! Tra-la! What ho!"

Put like that, it did seem reasonable.

"All my bally life, dear boy," Motty went on, "I've been cooped up in the ancestral home at Much Middlefold, in Shropshire, and till you've been cooped up in Much Middlefold you don't know what cooping is. The only time we get any excitement is when one of the choir-boys is caught sucking chocolate during the sermon. When that happens, we talk about it for days. I've got about a month of New York, and I mean to store up a few happy memories for the long winter evenings. This is my only chance to collect a past, and I'm going to do it. Now tell me, old sport, as man to man, how does one get in touch with that very decent bird Jeeves? Does one ring a bell or shout a bit? I should like to discuss the subject of a good stiff b.-and-s. with him."

• • •

I had had a sort of vague idea, don't you know, that if I stuck close to Motty and went about the place with him, I might act as a bit of a damper on the gaiety. What I mean is, I thought that if, when he was being the life and soul of the party, he were to catch my reproving eye he might ease up a trifle on the revelry. So the next night I took him along to supper with me. It was the last time. I'm a quiet, peaceful sort of bloke who has lived all his life in London, and I can't stand the pace these swift sportsmen from the rural districts set. What I mean to say is, I'm all for rational enjoyment and so forth, but I think a fellow makes himself conspicuous when he throws soft-boiled eggs at the electric fan. And decent mirth and all that sort of thing are all right, but I do bar dancing on tables and having to dash all over the place dodging waiters, managers, and chuckers-out, just when you want to sit still and digest.

Directly I managed to tear myself away that night and get home, I made up my mind that this was jolly well the last time that I went about with Motty. The only time I met him late at night after that was once when I passed the door of a fairly low-down sort of restaurant and had to step aside to dodge him as he sailed through the air *en route* for the opposite pavement, with a muscular looking sort of fellow peering out after him with a kind of gloomy satisfaction.

In a way, I couldn't help sympathising with the chap. He had about four weeks to have the good time that ought to have been spread over about ten years, and I didn't wonder at his wanting to be pretty busy. I should have been just the same in his place. Still, there was no denying that it was a bit thick. If it hadn't been for the thought of Lady Malvern and Aunt Agatha in the background, I should have regarded Motty's rapid work with an indulgent smile. But I couldn't get rid of the feeling that, sooner or later, I was the lad who was scheduled to get it behind the ear. And what with brooding on this prospect, and sitting up in the old flat waiting for the familiar footstep, and putting it to bed when it got there, and stealing into the sick-chamber next morning to contemplate the wreckage, I was beginning to lose weight. Absolutely becoming the good old shadow, I give you my honest word. Starting at sudden noises and what-not.

And no sympathy from Jeeves. That was what cut me to the quick. The man was still thoroughly pipped about the hat and tie, and simply wouldn't rally round. One morning I wanted comforting so much that I sank the pride of the Woosters and appealed to the fellow direct.

"Jeeves," I said, "this is getting a bit thick!"

"Sir?"

"You know what I mean. This lad seems to have chucked all the principles of a well-spent boyhood. He has got it up his nose!"

"Yes, sir."

"Well, I shall get blamed, don't you know. You know what my Aunt Agatha is."

"Yes, sir."

"Very well, then."

I waited a moment, but he wouldn't unbend.

"Jeeves," I said, "haven't you any scheme up your sleeve for coping with this blighter?"

"No, sir."

And he shimmered off to his lair. Obstinate devil! So dashed absurd, don't you know. It wasn't as if there was anything wrong with that Broadway Special hat. It was a remarkably priceless effort, and much admired by the lads. But, just because he preferred the White House Wonder, he left me flat.

It was shortly after this that young Motty got the idea of bringing pals back in the small hours to continue the gay revels in the home. This was where I began to crack under the strain. You see, the part of town where I was living wasn't the right place for that sort of thing. I knew lots of fellows down Washington Square way who started the evening at about two a.m.—artists and writers and so forth who frolicked considerably till checked by the arrival of the morning milk. That was all right. They like that sort of thing down there. The neighbours can't get to sleep unless there's someone dancing Hawaiian dances over their heads. But on Fifty-seventh Street the atmosphere wasn't right, and when Motty turned up at three in the morning with a collection of hearty lads, who only stopped singing their college song when they started singing "The Old Oaken Bucket," there was a marked peevishness among the old settlers in the flats. The management was extremely terse over the telephone at breakfast-time, and took a lot of soothing.

The next night I came home early, after a lonely dinner at a place which I'd chosen because there didn't seem any chance of meeting Motty there. The sitting-room was quite dark, and I was just moving to switch on the light, when there was a sort of explosion and something collared hold of my trouser-leg. Living with Motty had reduced me to such an extent that I was simply unable to cope with this thing. I jumped backward with a loud yell of anguish, and tumbled out into the hall just as Jeeves came out of his den to see what the matter was.

"Did you call, sir?"

"Jeeves! There's something in there that grabs you by the leg!"

"That would be Rollo, sir."

"Eh?"

"I would have warned you of his presence, but I did not hear you come in. His temper is a little uncertain at present, as he has not yet settled down."

"Who the deuce is Rollo?"

"His lordship's bull terrier, sir. His lordship won him in a raffle, and tied him to the leg of the table. If you will allow me, sir, I will go in and switch on the light."

There really is nobody like Jeeves. He walked straight into the sitting-room, the biggest feat since Daniel and the lions' den, without a quiver. What's more, his magnetism, or whatever they call it, was such that the dashed animal, instead of pinning him by the leg, calmed down as if he had had a bromide, and rolled over on his back with all his paws in the air. If Jeeves had been his rich uncle he couldn't have been more chummy. Yet directly he caught sight of me again, he got all worked up and seemed to have only one idea in life—to start chewing me where he had left off.

"Rollo is not used to you yet, sir," said Jeeves, regarding the bally quadruped in an admiring sort of way. "He is an excellent watchdog."

"I don't want a watchdog to keep me out of my rooms."

"No, sir."

"Well, what am I to do?"

"No doubt in time the animal will learn to discriminate, sir. He will learn to distinguish your peculiar scent."

"What do you mean—my peculiar scent? Correct the impression that I intend to hang about in the hall while life slips by, in the hope that one of these days that dashed animal will decided that I smell all right." I thought for a minute. "Jeeves!"

"Sir?"

"I'm going away—tomorrow morning by the first train. I shall go and stop with Mr. Todd in the country."

"Do you wish me to accompany you, sir?"

"No."

"Very good, sir."

"I don't know when I shall be back. Forward my letters."

"Yes, sir."

As a matter of fact, I was back within the week. Rocky Todd, the pal I went to stay with, is a rummy sort of a chap who lives all alone in the wilds of Long Island, and likes it; but a little of that sort of things goes a long way with me. Dear old Rocky is one of the best, but after a few days in his cottage in the woods, miles away from anywhere, New York, even with Motty on the premises, began to look pretty good to me. The days down on Long Island have forty-eight hours in them; you can't get to sleep at night because of the bellowing of the crickets; and you have to walk two miles for a drink and six for an evening paper. I thanked Rocky for his kind hospitality, and caught the only train they have down in those parts. It landed me in New York about dinnertime. I went straight to the old flat. Jeeves came out of his lair. I looked cautiously for Rollo.

"Where's that dog, Jeeves? Have you got him tied up?"

"The animal is no longer here, sir. His lordship gave him to the porter, who sold him. His lordship took a prejudice against the animal on account of being bitten by him in the calf of the leg."

I don't think I've ever been so bucked by a bit of news. I felt I had misjudged Rollo. Evidently, when you got to know him better, he had a lot of good in him.

"Fine!" I said. "Is Lord Pershore in, Jeeves?"

"No, sir."

"Do you expect him back to dinner?"

"No, sir."

"Where is he?"

"In prison, sir."

"In prison!"

"Yes, sir."

"You don't mean—in prison?"

"Yes, sir."

I lowered myself into a chair.

"Why?" I said.

"He assaulted a constable, sir."

"Lord Pershore assaulted a constable!"

"Yes, sir."

I digested this.

"But, Jeeves, I say! This is frightful!"

"Sir?"

"What will Lady Malvern say when she finds out?"

"I do not fancy that her ladyship will find out, sir."

"But she'll come back and want to know where he is."

"I rather fancy, sir, that his lordship's bit of time will have run out by then."

"But supposing it hasn't?"

"In that event, sir, it may be judicious to prevaricate a little."

"How?"

"If I might make the suggestion, sir, I should inform her ladyship that his lordship has left for a short visit to Boston."

"Why Boston?"

"Very interesting and respectable centre, sir."

"Jeeves, I believe you've hit it."

"I fancy so, sir."

"Why, this is really the best thing that could have happened. If this hadn't turned up to prevent him, young Motty would have been in a sanatorium by the time Lady Malvern got back."

"Exactly, sir."

The more I looked at it in that way, the sounder this prison wheeze seemed to me. There was no doubt in the world that prison was just what the doctor ordered for Motty. It was the only thing that could have pulled him up. I was sorry for the poor blighter, but after all, I reflected, a fellow who had lived all his life with Lady Malvern, in a small village in the interior of Shropshire, wouldn't have much to kick at in a prison. Altogether, I began to feel absolutely braced again. Life became like what the poet Johnnie says—one grand, sweet song. Things went on so comfortably and peacefully for a couple of weeks that I give you my word that I'd almost forgotten such a person as Motty existed. The only flaw in the scheme of things was that Jeeves was still pained and distant. It wasn't anything he said, or did, mind you, but there was a rummy something about him all the time. Once when I was tying the pink tie I caught sight of him in the looking-glass. There was a kind of grieved look in his eye.

And then Lady Malvern came back, a good bit ahead of schedule. I hadn't been expecting her for days. I'd forgotten how time had been slipping along. She turned up one morning while I was still in bed sipping tea and thinking of this and that. Jeeves flowed in with the announcement that he had just loosed her into the sitting-room. I draped a few garments round me and went in.

There she was, sitting in the same arm-chair, looking as massive as ever. The only difference was that she didn't uncover the teeth as she had done the first time.

"Good morning," I said. "So you've got back, what?"

"I have got back."

There was something sort of bleak about her tone, rather as if she had swallowed an east wind. This I took to be due to the fact that she probably hadn't breakfasted. It's only after a bit of breakfast that I'm able to regard the world with that sunny cheeriness which makes a fellow the universal favourite. I'm never much of a lad till I've engulfed an egg or two and a beaker of coffee.

"I suppose you haven't breakfasted?"

"I have not yet breakfasted."

"Won't you have an egg or something? Or a sausage or something? Or something?"

"No, thank you."

She spoke as if she belonged to an anti-sausage society or a league for the suppression of eggs. There was a bit of a silence.

"I called on you last night," she said, "but you were out."

"Awfully sorry. Had a pleasant trip?"

"Extremely, thank you."

"See everything? Niagara Falls, Yellowstone Park, and the jolly old Grand Canyon, and what-not?"

"I saw a great deal."

There was another slightly *frappé* silence. Jeeves floated silently into the dining-room and began to lay the breakfast-table.

"I hope Wilmot was not in your way, Mr. Wooster?"

I had been wondering when she was going to mention Motty.

"Rather not! Great pals. Hit it off splendidly."

"You were his constant companion, then?"

"Absolutely. We were always together. Saw all the sights, don't you know. We'd take in the Museum of Art in the morning, and have a bit of lunch at some good vegetarian place, and then toddle along to a sacred concert in the afternoon, and home to an early dinner. We usually played dominoes after dinner. And then the early bed and the refreshing sleep. We had a great time. I was awfully sorry when he went away to Boston."

"Oh! Wilmot is in Boston?"

"Yes. I ought to have let you know, but of course we didn't know where you were. You were dodging all over the place like a snipe—I mean, don't you know, dodging all over the place, and we couldn't get at you. Yes, Motty went off to Boston."

"You're sure he went to Boston?"

"Oh, absolutely." I called out to Jeeves, who was now messing about in the next room with forks and so forth: "Jeeves, Lord Pershore didn't change his mind about going to Boston, did he?"

"No, sir."

"I thought I was right. Yes, Motty went to Boston."

"Then how do you account, Mr. Wooster, for the fact that when I went yesterday afternoon to Blackwell's Island prison, to secure material for my book, I saw poor, dear Wilmot there, dressed in a striped suit, seated beside a pile of stones with a hammer in his hands?"

I tried to think of something to say, but nothing came. A fellow has to be a lot broader about the forehead than I am to handle a jolt like this. I strained the old bean till it creaked, but between the collar and the hair parting nothing stirred. I was dumb. Which was lucky, because I wouldn't have had a chance to get any persiflage out of my system. Lady Malvern collared the conversation. She had been bottling it up, and now it came out with a rush.

"So this is how you have looked after my poor, dear boy, Mr. Wooster! So this is how you have abused my trust! I left him in your charge, thinking that I could rely on you to shield him from evil. He came to you innocent, unversed in the ways of the world, confiding, unused to the temptations of a large city, and you led him astray!"

I hadn't any remarks to make. All I could think of was the picture of Aunt Agatha drinking all this in and reaching out to sharpen the hatchet against my return.

"You deliberately—"

Far away in the misty distance a soft voice spoke:

"If I might explain, your ladyship."

Jeeves had projected himself in from the dining-room and materialised on the rug. Lady Malvern tried to freeze him with a look, but you can't do that sort of thing to Jeeves. He is look-proof.

"I fancy, your ladyship, that you may have misunderstood Mr.

Wooster, and that he may have given you the impression that he was in New York when his lordship was—removed. When Mr. Wooster informed your ladyship that his lordship had gone to Boston, he was relying on the version I had given him of his lordship's movements. Mr. Wooster was away, visiting a friend in the country, at the time, and knew nothing of the matter till your ladyship informed him."

Lady Malvern gave a kind of grunt. It didn't rattle Jeeves.

"I feared Mr. Wooster might be disturbed if he knew the truth, as he is so attached to his lordship and has taken such pains to look after him, so I took the liberty of telling him that his lordship had gone away for a visit. It might have been hard for Mr. Wooster to believe that his lordship had gone to prison voluntarily and from the best motives, but your ladyship, knowing him better, will readily understand."

"What!" Lady Malvern goggled at him. "Did you say that Lord Pershore went to prison voluntarily?"

"If I might explain, your ladyship. I think that your ladyship's parting words made a deep impression on his lordship. I have frequently heard him speak to Mr. Wooster of his desire to do something to follow your ladyship's instructions and collect material for your ladyship's book on America. Mr. Wooster will bear me out when I say that his lordship was frequently extremely depressed at the thought that he was doing so little to help."

"Absolutely, by Jove! Quite pipped about it!" I said.

"The idea of making a personal examination into the prison system of the country—from within—occurred to his lordship very suddenly one night. He embraced it eagerly. There was no restraining him."

Lady Malvern looked at Jeeves, then at me, then at Jeeves again. I could see her struggling with the thing.

"Surely, your ladyship," said Jeeves, "it is more reasonable to suppose that a gentleman of his lordship's character went to prison of his own volition than that he committed some breach of the law which necessitated his arrest?"

Lady Malvern blinked. Then she got up.

"Mr. Wooster," she said, "I apologise. I have done you an injustice.

I should have known Wilmot better. I should have had more faith in his pure, fine spirit."

"Absolutely!" I said.

"Your breakfast is ready, sir," said Jeeves.

I sat down and dallied in a dazed sort of way with a poached egg.

"Jeeves," I said, "you are certainly a life-saver."

"Thank you, sir."

"Nothing would have convinced my Aunt Agatha that I hadn't lured that blighter into riotous living."

"I fancy you are right, sir."

I champed my egg for a bit. I was most awfully moved, don't you know, by the way Jeeves had rallied round. Something seemed to tell me that this was an occasion that called for rich rewards. For a moment I hesitated. Then I made up my mind.

"Jeeves!"

"Sir?"

"That pink tie."

"Yes, sir?"

"Burn it."

"Thank you, sir."

"And, Jeeves."

"Yes, sir?"

"Take a taxi and get me that White House Wonder hat, as worn by President Coolidge."

"Thank you very much, sir."

I felt most awfully braced. I felt as if the clouds had rolled away and all was as it used to be. I felt like one of those birds in the novels who calls off the fight with his wife in the last chapter and decides to forget and forgive. I felt I wanted to do all sorts of other things to show Jeeves that I appreciated him.

"Jeeves," I said, "it isn't enough. Is there anything else you would like?"

"Yes, sir. If I may make the suggestion—fifty dollars."

"Fifty dollars?"

"It will enable me to pay a debt of honour, sir. I owe it to his lordship."

"You owe Lord Pershore fifty dollars?"

"Yes, sir. I happened to meet him in the street the night his lordship was arrested. I had been thinking a good deal about the most suitable method of inducing him to abandon his mode of living, sir. His lordship was a little over-excited at the time, and I fancy that he mistook me for a friend of his. At any rate, when I took the liberty of wagering him fifty dollars that he would not punch a passing policeman in the eye, he accepted the bet very cordially and won it."

I produced my pocket-book and counted out a hundred.

"Take this, Jeeves," I said; "fifty isn't enough. Do you know, Jeeves, you're—well, you absolutely stand alone!"

"I endeavour to give satisfaction, sir," said Jeeves.

from Conversations with the Capeman
by Richard Jacoby

Salvador Agron was a member of a Puerto Rican gang that killed two white boys in a 1959 playground confrontation in the Hell's Kitchen neighborhood of Manhattan. Graduate student Richard Jacoby collaborated with Agron on Conversations with the Capeman, *which was published in 2000. The book included these selections from Agron's letters to Jacoby.*

B ack then the gangs were everywhere: Negro gangs, Italian gangs, Puerto Rican gangs, and white gangs.

I was involved with approximately four different gangs during the 1950's: the Junior Chaplains in Brooklyn, the Tigers in Puerto Rico, and the Mau-Mao's of the Fort Green Projects, and the Vampires.

I was not the president of the Vampires, like the newspapers said I was, but rather the war counselor.

We used to call the fights we had with other gangs, "rumbles."

Sometimes a rumble would start because someone had invaded our neighborhood. This was our territory, or "turf," as we used to call it, and anyone here who didn't belong on this turf would be taking a chance on getting a beating. At other times, a rumble might start because someone's girlfriend had been insulted, or "sounded," as we used to call it, by someone from another gang. Or it might start because of racial stuff, like an Italian gang going after a Black gang, or a Puerto Rican gang going after a white gang.

This was the 1950s, and New York City belonged to the gangs.

One gang in the Bronx was the "Sportsmen," and I think they used to wear red and black as their colors, and then there were the "Bishops" and the "Chaplains" out in Brooklyn, but with brother clubs in the Bronx. Then there was the "Hobo Lords," the "Heart Kings," the "Mau-Mau Chaplains," the "Imperial Hoodlums," and the "Enchanters."

Gangs were all over New York City, and many of the gang members had been picked up for one thing or another. Some were actually framed on charges which were false in an effort by the different boroughs of New York to clean up the streets to comply with the public and civic pressure being put on by the city. Repression landed many an innocent kid in the can and there was no one to complain to.

Some of the gangs used garrison belts and some of them used zip guns. These were home-made guns built from toy guns that you could buy in almost any toy store. We used to file them down in such a way that you were able to attach the antenna from a car into the barrel of the toy gun. Then you attached some rubber bands to the barrel, put in a .22 bullet and you were all set. But I didn't like using them because sometimes they would misfire and then you were in big trouble.

Other gangs used baseball bats, sticks, knives, or whatever else was available that could be easily used as a weapon.

When I attended public schools during the 1950's, I was pushed through grades 6, 7, 8 and finally sat as a semi-illiterate with the mentality of a twelve year old in the back row of the 9th grade.

The New York City schools were a failure before I ever became one. The whole entire system was a farce and I think there was the real fear of educating first generation Puerto Ricans due to the fear of the times. The prejudice against the newcomers and the systematic spite of the system against those who spoke a foreign language.

This was at Junior High School 117 in Brooklyn, without graduating, and in complete disregard for my education. The public school system did not believe in the education of a "spic" and the records of the schools I attended in the fifties can show this undeniable fact.

When we weren't going to war against other gangs, we just hung out on street corners, or at a neighborhood candy store. Talking, showing off to the girls, and getting high. We used to drink cheap wines, like "Thunderbird" or "Sneaky Pete. " Sweet wines that got us high without a hassle. Then we'd stand around and listen to music, mostly doo-wop music.

Some of us smoked reefer, but not that often because it wasn't that easy to get. So mostly it was wine and goofballs, or barbituates, the stuff that either put you to sleep or made you feel dopy.

Even though I was just a little boy when I first came to New York City from Puerto Rico, there was still pressure for me to become a gang member. But I still did not embrace the "gang concept" right away. This took time.

What I'll never forget about coming to New York City that first time was the bumpy airplane ride. I don't know what kinds of airplanes they've got going back and forth now but the one I was on was real bumpy, like we was always on the verge of crashing.

When we landed there was no one there to meet me.

From the very first moment that I walked into that apartment, there was trouble between me and my step-father. It was like he didn't want to have nothing to do with me.

I fell from the fifth story of our apartment into a yard with rocks, sticks, broken bottles, and empty beer cans. I was maybe eleven years old when this happened, and I broke my arm. The fire department took me to Bellevue Hospital where my arm was put in a cast. I was playing Superman on the fire escape when I must have jumped or slipped. People said I jumped. I was too caught up in the fantasy of playing Superman to really know. I was influenced by television easily.

At Bellevue, I refused to eat my peas and when I was ordered to eat the meal, I threw them on the floor. For this action, a net was put over my bed. It looked like a fishing net. I reached into a drawer on a stand next to the bed where I kept a razor blade and with the blade I cut the net to pieces. The nurses and attendants tried to grab me and I went near a window and threatened to jump out.

I was sent to the Youth House at the age of twelve for breaking into a neighbor's house, stealing cigars, some money, and a flashlight. We stole $7 and a flashlight. When we went inside the bedroom of my neighbor's apartment, he was in a t-shirt, lying on his bed, drunk as a stone. I took a cigar and put it in his mouth and we left out the window. I was caught because I tried to sell the flashlight to my step-father.

I spent about nine months in the Youth House. There I learned how to swim, play pool and basketball. At the Youth House I used to be taken out to the park to play ball, but I did not participate, always searching how to escape from my captors but never succeeding.

At the Youth House I was once punished for a fight by being put all day in a pitch black room. Being afraid of the dark, I cried like the eleven-year-old boy that I was. At the end of the day, I was taken out and sent to my room.

My step-father told the Children's Court judge that I was too much to handle, but I felt the same about him.

The Wiltwyck School was my next stop. I was sent there in 1955 by the juvenile court. There I went to school, but being a bit retarded I could not learn. I tried but my reading and writing was semi-literate. At Wiltwyck I got punished with straps for unruly behavior and I wound up more of a juvenile delinquent than when I went in. I was miseducated. I learned about crime and gangs. I was not given individual care and treatment for which Wiltwyck was successful and boasted for. It was all a public lie. I ran away from Wiltwyck two times and when we were taken to the circus at Madison Square Garden, I absconded, making my third attempt at escaping front my captors a success.

At Wiltwyck I picked up many bad habits, such as the knowledge of pot and smoking. It was supposed to be a home or institution for retarded and troubled kids, problem children, and I was considered such. I knew how to read Spanish a little and English also, but I had no comprehension of anything that I read. I even had trouble in comprehending the Dick and Jane reading books of the 1950s. "Spot jump. Dick run. Jane cry. This is Spot. This is Dick. He is a boy. Jane is a girl." Well, it was funny talk, but I still couldn't make any sense out of such stupidity and so I was considered a bit retarded.

My always sounding and acting like I was mentally retarded was not due to my mental state but because I did not get the parental affection necessary to develop normally. Also, those who were my judges and social worker, counselor, etc. were much more confused than I in that they could not give me the proper attention and care that I desperately needed. This almost distorted my sense of love in life and later on I had to teach myself what love was for me.

I can still remember my first day at Wiltwyck. I came up to Poughkeepsie by train and was picked up by a counselor at the Poughkeepsie train station. Mrs. Weiss, my social worker, handed me over to the counselor and also handed him a folder which today seems to be still following me around. I was taken to a car (a 1950 station wagon) and directed to the front seat by the counselor whose name I forgot.

As the car moved, I looked down the Hudson River trying to see if I could spot traces or signs that would lead me back to New York if I should ever decide to run away. The only thing that I could see that led back to New York were the railroad tracks. The counselor looked at me and said, "Don't look so sad, son. You'll get used to these parts and Wiltwyck is better than Warwick." But, deep in my heart I felt otherwise. I felt out of place. I felt lonely, rejected, unloved, like I was not worth anything, and the counselor was a big Black dude whom I already felt was a fucking liar and could not keep a straight face when he spoke.

"Don't call me son," I said defiantly. "My father is in Puerto Rico."

"Okay, kid."

"Don't call me kid," I said defensively. "My name is Salvador Agron. A-G-R-O-N."

"Okay, Sal. Now that I know that you can spell your name," he retorted as though trying to humor me. But I was not to be humored, and I just turned my head away and looked out the window. He kept his mouth shut the rest of the way and when he got to the Wiltwyck School property, he spoke.

"Well, Sal, we're already home, but you do not seem to be in a talkative mood."

"This is your home, not mine," I said rebelliously.

"Sal, you better start learning to get used to it because from your attitude I think that this will be a second home to you for quite a while." As he spoke, the car pulled to a stop in front of the cottages and straight ahead was the main office. To my right, the mess hall and to my left, on a hill, the wall and the mountains. It is a stone wall that does not enclose anything but which is just there and appears very much like a prison wall.

I got out of the car and walked towards the main building. I was processed, interviewed, sent upstairs, stripped and put through the regular institutional process. Upstairs I was issued my clothing, winter boots, and a coat with squares of yellow, red, and blue. Regular civilian clothes, yet with the institutional smell on them.

While in Wiltwyck, homosexuality was rampant. Attacks, con games, inducements, and the whole seduction process was there. My first experience came with a counselor. I went to see him one night for something and I had to go all the way to his room. He was sleeping so I knocked on the door. He said, "Come on in, Sal." I stepped inside and he ordered me to lock the door behind me which I did. I was standing, right there in front of him in my jockey shorts. I was about 12 or 13 and he was in his twenties somewhere, a calculation. I explained my problem. I think it was a stomach ache that I had. He told me to sit on the bed and so I sat there innocent to what was about to happen. The pervert put his hand on my stomach and began to massage my tummy with his hand.

He told me to lay back on the bed, which I did, and he came from under the sheets and he was nude. His penis was hard but I made like I didn't notice. He rubbed his face against mine and I could feel his rough stumps scrape against my hairless face. Then he slowly went to my chest. Now I could feel his cock rubbing up against my body, hot and hard, while his hand worked on my shorts till he pulled them down and began playing with my now erect penis. He took it into his mouth and then came up and kissed me right on the lips.

I felt disgust, but at the same time the perversion was arousing me. He gently guided my hand to his throbbing cock and placed it around it. I knew what the pig wanted so I played with it and he played with mine. He put them together and mine was sort of small next to his. He removed my hand from his hard penis and face-to face with me he placed his cock between my legs while pushing his hard penis against mine and his belly. His rod between my legs felt warm and hard and I was sort of enjoying this. Then warm liquid hit me and his ejaculation between my legs ran down my buttocks. I could not come but he drove me into a thrill with his mouth on my cock.

When I walked out the room I was still a virgin child in the sense that he did not insert his penis in my rectum and this he did not do because I was so young. I went back upstairs, got under the covers and cried mutely. Shame was in my conscience and I felt lonely, abused and low for what had just happened. And to think that he worked in this institution for kids. I said the Our Father out of guilt for enjoying such dehumanization at the hands of this counselor and I asked God, in the name of Jesus, to forgive me.

I was left with my guilt though and I doubted my maleness. I hated this counselor after this, but I did not want to show it. He treated me extra good after this and because of fear that I should say something, he would let me get away with anything. But he never did this again because he knew that once was enough of a chance.

I have been the victim too. I thought about becoming the hunter of those who made me what I became.

Wiltwyck is not the place that Claude Brown in his fictitious *Manchild in the Promised Land* makes it to be. Wiltwyck was a school of corruption, a school where I learned how to play strip poker from a female counselor who enjoyed watching us play while she literally played with her cunt and lustfully watched the kids in the nude. Wiltwyck was a house of lust, crime, and further disorientation of the boys and their sanity.

After leaving Wiltwyck I went to live in Brooklyn with my mother and step-father. We lived down by the waterfront, between Hudson and Water Streets. On the first floor of the building was the storefront Pentecostal Church. From down below every night came the loveliest of songs and hymns dedicated by the hallelujahs to the Kingdom of God. In this congregation the rainbow people, from ebony black to rosy pink clapped their hands in union to their god. I attended the services to feel some of the brotherly and sisterly love and look over the Pentecostal virgins as they danced around intoxicated by the Holy Spirit, with their tambourines and their beautiful dresses as though they were Garland virgins of dance and song, as a druid would say. At times I sat outside the church, or across the street, and listened to the strumming of the guitarist and the blessings of the congregation.

I was living in Brooklyn on 75 Hudson Street, and my hangout was the Farragut Projects around Sand Street. It was there that I joined a gang, the Junior Chaplains, after being released from Wiltwyck. This was when I met a kid named Jones for the first time, and we became good friends.

Jones was Black and also a member of the Junior Chaplains. He was a strange fellow in many ways. We would steal together, fight together, and eat together. However, he wanted to dominate the friendship we had and I felt the same way. This led to arguments and we would jump on the grass in the housing project and fight like two wild cats. But if anybody from the Junior Chaplains tried to intervene, we would both stop fighting and kick his ass.

The Junior Chaplains did not have initiations and one could join the gang just by hanging out. We were all Junior because we were trying to imitate the older kids from the Fort Green projects. There was a president, but he did not care much about the gang and so it was a rather disorganized gang—a sort of mimicking of the Fort Green Chaplains who we looked up to.

We were considered to be the "little people" of the Chaplains and we usually fought against the little people from the other gangs, like the Bishops or the Sand Street Angels. The little people were actually most of the time the brothers and sisters of the above fourteen year olds belonging to the older gangs which ranged from age 15 to 21. Usually when a gang member became 18 or 21, he or she would quit the gang and become a "coolie," meaning that he was in no gang or had stopped bopping or gang fighting.

Coolies with gang reputations were usually challenged by gangs all over when spotted in their neighborhood. They either walked away or defended themselves or went to their house, put on their colors (jacket with gang insignia) and fought to maintain their reputation. The cycle was always present and some who tried to go straight never made it out of the vicious cycle.

We all saw a knife duel one time between two coolies. They cut each other up real bad. It was a tough cat from the Chaplains and one from the Elderly Bops. They were at a party in Fort Green when they started arguing over a girl. Both had retired from gang busting, but that night in the heat of argument, they both went home and stepped out flying their colors.

When a coolie goes to his closet and takes out his outfit and comes out flying his colors, it means that he is ready to kill and die. When these two coolies confronted each other in the park near Fort Green, we all watched. Both had to be taken to the hospital from the knife cuts they inflicted on each other.

One day, as I remember now, a young guy named Bone came and rounded up the whole of the Junior Chaplains. Bone was one of the leading members. We all went and fought the little people of the Sand Street Angels. That night I stabbed two kids. It was a bloody fight and we were victorious. One white boy came at me with a chain and hit me across my chest. Luckily my leather jacket was closed. It stopped the impact, but I hit the ground and not being able to breathe, gang members were scrambling all over. I was given a knife (an extra) by Tom and when I got up, I looked for the guy with the chain. When I saw him, I screamed, "You guinea motherfucker. I'm still breathing." I ran to wack him with a tin garbage can to prevent him from hitting me with the chain again. The chain hit the garbage can top to prevent me from hitting him with the chain again. The chain hit the can top as my hand came from under it and he held his guts calling me a "dirty low-down tropical monkey spic." I stabbed the other two who tried to hit me. When the police cars came, we all ran in different directions.

The next day the older kids from Sand Street were looking for me to kill me, but when the Chaplains of Fort Green got word of it, they came down from Fort Green and told the Sand Street Angels not to interfere in the rumbles of the little people. Otherwise there would be an all-out gang war. They argued about how dirty I was and the Chaplains told them that their little people were just as vicious.

After much consultation, the older guys decided that it was better to leave the rumbles of the little people among the little people. I was saved from the vengeance of the kids' brothers—big Italian guys. But I never forgot what they said. "You let that spic punk know that as soon as he becomes fifteen and joins the Chaplains or Mau Mau's, we're going to get him. I was about fourteen then. I got out of Wiltwyck when I had just turned fourteen. It was difficult going to school. I had to carry a stiletto with me all the time and look over my shoulder.

Being that I was getting picked up for street rumbles and did not attend school, my mother asked me one day, "Son, why don't you go to Puerto Rico for awhile? I looked at mom and agreed. "Yes," I told her, "I should go and visit my father."

This gang atmosphere was one of the main reasons that I left for Puerto Rico.

I left at my family's request.

My father and I got on the plane leaving San Juan for New York. In order not to be recognized by anyone looking for me from the reformatory, I combed my hair and parted it in the middle like I was taught when I was a kid at the poorhouse. That was when my hair was bleached blond from the sun, and long, almost down to my little ass. I also wore dark sunglasses and turned up my collar in case someone was watching for me at the airport. As soon as we landed in New York, I took off my glasses, went into the men's room and combed my hair again in the Tony Curtis style, but I kept my collar up in the Elvis style.

When I got back to New York City in 1958, my sister was living in Manhattan on 124th Street on the East Side. My mother was living in Brooklyn on 75 Hudson Street where she would take care of Madelyn, my niece.

My other niece Rosie was staying with Aurea. I was welcomed when I got to Brooklyn by my step-father and my mother and the brothers and sisters of the Pentecostal Church. The kids and people in the neighborhood would say, "Hey, Sal is back."

As I walked in the neighborhood with my eyes wide open, I saw that things had changed. There were some new gangs, and the old ones appeared tougher. The first gang I ran into was the Sand Street Angels. Their girls were still pretty as ever. They had matured more and wore the new styles. There was the blonde and the one with black hair, very Italiana, who I would eye all the time, but something separated us. The Sand Street Angels still had their mean look and their black leather jackets. Of course I was afraid of those whiteys because I knew they were vicious with their stillettos.

I came back from Puerto Rico smarter and tougher; but now I was trying to be cool.

In the Farragut projects there were no more Junior Chaplains. It was now the Fort Green Chaplains and the Farragut Chaplains. You were one or the other. They were now under the leadership of Big John the Bop. I walked by and checked in as a "coolie." They would laugh and say, "Sal is now a coolie." That was their magic word for non-gang members and it was like a passport to walk around the neighborhood. It actually meant you were "cool" and did not come to fight, that you would not disrespect the gang or the girls.

A coolie had more license to look, talk, and dance with the "debs," but with respect. Otherwise he could get his ass kicked. As I walked over to Fort Green, which was a more vicious place than any other, I

saw a gang pass by with their leather jackets with two M's on the back.
They stared at me as I looked back and one of them said, "The Mighty
Mau-Maus!" I immediately identified myself, "A coolie from the turf."
They kept walking and I burst out laughing, thinking to myself, "Que
los Mowmows! Cono, even the suckers are around . . . The Mighty
Mowmows! . . . They must be out of their minds."

After being a month back in Brooklyn, I decided to go back to
school at P.S. 117. I told my mother that I wanted to start school again
in order to get my high school diploma. She thought it was the best
thing that could happen. I went to see the people at Wiltwyck. They
had their offices on 125th Street. When I went in, I asked to see Mrs.
Weiss who was my social worker. She was happy to see me and com-
mented on my change, saying that I looked a little more mature.

I told her that I had just come from Puerto Rico and that I was ready
to start school and try to graduate. I told her that I needed help—that
they could tell me what I should do. She picked this young Black man
and told him the problem. He was a social worker. They decided to
take me to a place in Brooklyn where I could be assigned a school. We
went to Brooklyn together and he got me enrolled in P.S. 117 between
Willoughby and Franklin Avenue.

Members of other gangs were also going to P.S. 117.

One day as I came out of school, a group of Marcy Street Chaplains
were waiting for me. I already knew they had something for me. I sensed
their vibes. As I stepped to the sidewalk they surrounded me and
demanded money. It was a shakedown. I saw a couple of switchblades
in the hands of some of the guys. Not being armed myself, I went into
my pocket and pulled out the only $3 I had and handed it over to the
head of the group. As I gave him the money, I said, "Remember this, my
man. I'll be back for my money." They were eager for a fight then since
I had given them an excuse to beat me up. In the back of my head I
thought, "Wait till I catch them alone! I'm gonna cut some faces and
necks." They were about to beat the hell out of me. As this was going on,
there were two Mau-Maus at the street corner—Tito and someone else.
When Tito saw what was happening, he ran over to the group and

screamed, "Mau-Maus to the heart!" He told them to give me my money back and they did it. One guy said, "Tito, he's a coolie. Why do you stick up for him?" Tito said, "Because he comes from my territory."

Tito was war counselor of the Mau-Maus and had the power to declare a gang war on the group or any other gang, but the Marcy Chaplains were a brother club. I was amazed at the power he had and the way the group feared his threats. Tito explained that the president of the Mau-Maus had a brother who was my friend. The president of the Mau-Maus was Carlos and his brother was a church attendant. I took the money back and said to the kid who took my money, "Now, how do you want to fight me? With a knife or with your fists?"

He was a bit nervous and backed up, not knowing what to say. When I turned to Tito, I asked him for a knife. Tito looked at me when he saw that the kid did not want to have it out and said, "Sal, forget about it. They are a brother club. It was a mistake." I listened to him, but at the same time while I held the knife in my hand, I stepped closer to the kid and gave him a back hand across his face which knocked him to the ground.

Tito grabbed me by the arm and pulled me away saying, "You crazy motherfucker, Forget about it!" He helped the other kid up and said to him, "Forget this or face a rumble." The kid said that he already had forgotten this whole incident. We shook hands and I warned him, "If you ever pull this shit on me again, I will have to kill you. And prisons do not scare me!" Tito and I walked home.

When we got there, he told the Mau-Maus how I handled myself. Tito said it came close to declaring a gang war. One guy said, "Those punks want trouble. Tomorrow I'm going up there and tell those idiots not to bother anyone from the Fort Green area without first asking the Mau-Maus."

Tito began to introduce me to the members of the gang—Gago, Carlos, Israel, Chino, Priest—and to the Mau-Mau debs—Delores, Vicky, Bernice, Cookie, Carmen. It was a friendly atmosphere. Israel and Carlos asked me if I wanted to join and I said, "Yes." They explained the rules:

One, if you hurt a Mau-Mau, we will hurt you. Two, if you kill a Mau-Mau, we will kill two of you. And any Mau Mau that turns stoolie will be hanged in the park by his feet and beaten to death. When one had money, he should give the treasurer a couple of bucks to buy the gang outfit with all the colors, or for any purpose deemed necessary by the President, Vice-President, War Counselor, and Treasurer. Without a full vote, no money could be used. The vote was among the four heads and it had to be a unanimous decision.

They explained to me that I would have to go through the "initiation" to be a Mau-Mau.

The initiation was either to stand against a wooden wall and have the most nervous guy throw a knife at you. Blind Man was usually picked for this because he could not see too good when he took off his glasses. Or one could take a beating from the gang without screaming or crying one word. It was decided that I should meet them at the Willoughby Center in the Farragut Projects. After I agreed and picked the beating as the safest initiation, I was told this, "Never, as long as you live forget this: Once a Mau-Mau, always a Mau-Mau." These were unwritten laws of the concrete jungle.

This process of selecting members for the gang made the Mau-Mau's the most dangerous gang in Brooklyn.

A lot of Mau-Mau's were already at the Center when I arrived, and they were touching their knuckles as though they had not initiated someone in a long time. My mind raced back to El Cano de Moca who had gotten a beating by the leaders in La Correctional just like I was about to receive. I looked at them real good. They were happy to initiate another member, but they were expressionless. The president Carlos said, "Big Foot, it looks like you're ready. It won't last long!"

I was told to go into the bathroom and me and the Mau-Mau's all crowded in. They were calm. I was nervous as hell. One walked over to me and said, "My name is Terror and I'm going to terrorize you right now." As he said this, he took his fist and hit me right in my stomach with a real hard blow. But having trained in Puerto Rico, I breathed in really hard and tensed my body. I raised my hands, but before making any defense about twenty Mau-Mau's fists were all over me. I was hit everywhere. One shot landed on my eyes, another on my nose, and one on jaw. The rest was foggy.

All through the initiation I did not utter one word. I thought I had woken up in heaven with the angels. I went home, an initiated Mau-Mau. When I got home, my sister was a bit puzzled about what had happened. My mother asked me, but I told her I had just had a fight. I went inside my room, opened the window, and leaned out while I lit a "yerbo" and turned on the radio. I smoked my joint, lit an L & M and sat there quietly.

The Mau-Mau's were fighters.

So one night it was time to "go down" on the Bishops from South Brooklyn. I pulled out my bayoneta from out of its holster which I had inside my pants and said, "Ready any time. Ready to leap tall buildings at a single bound. It's a bird. It's a plane. No, it's the tempered steel!" Everyone laughed and the war counselor said, "Okay, give the girls your weapons and walk cool as though we're going to a party. Try not to stay all together." I had no one to give the knife to. I turned to Barbara and she smiled and said, "Why don't you give it to Vicky?" I replied, "She carries Carlos Apache's knife, not mine." I winked at her as she took the bayoneta and hid it under her blouse. However, she seldom went to fights with us. She used to stay home.

That night there was a fight. I chased a group of white boys with my knife, while beating up others. I always used the bayoneta to scare my opponents in the rival gang and seldom stabbed someone. I mostly used to stab people on their shoulders or their thighs, not really wanting to kill someone, but I always wanted to hurt them— hurt them real bad. I had anger and hate in my eyes.

The gang broke up after the Mau-Mau's shot a boy in the Penny Arcade near the Paramount Theater. After that, I was chased out of Brooklyn by the Sand Street Angels who actually wanted to kill me for what happened with their friend Anthony at the hands of the Mau-Mau's. But me, Big Foot Machinegun Sal was not going to stay around and get killed. I headed towards the bridge. When they spotted me, I had to run across to Manhattan. When I got to the other side I went up to 125th Street to live with my sister. I began to take walks all over Manhattan. I would come down Broadway at times with a cane like Bat Masterson in tuxedo outfits looking like I was Howard Hughes' own rich son. In my imitations of white middle class Americans, I always used to gravitate towards the English, as though I were Winston Churchill or one of the knights of the round table. I frequented the 80's and 70's on the West Side and passed my time in the park.

One day Vicky, Cookie, Carlos and myself spent a whole day playing around in the park and rowing a boat. Carlos, having been in the Dragons, used to come from Brooklyn. We would walk all over Spanish Harlem and Black Harlem. Junior used to come also and I would take Junior up to my sister's house and relax up there.

After that I met Tony Ralph from the uptown Diablos. Tony and I got a $7 a week room on 77th Street where I was one night stripped of all my clothing as I slept in a drunken stupor. I was initiated by Tony into a Diablo. This was done by putting Red Devil hot sauce up my nose, in my mouth, my ass, my balls, so that when I woke up I was red all over and burning from the hot sauce all over my body. It was here that Tony found out how wicked I was. I went through a whole set of kitchen knives in a week's time. Tony came with me to the park and we would hold up people. In the long run, we turned into a gang, known as the Vampires, with aspirations of controlling the west side of Manhattan.

It was August 29th, 1959, and earlier in the day it had been raining.

I was living back then on 77th Street between Columbus and Amsterdam Avenues. I was living in a seven-dollar a week room with two other friends: Anthony Hernández (the Umbrella Man) and another boy whose name was Ralphie. From hustling on the streets we were able to pay the rent, eat, and buy our clothing. All of us had left our homes, and Tony was the only one who still maintained any kind of contact with his family.

Saturday night and from Seventieth Street to the Eightieth Street the night life was taking its usual course. Young Puerto Ricans on the West Side of the City of New York would congregate earlier in the evening, drink the cheap wine, and share it with the different gangs that were considered "brother clubs." It was a typical night during the 1950's. Gangs, clubs, and social groupings of youths has always been a reality of New York City—a youth would either be a loner or be in a group. Some groups are more violent than others. Some liked to dance. Some liked to smoke marijuana. And others like to fight. There is not much good to be found in cities such as New York, and even more so during the 1950's.

That night I walked from my room to 76th Street. Once I got there drank about six beers. Later on I walked over to 72nd Street to see if I could hustle up some more money. And when I did have some more money, I found someone willing to sell me some goofballs. I took two of the goofballs, and then I walked over to the park, where I sat for awhile before returning to hang out with some other gang members on the corner of 72nd Street.

It was about 9:30 p.m. when a call was received from one of our brother clubs down in the Forties. One of our gang members went over and picked up the telephone that rang on the corner of 73rd Street and after talking with someone, he walked back over to us and said that some people from a gang who called themselves, "The Norsemen," had beaten up some Puerto Ricans, and that someone had tried to sell marijuana to someone's mother. It was a confusing story. Gangs seldom check out thoroughly before acting anyway, so that the phone call had already sparked the desire for a rumble.

The fellow who answered the telephone told me to wait a little while before a reply could be given. He came over and after I had asked him what was really happening, I went over and spoke to Frenchie.

"Who is this?" the voice on the other side of the line asked.

"It's me, Frenchie."

"Qué pasa, man?"

"We got trouble with the Norsemen, man, and we need some help. Some of those guys beat on some of our guys."

"Hey, no problema, man, I'll call some of our people and we'll meet you down at the playground on 46th Street."

Then I called some of our brother clubs, like the Hell Burners, and the Mau-Mau Chaplains. Everyone agreed to meet us later at the playground. From the playground we would proceed to Fiftieth Street for the rumble of the century.

The gang that was down at the Forties was the Heart Kings, our gang up in the Seventies was the Vampires, and on Eightieth Street were the Buccaneers and further up were the Young Lords.

Central Park was our home away from home.

The Heart Kings had recently become a brother club of the Vampires and the others. The Vampires had already been in existence for about eight months.

I started the Vampires in order to fight back those other gangs that would otherwise try to control the section between 60th and 80th Streets. At first we received opposition from the nearby gangs (like the Buccaneers and the Young Lords) but it did not take long to establish our boundaries and the fact that we were all predominantly Puerto Ricans created a sort of brotherhood. Fiftieth Street and Ninth Avenue was the territory of the Norsemen and down Fortieth Street were the Heart Kings who had territory from 30th on up but who were constantly in trouble because of the race problem existing between Puerto Ricans, Italians, Irish, and others. As for Black gangs (known at that time as Negro gangs) there were not many around those parts. In the Vampires, there were more Puerto Ricans than in any other group. We did have a few Italians, a few Irish, and a few Blacks, but they mostly stayed with us because they lived around those parts.

I had an umbrella, which I gave to Tony Hernández, and he gave me his black cape with a red, satin lining. I put it on. Weapons were given out and I chose a Mexican dagger. This had belonged to our President, Manny Ortega, and it was the same dagger used when we took our oath months ago in Central Park. An oath taken underneath a full moon, and so named our gang, the Vampires. The oath was taken by lifting the dagger up to the moon and swearing that we would from that day onward defend one another as brother and fellow Vampires.

That night we also swore that we were going to kill someone in Central Park in order to confirm the oath with blood. But now, here it was August the 29th, 1959, and nearly nine months to the day that the oath had been taken.

Some would walk to the playground on 46th Street, some would take a cab, and some, like myself, would take the subway.

I remember entering the playground, sitting in a corner with my Mexican dagger. Then a fight broke out (this fight was supposed to occur on 50th Street and not on the playground).

I remember running around the playground using the term, "gringo," and trying my best to get out with my knife in front of me.

I remember getting out and while walking fast, wrapping the knife in my cape which I had taken off.

It was dark in the park, there weren't any lights, and when we ran outside the gate everyone took off in a million directions.

But I swear by all that is holy, I do not remember using the knife that was in my hand.

I started running to the subway station but then someone grabbed my arm and said, "Let's take a taxi uptown, it'll be a lot quicker."

Then we ran over to Ninth Avenue to where there were lots of cabs, and after we hailed down a cab, six of us got inside.

Someone in the cab told the driver we wanted to go to 72nd Street but when we started getting these funny looks from the driver, we all got off instead at Fifty-second Street.

From there we divided up. Some of us took the subway to 72nd Street and some of us walked. We were all hyped up from what had happened in the playground, this I do remember.

When we got to 72nd Street we went to someone's apartment and listened to the news of what had happened over the radio.

As soon as we heard the news about the killings I knew there was no way I could keep hanging around 72nd Street because when they found out it was me down there, the first place they'd be looking would be right in this neighborhood.

I went up to the Bronx with Tony and another guy. We stayed where we could, but mostly we slept in the hallways of apartment buildings, or on the roofs.

And we took food from garbage cans.

Then two cops in a patrol car called me over. It was late, I think after midnight, and when they asked me what I was doing out so late, and where did I come from, I told them that I was from Brooklyn, and that my father was a minister and we lived in an apartment over a grocery. I told the cops I was visiting with friends in an apartment nearby and then they took me over to see if this was the truth.

The people we had been with said, "Yeah, he was here a few hours ago, like at seven or so." But when the cop said something about me being a long way from Brooklyn, the kids said something like it was their understanding that I came from 76th Street in Manhattan and not from Brooklyn.

The cops must have gotten suspicious because right away they took me down to the station house and started questioning me, and that's when I told them, "Well, you're going to find out anyway. I'm the guy you're looking for."

I was the first to be arrested, and then they picked up Tony a few hours later.

They took us from the police station in the Bronx to the 16th Precinct on West 47th Street and that's when they started questioning us about what had happened at the playground.

Maybe some people like police stations, but I never have.

The 16th Precinct was just like all the rest of them. Nothing but sad places with people in handcuffs going to jail.

Handcuffed to Tony, we're taken upstairs. Reporters and photographers are everywhere.

The room smells like someone just died inside. One of the cops tells us to take a seat and when we do he unlocks one of our handcuffs and puts it through one of the wooden bars of the chair. Locking it shut, me and Tony are both tied to our chairs.

I don't know how long me and Tony were handcuffed to those chairs before one of the detectives came in to see me.

"Sal," he said, "your mother's here, and she wanted you to have this."

What he's got is a Bible, and before I can even think about what I'm saying, I'm shaking my head and telling him "No way, I don't want nothing like that."

"Are you sure?" he says. "Because your mother really wants you to have it."

I don't even answer him, and after waiting a second or two, he turns around and leaves the room.

He takes the Bible with him.

There were two knives on the desk, one was my Mexican dagger and the other was a bloody white-handled knife which was closed.

I told the cops that I used the knife but that I didn't know anyone had been killed until I heard it on the radio later that night.

"Sal, which is your knife," said the detective behind the desk while the District Attorney and other detectives looked on.

"This one," I said, pointing to the dagger.

"Why," asked one of the detectives, "isn't there any blood on it?"

This was a puzzling question, but since I had already admitted to the stabbing of five people altogether, I just said, "Well, when you stick it in fast and pull it out fast, it leaves no blood on the blade."

They all stared at me for a while and the detective behind the desk asked,

"Then whose knife is this?" He asked this pointing indignantly to the blood stained knife on the desk.

"I dunno, I dunno, man."

"This knife was found in the park, you must know whose knife it is—you are obviously the leader of these cutthroats," he said.

"Get the spic punk out of here," ordered the detective behind the desk.

They questioned us for a long time and at one point I remember signing some papers that someone put in front of me, and that's probably when I said that stuff about, "I don't care if I burn, my mother can watch me." There were lots of newspaper reporters around and I guess someone was listening when I said it.

Later on when they took me and Tony outside, there were hundreds of people all over the place. Lots of them were in front of the police station and the rest were up and down the streets, all over the place.

Lots of them were screaming at me and Tony. They was saying stuff like, "Kill the spics! Kill 'em all!" Fists were being waved at us, and some people were yelling, "Murderers!" and "Killers!"

Afterwards, when they took us outside, there were lots of reporters and people with cameras trying to take our pictures.

We were handcuffed and we were waiting for a paddy wagon, and I recognized one of the people who was yelling questions at us. It was Gabe Pressman, and I recognized him from seeing him on television.

"Tell me why you want to be president of the Vampires?"
"I don't wanna be no president."

"How do you feel about killing those two boys?"
"Like I always feel."

"How's that?"
"Like this, like I am right now."

"Do you feel sorry for those two boys?"
"That's for me to know and for you to find out."

"Why do you think kids are in gangs today?"
"That's also for me to know and for you to find out."

"Would you kill more if you could?"
"You're wasting your time."

"You feel like a big man today?"
"I feel like killing you, that's what I feel like."

"How do you feel about your mother and father?"
"That I'm sorry about, but nothing else."

The High Life and Strange Times of the Pope of Pot

by Mike Sager

Mike Sager has written about crack gangsters, Vietnam veterans, pit bulls, Palestinians, Aryan Nation militiamen, and Tupperware saleswomen. His article about Mickey Cezar appeared in Rolling Stone in June 1991.

There's a knock at the door and Mickey the Pope, the Pope of Pot, stubs out a joint and stashes it in a drawer. "Gotta go now, toots," he rasps, smoke leaking from his chipmunk grin, and then he laughs, "*Ah-ha-ha-HA*" and then he coughs, a deep black hack that shudders his shoulders. He swallows hard, wipes a tear, shrugs, smiles. A trickle of blood reddens the groove between his two front teeth.

Mickey hangs up the phone, writes a number in his little book with a green pen. His entries aren't alphabetical—more experiential, like life, taken in the order that comes, always in alternating colors. He likes things around him to be beautiful, the way God intended. He closes the book, puts a finger to his lips, concentrates. Something to do . . . What was it? . . . Hmmm . . .

Mickey pans the room, in search of a clue: a refrigerator, a stack of chairs, a poster of the Italian rock & roller he has taken off the street, a hot plate with one coil glowing, his desk, a pile of bills, a birthday card. *Birthday!* Today is Mickey the Pope's birthday. He is forty-nine years old. Today is also the day before the winter solstice, the last short-ening day on the calendar of seasons. This is significant somehow to Mickey the Pope, who's facing fifteen years in the slammer.

Since the bust, sales are down by more than half. Expenses, how-ever, remain the same. It looks like Mickey will have to get a loan. He'll have to ask his little brother to cosign. His brother, of course, will insist that Mickey write something besides pope on the section marked EMPLOYMENT. He thinks Mickey is meshugge. He may be right. But the fact is, Mickey can't stop being pope just because he has no money. When you start your own church, take the top spot, register it with the City of New York, you make a lifetime commitment. You have respon-sibilities, toots: You have to tend the flock, buy and dispense sacra-ment, hire couriers—people you can trust. And then there is operations: two apartments, two offices, the church, the handouts to unfortunates, the food and the dental plan for employees, the tele-phone lines, 800-WANT-POT. Give the pope a call if you live in Man-hattan. Leave your address, your first name, a description of yourself. Your pot will arrive by bicycle in forty minutes or less.

Mickey spies his papal miter, a high, white, John Paul crown, with underwires shaped to a peak, a nine-inch marijuana leaf pasted on the front, lace trailing from the sides. He dons it, tying the polka-dot ribbon beneath his chin. He wears the miter for all public appearances. The May Day Smoke-In at Washington Square, the Halloween parade in Greenwich Village, ACT-UP demonstrations at City Hall, Wigstock, in Tompkins Square—any occasion that requires his high-camp popely presence, any opportunity to stroll the streets, preach the gospel of marijuana and hand out free joints, the sacrament of his Church of Realized Fantasies.

Mickey the Pope swivels around in his chair, grinning, mouth agape, glasses glinting in the fluorescent light. *"Ah-ha-ha-HA!"*

The door again. Knock, knock.

Oh, yeah. The door. It is made of metal. It is very heavy. Mickey shambles over and yanks. His arm boings like a rubber band. The door doesn't budge.

Mickey giggles, shrugs. What, me worry? Used to be Mickey weighed 300 pounds. He's down a bit lately. A lot. He's a little weak. This diabetes shit. The bleeding gums, the fading eyesight. And all the time drink-and-piss, drink-and-piss, the other day he wet his pants. It was an accident. People have accidents. It'll be all right. The winter solstice is upon us, and the days will be longer, the world will be brighter. This is nature. We know this for a fact. Just as we know that when his church hits 1 million members, he'll have the best medical care available. Just as we know that when his case comes up, the jury will acquit. Some juror, the pope is sure, will know what he knows: that to follow an insane law is to be insane yourself.

Things may look bleak, but Mickey the Pope will find his way clear. He always has. He speaks with the voice and the authority of God. He'll tell you that himself. He also has experience on his side. Twenty years in the pot business, a dozen arrests, seven gunshot wounds, three years in jails, one deportation and all those men, toots, so many beautiful, wonderful men. The counselors at camp. The kids in his bunk. Ten percent of the crew of the U.S. Navy carrier *Intrepid* in the spring and summer of 1959. Two at once on public-access television, a salt-and-pepper team, the black one so big he could do it to himself if he wanted.

And then there was the guy in Amsterdam. He was hired to kill Mickey. As it was, Mickey was just wounded. Mickey was really fat then. The shot passed through the fleshy part of his right arm, down into his belly and out again. What Mickey remembers is that oil oozed from the wounds. It looked like chicken fat, nice and bright and yellow. "I felt like an oil sheik," he says. "*Ah-ha-ha-HA!*"

In the end, the guy who tried to kill him in Amsterdam became another of the many and varied lovers of Mickey the Pope. Amsterdam, that was the place, those were the days. During the Seventies, Mickey the Pope was known in Amsterdam as Da Paus Maus. He was the No.

1 pot dealer in a city of heads, unloading nickels, dimes, lids, to the tune of seven kilos a day, selling out of a room in his five-story house-boat on the Amstel River, the front hatch of which was painted to resemble a giant pair of red lips. You had to come through the lips to meet the pope.

The knock again. Mickey the Pope pulls hard on the door.

Late December in the meatpacking district in New York, the sun-light leaning into the West Side afternoon. In a few hours the crack boys will stir and the curbs will be deep in transvestites, and effem-inate men wearing leathers and lots of keys will come jangling down the block holding hands, headed for a basement club called the Hellfire. Now, though, things are almost serene on this corner of Thirteenth and Hudson, just in sight of the river. Mothers push strollers, delivery trucks come and go, old Irish ladies promenade—constitutionals taken daily since the boom days on the waterfront when corners like Mickey's were given over to pubs.

The pope's place, his Church of Realized Fantasies, is painted yellow in its present incarnation, a bright beacon against dark, slick streets and dirty brick. It's an old comic-book store—Dick Tracy painted on one side—with eight big windows, so good for his plants. Mickey the Pope loves plants.

Two men stand flat-footed outside the church. One wears a pom-padour and a trench coat. He looks like a mobster. The other carries a pad. He looks like a balding Irish guy in a leather jacket trying to look like something other than a cop. The door swings open. "Michael Cezar?" asks the guy in the leather jacket.

"Howdy, honey, howdy!" rasps Mickey the Pope, beak nosed, red faced, wearing his marijuana bonnet. He giggles, raises his hands—palms out—and rubs tiny circles in the air before him, the papal greeting.

"Internal Affairs," says the guy in the pompadour.

Back now to August, earlier in the year. Across the Americas, from Bogota to Harlem, the drug war is raging. Though the government has proclaimed drug use on the slide, curbside dealers are trading briskly in cocaine, prices are down, supply stable, the rat-a-tat-tat of automatic-weapons fire rings across the ghettos like cash-register bells. Sales are also strong in heroin, an old drug making a resurgence as an antidote to crack. At first the police notice a sudden infusion of high-grade, low-price H into the cities. Later it is revealed, but not widely reported, that most of the stuff is China White from Asia's Golden Triangle, moved into America by Triads, many of whose members have recently emigrated from Hong Kong. What fools the police is ingenuity: Chemists are processing different batches with different recipes out of the international heroin cookbook, making some of it look like Mexican, some like Lebanese.

Meanwhile, potheads across the mainland are mourning. It is the time of the drought, the great marijuana drought of 1990, the summer of scrounging, of smoking roaches and cleaning seeds and finally just giving up. Film at eleven shows bonfires of prime buds and old tires sending thick black smoke into the ecosystem. County sheriffs in camouflage fatigues stand around smiling, pitchforks or shotguns in hand. In the cities, the police and legislators launch a massive assault on head shops. Mail-order companies are also targeted. The police seize records, mailing lists, stock. It becomes impossible to buy a bong.

One fine summer day in the midst of all this, a New York radio personality named Howard Stern—the drive-time attitude idol of the bridge-and-tunnel crowd—is sitting at his desk at the station. He's paging through a New Jersey newspaper, looking for material for his talk show, when he spies an ad. He blinks in disbelief.

"Call 1-800-WANT-POT."

The next morning, live before 2 million listeners in three Eastern cities, Howard calls Mickey the Pope.

"Hey, dude!" Howard says. "You're on the air!"

"Howdy, honey, howdy!" rasps Mickey. "I'm the pope. The Church of Realized Fantasies."

"So what do you do, sell pot?"

"Oh . . . see . . ., " says Mickey. "We give out sacrament for those who need it."

"You don't think it causes any—"

"No," interrupts the pope. "It cures everything. Even AIDS."

"It gives you breasts," blurts Howard. "How's your breasts?"

"My breath may stink a little. I didn't brush my teeth."

"No! Your breasts!"

"They're fine," says the pope. "They get erect, I suppose."

"So," says Howard, changing the subject. "You make a lot of money doing this?"

"I'm living on the Upper East Side. I'm comfy. And I have a palace in New Jersey."

"Really? All from just dealing pot?"

"Well, from being the pope. A lot of people admire the pope."

They talk a while longer, then Howard says goodbye.

"You know," Howard says to his sidekick, Robin Quivers, "I had seen the number in the newspaper, and I thought, 'This is kinda cool.' I mean, I don't think it's cool that he's a drug dealer, but it's kinda cool that he's getting away with it."

"It seems it would be pretty easy to catch him, wouldn't it?" says Robin. "You just call him up, make an order, he shows up, you book him."

"He ought to change his number to 1-800-ARREST-ME," says Howard.

Mickey the Pope was born Michael Ellis Cezar, in New York City's Greenwich Village, the eldest child of a Jewish engineer and his wife, the daughter of a former postmaster general of Jamaica who was the scion of an English colonial family that had made a fortune mining bauxite. Mickey's father owned an electronics factory in Paterson, New Jersey, which built transformers for radar, the space program, nuclear-power plants. Mickey's little brother runs the factory today. One sister is a real-estate agent, the other, a ceramics teacher who lives in the family "palace," a large house in Morris Plains, New Jersey, which has been stripped of all its furnishings to pay the family bills.

Mickey dropped out of high school after his father went bankrupt.

Starting over in a new plant, Mickey built tables for machines, hooked up the electric and the plumbing, did everything from filing and drilling to sweeping the floor. Later, after a stint in the navy, he feuded with his father, who in turn disinherited his son and committed him to a mental institution. Upon his release, Mickey fled to Europe.

One day in the early Seventies, Mickey took the fabled Magic Bus Tour of Amsterdam. When it stopped at the Lowlands Weed Company, says Mickey, "I knew I'd found a home."

Lowlands Weed, it turned out, was owned by a bunch of Dutch Provos, anarchists who renounced the concept of work. They were known for their be-ins, demonstrations during which they sat around and did nothing but be themselves. The Provos also advocated the legalization of marijuana. They were the original potheads of Europe, the Continent's largest dealers. They would eventually place several of their number on Amsterdam's city council. Oddly, after achieving their political foothold, the Provos disbanded. It was probably the shock. Having won, these devout anarchists found themselves in charge of legislating societal order.

"They were a bunch of crazy people," says Mickey the Pope. "This one guy threw smoke bombs at the marriage of some Dutch aristocrat. He used to have sex with women and their kids. I'm telling the truth. I had people take shits on my floor. I had other people come in and eat it.

"In the beginning, they sold pot by the plant and seeds," the pope continues. "I convinced them to sell the smokable product. Buses would pull up and three-quarters of the passengers would flow into the shop to buy pot."

Soon, Da Paus Maus moved out of Lowlands and founded his own retail operation, selling out of a series of ever-larger houseboats. A port city, Amsterdam had an almost inexhaustible supply of drugs. Da Paus would get the list of ships from the harbor master, then go down to the docks at three in the morning. He'd fall into step with some sailors, say, "Howdy, toots!" and offer to share a joint.

"And then you'd go on board and there were tons of smoke pouring out of the ship," Mickey says. "Everybody had the stuff. So I'd give them a good price and they'd throw it down on the dock, and then I'd drive out, waving to the customs guy. He knew everything. The whole government was in on it. I was once visited on my houseboat by some secretary of state. He said, 'Keep up the good work. It's great for the tourists!' "

Amsterdam had always been known for its coffee bars and hashish, but the pope saw an opening and set about creating a market for marijuana. He kept long hours, stayed open seven days a week and sold at a tiny profit—even advertised in the yellow pages as "Hennep Producten." Pretty soon, says the pope, the Cosmos, the Milkyway, Paradiso, all the big clubs were selling Mickey's finest. "I was making, like, $20,000 a day," remembers Mickey.

Mickey lived the good life for a while, spending the guilders as fast as they came in. A new boat, an old school to house his forty workers, medical and dental plans and always the handouts. Then Da Paus Maus was busted. After seven years in business, Mickey was kicked out of Holland.

Penniless, still estranged from his family, Mickey landed on New York's Lower East Side in 1979. He met up with some anarchists, moved into a little apartment at First Street and First Avenue and began selling loose joints. Soon he started his first telephone delivery service, 777-CASH.

And thus began the pope's delivery empire. He serviced UN diplomats, rock stars, whorehouses, nightclubs, night watchmen, magazine editors, yippies, yuppies and punks. For a time the pope had a diner. For a time he operated a storefront on First Street, selling bags brazenly to all comers. When that store was busted in 1981, the pope did eight months in Rikers Island Prison, whereupon he returned to the Lower East Side and started all over again, this time at Eleventh Street and Avenue B.

"People lined up outside to buy pot all day long," says a longtime associate. "They were taking the money out in garbage bags, but the cops were so busy with all the heroin in the neighborhood they didn't really have time to fool with Mickey."

The mid-Eighties saw the pope battling the underworld. First came a Puerto Rican gang called the Hitmen Club. When Mickey refused to pay protection money, the gang members forced their way into his telephone center, holding the workers at bay with a .357 and a straight razor, taking $500. The next day they came back, demanding $1000 a week from the pope. When Mickey refused, they ambushed him later on the street, shooting him six times with a .22. "He was so fat they didn't hit any vital organs," says the associate. "The ambulance guy didn't even believe Mickey had been shot until he opened up his coat and showed him the bullet holes."

Later the young sons of some Italian mobsters would try to muscle in on Mickey's operations. They cut the phone lines, waited outside to break Mickey's legs. Meanwhile, inside, Mickey the Pope was alone, in pain from a bowel obstruction, a complication from the Puerto Rican ambush. Weak, sick, determined, he held the fort for five days. In the end he was rescued by his father. "Well, I guess if you're dying, I can take you to the hospital," the old man said.

Over the years, Mickey estimates, he has presided over phone operations in more than forty different locations, always with modest success. Then came the summer of 1990, the drought. Nobody could find any pot except for Mickey. Business boomed.

Each morning, the bicycle couriers would meet at a secret location and check out stock for the day, four-gram bags of brown-green commercial Mexican, packaged in sealable glassine inside white paper envelopes. The couriers would hit the streets by 10:00 a.m. As calls came in, telephone operators would take down locations in logbooks and then beep the couriers, who would deliver the goods within forty minutes. Each bag cost the consumer $50. Delivery was $10 extra. At twenty-eight grams to the ounce, the pope's medium-grade pot was expensive, selling at about $350 a lid. But it was the only pot available. One hundred or 200 calls a day were not unusual.

By eight each evening, the couriers would check back in and pay up. No business was done after dark. That's when the real criminals were out, and couriers were often taken down by street thugs or fake cops with Chinatown shields. Mickey worried for his people. Usually, at night, the pope would gather around him a number of his flock and somebody would cook a big dinner. It was a happy family, mostly. And why not? The pope provided food, a dental plan, money to fix a broken bike. He gave out free pot, sometimes paid the medical bills of people he knew with AIDS. He'd even let you live in the telephone center or his extra apartment if you needed a place to squat. The police say Mickey was doing $40,000 a day. Mickey says he was probably making about half that much.

In any case, as quick as it came, it went. As Mickey says, "Money is like manure, toots, it's meant to be spread around."

Then, as the church was hitting its stride, the New York police did exactly what Robin and Howard had suggested on their radio show. On September 22nd, 1990, the cops called the pope's 800 number. As guaranteed, a courier delivered. The police did the same again on October 12th and 26th. A few days later, during the massive Halloween parade held each year in the West Village, the pope gave a joint to an undercover cop. Handing it over—as he had to so many others that evening—Mickey giggled and declared: "I'm the Pope of Pot! If you want pot, call my number!"

That was it. The NYPD labeled Mickey the Pope a high priority. "There comes a time when you have to let people know that you are serious," said Special Narcotics Prosecutor Sterling Johnson. "He defied the authorities. He threw down the gauntlet."

On November 14th, with the press in tow, the cops raided the Pope of Pot. It was, said the *Village Voice,* "a police operation worth of *America's Most Wanted.*" The bust made all the news shows the next day and all the papers, even the *New York Times.* The *New York Post* played it on the front page with the headline COPS NAB PHONE 'POPE OF DOPE.' Police officials were quoted as saying that Mickey was taking 360 calls an hour on six telephones.

Mickey was brought out of his yellow church to a fusillade of flash-bulbs and questions. Handcuffed, red faced, blood pressure soaring, the pope had time to rasp only a quick "Howdy, honey, howdy," before he was piled into a police car. Over in the shadows across the street, crack dealers and transvestites watched in amazement. They knew Mickey. On cold nights, he sometimes let them into the church to get warm. He gave out hot chocolate.

Then a cop in a suit, Assistant Chief John J. Hill, stepped forward into the klieg lights. His public statement: "We seized here a total of five messengers, two people operating the phones and the pope himself. Also seized were seven pounds of marijuana."

Nighttime now at the Church of Realized Fantasies. In an hour or two the doors will open at a club called Mars, and a benefit will commence, a bailout throw-down for Mickey the Pope. Meantime, some of the inner circle have gathered to wait. They smoke joints, watch a video of the pope, eat spongecake, drink hot chocolate.

Soon after his arrest and release, Mickey was arrested again, this time for participating in an ACT-UP protest. Radical gays, demonstrating for a city-sponsored needle exchange for addicts, collected dirty syringes in a bucket. The pope was snatched when he attempted to turn the needles over to the police. Later he was arrested again for selling a half an ounce of pot to an undercover cop who came calling at the "palace" in New Jersey.

So it has gone. At the moment, the Pope of Pot is, to put it simply, destitute. All the change from the Mason jar in his apartment has been spent. He doesn't even have a subway token in his pocket. He has plenty of church currency—poker chips in various colors stamped in gold with his sickle and marijuana leaf insignia—but nobody wants it. MCI has cut off the 800 number; New York Tel is threatening his other accounts. Landlords are clamoring too. And, of course, there are the lawyers.

Hence the benefit, this gathering at Mickey's church. They are an odd bunch sitting on stackable plastic chairs, about two dozen of the 5000 that Mickey claims as followers, having crawled this night from the belly of an F train from the Lower East Side, descendants of Burroughs and Ginsberg and Huncke the Junkie, of Madonna, Andy

Warhol and Kenny Scharf, the ever-changing members of the cult of near-fatal hipness that has thrived for so long in the East Village.

Quite a collection tonight. A guy in a Burberry raincoat, a silk tie, one eye stitched shut. A Russian Jew. A singer who is famous for looking like John Lennon. A man who looks like Charles Manson. A man named Mighty Man. One guy wears a black turban and little, square red plastic sunglasses. Another wears striped pants, a plaid coat, a Siberian fur hat. No one says a thing. Not a word. They sit, dumb, passing a joint.

Over in a corner, near the hot plate that heats the storefront, Mickey the Pope is being videoed as he watches the video of himself. An artist named Clayton has the minicam. He takes the thing everywhere, its red eye glowing, recording for a documentary what's been known for years in its many and varied forms as "the scene." Clayton made headlines in 1988 when he refused to surrender some footage to city authorities. His film showed cops, badges removed, beating homeless men and local residents with nightsticks during a riot in Tompkins Square Park. Clayton also has a storefront on the Lower East Side, on Essex below Houston, next to a kosher Chinese restaurant, in a Puerto Rican neighborhood known to Caucasian druggies from New Jersey as a good copping spot for Percodan. Clayton's mustache looks like two caterpillars inching along his lip toward his nose. His goatee is long and thin like a Three Musketeers'. The hair along his two frontal lobes has been shaved. The rest hangs long in the back.

To Clayton's left is Mickey the Pope, who is being pumped by a woman for information about a friend of hers named Danny Rakowitz. Rakowitz is a Lower East Side artist and short-order cook who was arrested for cutting up his girlfriend, cooking her into soup, serving the soup to the homeless, leaving her skull and bones in a five-gallon bucket filled with Kitty Litter in the baggage claim at the bus station.

Rakowitz's friend is a tiny black woman with ashen skin and a shock of nappy hair. Her leather jacket is decorated with skull buttons. She looks like a skull, all cheekbones and sunken eyes and this thick top lip that flies up and to the left with every third word, a dancing sneer, a sort of visual "Fuck you." She is sure her friend didn't kill Monica. She's been interviewing people for months, gathering evidence. There's a plot. She knows this. Everyone is involved.

"But Danny had no reason to kill Monica," declares the skull lady.

"What's the difference?" asks the pope. "The girl saw the body in the bathtub."

"Doesn't that seem strange to you?"

"Of course it does."

"Why wasn't there any blood!" asks skull lady. "Where was the blood?"

"An awful lot of cleaning, dear," says the pope, lecturing. "Put her in the tub. Cut her up. Run the water, toots. *Ah-ha-ha-HA!*" He raises his palms, rubs tiny circles in the air before him. "The guy is crazy. He even had a sign on the door: SOUP KITCHEN. Everybody knew it."

"Well, why didn't anybody call the cops?"

"Why didn't anyone call the cops?" repeats the pope, begging the question. He snorts, giggles. "What do you expect? It's the Lower East Side."

Only in New York, only on the Lower East Side, could somebody like the pope be the pope.

Three centuries ago, the Lower East Side was farmland and aboriginal hardwood forest, and the Bowery—now the western edge of the district, changing to Third Avenue just north of Houston Street—was a trail, used by Native Americans in their sorties against the occupying Dutch colony of New Amsterdam. Today, this jumble of factories, tenements and store-fronts strewn from Astor Place to Alphabet City and from Fourteenth Street to Chinatown remains the wilds of Manhattan—a campground from which the natives, with their alternative lifestyles, still launch assaults on the tastes of the mainstream uptown.

The late 1800s on the Lower East Side saw the first flowering of the immigrants. Millions of Turks, Greeks, Italians, Poles, Germans, Ukrainians and Jews came through Ellis Island to the world's newest urban frontier. It was a dense ethnic soup, the original American pepper pot—a world, according to a WPA guidebook, "of politicians, artists, gangsters, composers, prizefighters and labor leaders."

World War II, the Fifties, the early Sixties, saw new waves of immigration. Jews gave way to Puerto Ricans, winos to junkies. The Beat era was upon the East Village, a dark time of morphine, heroin and speed, of caffeine and marijuana, of bongos, berets, turtlenecks and homosexuality. Starting with writers William Burroughs and Herbert Huncke, poet Allen Ginsberg—continuing with Jack Kerouac, Neal Cassady, the Merry Pranksters, hallucinogens, communal living, free love—a new kind of culture, expressed in the widest range of perverse and irreverent and star-crossed possibilities, grew in the shabby far reaches of the Lower East Side.

The Seventies saw the rise of the club and art scene. There were punk rockers, hip-hoppers, new wavers, performance artists, fashion designers and drag queens. The club of the moment was CBGB; the musicians were Lou Reed, Patti Smith, Debbie Harry, the Ramones. Andy Warhol and his Factory were the spiritual center of the art world. Around him would revolve the likes of Keith Haring and Jean-Michel Basquiat.

"Although they sprang from varied backgrounds, the artists [who came to the area] shared a collective media-drenched consciousness, the heritage of the suburban teenager," writes Steven Hager in a book about the East Village. "In the Sixties, this pampered upbringing was frequently a source of guilt, but in the Seventies, it was dissected and rearranged, and eventually regurgitated into new forms."

In the last few years, with the fall of the economy and the rise of a new era of American Prohibition, the Lower East Side has hit hard and seamy times. "Every year it's been a different thing," says Clayton, the video artist. "Some years it's been drag queens. Other years it's been skinheads, the police, squatters, homeless. This year seems to be, you know, there's a depression happening in the country, a lot of uncertainty. They're trying to close our fire department, that's big for us. There's Mickey's bust, the Rakowitz murder, AIDS, crack. It changes down here, but it never changes. A lot of these fuckin' people are geniuses. A lot of them are nuts."

"So what's up with the telephone center," asks the hippie. "Is it cool or not?"

"I don't know," says Mickey the Pope.

"Well, we're only doing twenty deliveries a day, and that ain't shit!"

"Put me on PR!" chimes in Bartman. "Give me a minimum budget! Give me no budget!"

The pope eyes Bartman, shakes his head in sorrow. Bartman, Freddie Redpants, Larry the Libertarian . . . Why can't he find some help? Why must he do everything himself? Here in the church, a few days before his birthday, Mickey the Pope is in ruins. The other night at the fund-raiser at Mars, 700 people crowded all four floors. It was a raging success. There was so much support for the pope that you couldn't move across the room. Unfortunately, nobody at the benefit thought about collecting any money.

Mickey the Pope lost forty dollars.

So now he has gotten himself a new partner. Call him the hippie. He is bald on top with a fringe of shoulder-length hair, a gray beard cascading down his chest. He is hyper, creepy. He keeps looking all around him. Toward the windows. The back room. Under the papers on Mickey's desk. "So what about the phone center?" he asks again, picking up the trash can, checking the bottom, putting it back down. "Is it cool?"

"Well, there wasn't a big investigation," interrupts Bartman. "They didn't freeze his bank accounts. It was just—"

"Baaaaaart!" chides the pope.

"Listen, you little turd!" says the hippie, eyes suddenly wild, finger in Bartman's nose. "What you gotta do is one thing. Meet Red each morning, pick up, work. No more talking. Got it?"

"I've cut it back about twenty percent," says Bartman. "I'm definitely talking less. I'm gonna—"

"You're gonna do what you got to do!" hollers the hippie, puffing up, ballistic, a vein popping in his right temple. He zeros in on the hapless Bartman. "Look, I got a lot going for me right now. I can't have some little pussy to fuck it up. If I'm gonna go to jail for conspiracy, I'll kill a fucker and go to jail for the same amount of time!"

"I'm with that!" says Bartman.

"You know what I'm sayin'?" asks the hippie.

"Fuck! I swear!"

"Now, now, boys, boys," says the pope, batting his eyelashes, an aging coquette with a curly gray beard. "This is the sacrament we're talking about. Please. . . . Respect. *Ah-ha-ha-HA!*"

The pope is at home now, his Upper East Side studio, a second-floor walk-up. He's not feeling too well, lying shirtless on his unmade bed amid a clutter of plants and clothes and videos with titles like *Hot Rocks II*, his scars and his bullet wounds pink and ropy amid a forest of fine graying hairs.

Over in the kitchen, a friend of the pope's is scouring the oven. The sink is filled with dishes. A flesh-colored marital aid pokes up out of the soapsuds. The friend has just been released after twenty years in prison. He doesn't want his name mentioned, but he intimates that he had something to do with an art heist and a murder at a big museum in New York City. He met the pope in prison. All the Jewish guys in there knew each other. He looked out for the pope. They also took ceramics together. The pope is letting him crash in a basement apartment while he looks for a job in his old field, public relations.

It is time now for a papal audience. Why? the pope is asked. Why is he setting up business anew? Why is he letting a reporter see all this? Does he have to have an 800 number? Couldn't he just chill like the other eleven delivery services in Manhattan, do a thriving underground business? Perhaps Howard Stern is right. Is he begging to go to jail?

"I'm the bringer of wisdom and truth," explains Mickey the Pope. "I'm doing what's right. I'm the kind of person, you're not gonna intimidate me. Marijuana is the saving plant. It should be legal. People want it that way. The voice of the people is the voice of God in a democracy. If you get enough people into it, the politicians have to listen. I think what we should do is, sort of set up our own society and do our own thing. Let all the others go do what they will. We're doing what's right and proper and screw 'em, our little group should live better than they do. We should win by example."

With that the tape recorder clicks off. The pope takes a long slow drink from a gallon jug of water, then grins, bats his lashes. "So how'd I do, toots?" he asks. "This is serious. I don't want to go to jail. I really don't want to go to jail."

Now it is Mickey the Pope's birthday, the day before the winter solstice, the last shortening day on the calendar of the seasons. There's a knock at the church door, and Mickey opens up and finds two undercover cops. One wears a pompadour and a trench coat. The other carries a pad.

"Oh! Internal Affairs!" giggles Mickey the Pope, remembering the appointment he'd scheduled. "I called you, didn't I?"

"Yes, sir," says the cop with the pad. He regards Mickey for a moment, beak nosed, red faced, wearing his marijuana bonnet. Then the cop rolls his eyes to the heavens. "Mind if we come in?"

"Of course, toots," rasps the pope, bowing, gesturing, showing the guests to some chairs.

"So what happened?" asks the cop with the pad.

"Well, when I was busted, there was this big media thing, you know, and John J. Hill said there were seven pounds confiscated in the raid."

"John J. Hill?" asks the pad.

"Yeah, he's an assistant chief."

"Oh! Chief Hill!" exclaims the pompadour, leaning forward.

"He said there were seven pounds?" asks the pad.

"Right there on the news," says Mickey.

"Oh," says the pompadour.

"So how many pounds were there?" asks the pad.

"Close to five."

"So, close to five pounds were taken into evidence by the police?"

"Right," says the pope.

"So, what's the problem?" asks the pompadour.

"Well, I was only indicted for two and one half pounds."

"So what's the problem?" asks the pad.

"See," says the pope, grinning. "Two and one half pounds are missing! Cops shouldn't be stealing the evidence. I mean, I don't steal. I don't jump turnstiles, none of that shit, I really don't. I live the pure life. I don't take from nobody, and that's the truth."

"I see," says the pompadour.

"The thing is, if the cops want pot, they should have to buy it like everyone else," says the pope. "If you're not gonna charge me for it, I want it back. After all, it's the sacrament. This is the church. The marijuana church. The Church of Realized Fantasies."

Marisa and Jeff
by Calvin Trillin

Calvin Trillin (born 1935) has published much of his work in the New Yorker, *which ran this piece in July of 2000.*

arisa Baridis, a control-group analyst at Smith Barney, was part of what Wall Street people call the Chinese wall. The wall is an administrative structure that a large securities firm erects to keep its trading operation shut off from the activities of its investment bankers, who routinely acquire a lot of inside information that would be illegal to use in buying and selling stocks. Since the first step in detecting leakage of inside information is to find out what information the firm has, Marisa Baridis and her colleagues talked constantly to investment bankers and noted on a confidential "watch list" exactly where each deal stood and when an announcement that could affect the stock of any of the companies involved was expected. Then, as she once summed it up, they would "look for trading that was in line with what we knew was going to happen." On Wall Street, a Chinese wall is festooned with security precautions—

paper shredders, separate computer servers, segregated trash pickup—
because another way to think of the watch list is as the mother lode of
inside information.

When Marisa Baridis joined Smith Barney, in 1993, she was in her
mid-twenties. A business-administration graduate of Boston University, she also had a law degree from the Touro law school, on Long
Island, although she had never taken the bar examination. She
wouldn't have struck someone on first meeting as part of an enforcement operation. A petite young woman with pale skin and jet-black
hair, she gave the impression of a certain fragility. Although the
nineties bull market was gathering steam when she joined Smith Barney,
control-group analysts were not among those young Wall Street types
who were beginning to indulge their tastes for high-performance
sports cars and staggeringly expensive co-op apartments. Marisa
Baridis's starting salary at Smith Barney was about forty-five thousand
dollars a year. Still, she was hardly poor. Although she had often quar-
relled with her father, a Greek immigrant who was a bridge-painting
contractor in Philadelphia, he took care of the rent on her apartment,
on the Upper East Side, as he had taken care of whatever she needed
in college and law school. He also pressured her to take the bar exam.
At one point, in order to make him think she'd taken it and failed, she
sent him a doctored-up rejection letter received by someone else from
the New York State Board of Law Examiners.

Even without the burden of rent, Marisa Baridis had no trouble getting rid of her salary. In fact, a couple of times she was feeling so
pressed that she told the credit-card company that an item she'd actually purchased had appeared on her monthly bill in error. She led the
sort of singles life in Manhattan that included regular appearances at
late-night clubs and memberships in fitness centers and shares in
summer rentals in the Hamptons. In conversation, she sounded like a
lot of other young people who worked in, say, the financial industry or
the real-estate industry and lived in high-rise boxes on the East Side
and worried a lot about their social lives—so that she could summa-
rize a relationship that didn't work out by saying, "I'm like, 'Weren't

you supposed to call me?' He's like, 'Yeah.'" She spent a lot of time E-mailing—not just questions to investment bankers about where a prospective merger stood but also the jokes that get passed around Wall Street electronically and messages like "Virginia just called. She said Michael and all those guys are going to dinner and then to some bar that Howard Stern is having a party at."

At Smith Barney, her performance appraisals occasionally mentioned problems like absenteeism and lack of focus. She seemed proud of holding such a responsible job in such a prestigious firm, but she wasn't getting along with her supervisor, and she sometimes found the work a strain. From the time she started with Smith Barney, she had been on Valium, prescribed by a psychiatrist. In the psychiatrist's view, Marisa Baridis had problems that went beyond a stressful job. Her parents had split when she was an infant, and she spent most of her childhood living with her mother, who was apparently physically ill much of that time and depressed to the point of inertia. After her mother died of breast cancer, when Marisa was fifteen, Marisa moved in with her father and his second family, but she hadn't felt truly welcome, despite the material objects her father gave her. Marisa Baridis's psychiatrist had concluded that she was suffering from low self-esteem, even self-hatred. Although she was an attractive young woman and had some good female friends, she tended to have miserable relationships with men. Her life, the psychiatrist said at one point, was an all too successful search for men who would abuse and betray her.

Marisa Baridis had heard of Jeffrey Streich before she met him. This was in the summer of 1996. For a couple of years, she'd taken a share in a Hamptons summer house run by a former girlfriend of Streich's named Tina Eichenholz, who told stories of her old beau's extravagance: on the third date, as Baridis remembered one story, Streich had given Eichenholz a five-thousand-dollar diamond bracelet. A dark-haired young man from Commack, Long Island, who had gone to community college and the State University of New York at Brockport, Streich was also involved with the securities business, but in an aspect of it that wouldn't have been familiar to the Ivy League investment bankers Marisa Baridis spoke to every day about mergers and acquisitions. He had begun his Wall Street career in what people in the trade call a bucket shop—a type of operation that Streich himself once summed up succinctly as "the bottom-of-the-barrel stock firm." A bucket shop generally pushes one or two stocks at a time—stocks that tend to be distinguished by how much the bucket shop itself owns of them and how little there is of substance to the companies that have floated them. Through high-pressure selling and reporting gimmicks and such devices as parking blocks of stock in the accounts of customers without authorization, the bucket shop keeps the house stock at an artificially inflated price. At some point, the house has its money and its customers are stuck with a stock that in the conventional market is impossible to sell.

"Before I was a broker, I was a normal human being making an honest living," Jeff Streich once said. "The only thing illegal I did, I think—when I was young I used to steal Pop Rocks." After he was a broker, he went a good deal beyond Pop Rocks. His first boss, Brett Hirsch—this was at a bucket shop called D.H. Blair—is Streich's contemporary, but he has been described as a sort of Fagin figure, who trained young men in a variety of securities scams. The thirty or so brokers and cold-callers clustered around Brett Hirsch wanted what he had—a flashy car, a flashy girlfriend, the wherewithal to toss thousand-dollar chips on the table in Las Vegas—and they worked hard to please him. On his team, they led a sleazeball version of the high life—regular visits to a strip club in the East Sixties called Scores, a ready supply of cocaine, bachelor parties in Las Vegas, a trip to Rio for New Year's. Streich began as a cold-caller, making three or four hundred calls a day off microfiche lists of prospects bought from people who'd stolen them from more respectable firms. Among members of the group, Streich was known as Heckel, a summer-camp nickname. The most inept cold-caller in the crowd became Schmeckel. Another broker was called Murray the Crook—although calling someone Murray the Crook in the Hirsch group was more or less like calling someone on an N.B.A. team Joe the Tall Guy.

The Hirsch group, in fact, could be described as too crooked—or at least too blatant—for the bucket shops. More than once, the daytime activities of the merry band included being escorted out onto the sidewalk en masse by company security guards. Jeff Streich, a smooth talker who seemed unburdened by compunctions, could be described as too crooked—or at least too blatant—for the Hirsch group. When the group moved from D.H. Blair to a firm called A.R. Baron, he was told that the multiplicity of complaints lodged against him with the National Association of Securities Dealers had made him too much of a liability to keep on board. Baron was hardly a pillar of rectitude itself. One of its officers at that time sticks in the mind of some law-enforcement people as a man who sometimes managed to spend twenty thousand dollars in a particularly festive evening at Scores.

Being left out of Baron didn't mean that Streich had run out of moves on Wall Street. First, he joined A.S. Goldmen, where he was fired after four months for unauthorized trading; then he was briefly at a firm called Gruntal, where he was fired for telling customers that they wouldn't be responsible for losses if the initial public offering he was pitching went down instead of up; and then he went to Beacon, where he was fired after an N.A.S.D. complaint over his handling of the account of a semi-retired man from Chicago named Shy Glass. When Streich took over the account, Glass, who was in his seventies, had a four-hundred-and-forty-thousand-dollar portfolio dominated by Amgen, an early biotech company whose stock was solid and, as it happened, about to become even more valuable. Through unauthorized trading and forging a margin-account application, Streich transformed the portfolio into house stocks that had the advantage of paying him a cash kickback but the accompanying disadvantage of becoming worthless. When it was all over, Shy Glass's portfolio amounted to thirty thousand three hundred and sixty dollars.

After Beacon, Streich put together his own "private placement"—the sale of a stock issue to a limited number of buyers, without a public offering. The company Streich had for sale, LJS Holdings, was what he described as a "laundromat-slash-café," although not the sort of laundromat-slash-café that had, say, a business plan or employees. The money Streich raised for LJS—two hundred thousand dollars or so—went straight into his pocket and out again in a matter of months, spent on drugs and expensive presents for women and gambling on sporting events. By the summer of 1996, Streich was by way of being a private investor, although not one with any money to invest. He was working out of an office maintained by a young man named Vincent Napolitano, in an apartment on East Sixty-fourth Street, helping Napolitano invest in initial public offerings. Brokers ordinarily ration out I.P.O.s among their best customers, so Napolitano had opened eighteen accounts under the names of various individuals and dummy corporations with tony titles like Synergy Plus, Inc.

Streich was living in a series of apartments on the Upper East Side, sometimes a step or two ahead of an eviction notice; his policy on rent seems to have been that it was the first month's that counted. That summer of 1996, he was running a group house in the Hamptons, which can be a business for somebody who isn't squeamish about how many people he assigns to each bedroom. He carried a lot of cash. In a group, he was the sort of person who wouldn't allow single young women to pay their share of a check. To them, he seemed protective, expansive almost like a particularly generous big brother. "You get used to these cheap guys who want to go Dutch or worry that you ordered too many appetizers," a friend of Marisa Baridis has said. "Jeff was more like 'Let's get champagne!' " Marisa Baridis later described Jeff Streich this way: "He's the kind of guy that, you know, if you, like, asked for a pack of cigarettes he would, like, give you fifty dollars and tell you to keep the change." She meant it as a compliment.

Jeffrey Streich did have a drinking problem and a cocaine problem and a gambling problem and, of course, a lying problem. Marisa Baridis met him at drinks with a group of people at a casual Hamptons spot on the water called Dockers, in a summer-house atmosphere that made no great distinction between the Wall Street of Smith Barney and the Wall Street of fly-by-night bucket shops. He was in a wetsuit, apparently having come over by Jet Ski from the house he was running. This was early in the summer—before he was ejected from the house because the agent discovered that the new tenants were not two couples but forty groupers, before the marine-supply store sued because the check for the Jet Ski bounced. "She liked his style—she found him exciting," a friend of Marisa's has said. To friends, Marisa expressed surprise that somebody as sophisticated as Jeff Streich was interested in her.

Jeff Streich was not the first person to have suggested to Marisa Baridis—in that joking way which leaves open the option of being taken seriously—that she and a careful partner could trade profitably on her access to the Smith Barney watch list, although he was the first to describe the potential enrichment in terms of matching Mercedeses. Four or five other people, including the husband of her best friend from college, had brought up the subject, and she had dismissed it. But as she and Streich saw each other over the summer—always as part of a group—she began to consider his offer.

Although Marisa and Jeff were supposedly just pals, two people in a jolly crowd sharing an order of chicken fingers on the weathered deck of a bar in the Hamptons, or downing shots of Jägermeister during happy hour at a bar on the East Side of Manhattan, her friends sensed from the start that she had a crush on him. (They also sensed that he remained enamored of Tina Eichenholz.) Marisa had always had a weakness for big spenders and extravagant flatterers. "He knew exactly how to play her personality," one of her friends has said. "He'd tell her she was in a different category from everyone else. I think a lot of people would be like 'Give me a break,' but she believed him." When Marisa Baridis herself was later asked why, after spurning other opportunities, she began thinking about giving inside information to Streich, she said, "I don't know if I thought that was the way I could get him or power over him, have a relationship with him. It was probably the only way. If I didn't have my position, I don't think Jeff and I would have had a relationship." In August, Marisa and Jeff went out to dinner alone in New York for the first time. Before the meal was over, she'd told him that Square Industries was going to be sold in a couple of weeks and could go up twenty per cent.

Eventually, they agreed that she would leak him information and he would do the investing, observing some safeguards to avoid drawing attention—tell no one, trade moderately, stay away from options trading. They would split the profits. Matching Mercedeses were not immediately forthcoming. Sometimes, even after an entry on the watch list said that the deal was going through, some accounting or legal problem held it up. Sometimes the deal didn't have the effect on the stock that might have been expected. Then, a few days before Thanksgiving, Marisa went to a phone booth outside the offices of Smith Barney and called Jeff to say that Owen Healthcare, the world's largest manager of hospital pharmacies, was about to be taken over by Cardinal Health. A few days later, that was precisely what happened, and the stock jumped from fifteen to twenty-five. The various accounts controlled by Vincent Napolitano made a hundred and seventy thousand dollars. Streich made nearly thirty-five thousand dollars in his own accounts, partly by free riding—buying without putting up any funds—with brokers he knew from bucket-shop days or from Hamptons shares. Something had presumably gone wrong with the safeguards, though: in the day or two before the sale, the volume of Owen stock being traded had jumped more than four hundred per cent.

That is the sort of activity that tends to draw the attention of the market-surveillance division of the New York Stock Exchange. The exchange has computers that can illuminate clusters of traders in the same zip codes or traders with particularly large buys or traders who have multiple accounts and a sudden interest in the hospital-pharmacy industry. A report was sent to the Securities and Exchange Commission, and an attorney in the S.E.C. enforcement division put in a call to Vincent Napolitano. Eventually, Napolitano provided some trading records and appeared for a deposition. In the deposition, he said what most people accused of insider trading say—that he'd made his trades on the basis of his own research and what he'd heard around town. The investigation didn't go any further. Napolitano had mentioned Jeffrey Streich to the S.E.C. attorney only in passing, when asked to name people who often came to the office on East Sixty-fourth Street. Marisa Baridis's name had never come up.

An inside trader who uses a partner to do the investing has a built-in problem: keeping track of the partner is virtually impossible. There is no way to know whether the partner is tipping others. There is no way to know how much money the partner has made by trading on the inside information. The problem is exacerbated, of course, if the partner is someone like Jeffrey Streich. Streich was essentially using Marisa Baridis's inside information as currency. He traded tips to brokers in return for allowing him to free ride. He met with Brett Hirsch to see about trading tips for I.P.O. lists. He gave tips to brokers for a share in their profits.

Streich was constantly being warned by Marisa that widening the network, and thus the volume of trading, could only bring suspicion, and he was constantly assuring her that he'd been keeping the information to himself. In fact, there were at least a dozen people getting inside information from Streich, some of them so routinely that when a tip hadn't come along for a while they'd phone and say, "Any pickles coming?" A pickle was information from the Smith Barney watch list. Streich assumed that Napolitano was also passing along Baridis's information to other people. For that matter, so was Marisa Baridis. In January of 1997, about six months after her first tip to Streich, she had started tipping the husband of her best friend from college.

She suspected that Streich was cheating her on the split, and she was right. Streich lied about how much he'd bought. He lied about what the price was when he'd bought it. At one point, he convinced two brokers that they ought to chip in for a payment to the source of the inside information—he collected eighteen thousand dollars from them—and then he kept the money himself. For Marisa, getting any money at all from Jeff required constant badgering. At times, she threatened to quit providing information, but in April of 1997, when she moved from Smith Barney to a nearly identical job at Morgan Stanley—she was now making about seventy thousand dollars a year, working for the one old-line, white-shoe firm that had emerged from the changes of recent decades as a power on Wall Street—her arrangement with Streich remained unchanged. At around that time, she had dinner with Tina Eichenholz, who told her that Streich was playing her for a fool—that he and his friends were making an enormous amount of money and cheating her. Jeff denied it. "Did I believe Jeff that other people, his friends, his best friends, weren't involved in the trading?" Marisa said later. "I don't know if I believed him a hundred per cent, but I decided to ignore what Tina had told me."

For a year or so after that first tip about Square Industries, Jeff and Marisa had been involved in an intense but platonic relationship; they were, at least in Marisa's view, best friends. During most of that period, she had a more or less steady boyfriend, someone who had a lot of problems of his own, and their relationship was stormy. She once estimated that she and her boyfriend had broken up thirty or forty times—one time with so much gusto that the police had been summoned.

Then, in September of 1997, Jeff and Marisa went to the Mirage Hotel, in Las Vegas, with Marisa's college friend and her husband—a party of four that included two people who, unbeknownst to each other, were receiving inside tips from a third. At the Mirage, Jeff and Marisa became more than best friends. That didn't mean that they walked off into a life together while the theme music played. For one thing, he'd stuck her with the hotel bill. She went straight from Las Vegas to Hong Kong for a three-week stint in Morgan Stanley's office there, and when she returned to New York, in October, she E-mailed a friend about Jeff. "He didn't pay the bill from the hotel in Vegas. It's two thousand dollars. He has been ignoring my phone calls and when I saw him out Friday night he completely ignored me. He keeps making derogatory comments when we speak. I have to borrow money to pay the Vegas bill. I fucking hate him."

But they seemed friendly enough when they finally met for dinner one evening in late October. This was at C.S. Barrington's, on Fifty-fourth and Second. Barrington's was a place that had one of those all-glass arcades built out onto the sidewalk, so that some diners—Marisa Baridis and Jeffrey Streich among them that night—seemed almost to be eating in a show window. Over a meal of chicken fingers and fried clam strips and spicy French fries and Southwest potato skins and something called Buffalo calamari, they talked about her love life and his housing problems and her tax problems and his tax problems (both of them were dealing with I.R.S. liens) and her fears that they would get caught at insider trading. What had happened between them in Las Vegas was not mentioned, although the hotel bill was. Jeff discussed the hot prospect he was about to see in his new job as a broker for water-proofing contracts ("I think I'm just going to take him to Scores, make sure the girls give him a nice little time"). Marisa shared some of her impressions of Hong Kong ("It's like Madison Avenue—Armani, Versace, Moschino. The price isn't that different. . . . It's not like you're in Italy, where you're getting Prada for cheaper"). They exchanged views on whether a club called Envy was hot and a club called Opera was good on Tuesdays and a club called Two Rooms was over. They talked about the relative merits of Belvedere vodka and Ketel One vodka—a subject of some immediate interest to Streich, since in the time they were together he had six Martinis.

Eventually, they talked about her split of the profits and about her suspicions that he was holding out on her. When Streich wanted to underline his sincerity, he'd say, "I swear on my mother's ashes." When Marisa Baridis wanted to do the same, she said, "I swear on Heather's life." Heather was a Yorkshire terrier. "Why wouldn't you trust me?" Streich said at one point. "I never gave you a reason not to." (By then, Streich and Napolitano had each made about a quarter of a million dollars on Marisa Baridis's tips, and the other people they tipped had made hundreds of thousands of dollars more; Marisa Baridis's even split had come to about twenty thousand dollars.) Finally, he handed her twenty-five hundred-dollar bills—a down payment on thirty-six thousand dollars he assured her she would soon get. In a van parked just outside C.S. Barrington's, Investigator Walter Alexander, of the Manhattan District Attorney's office, trained a video camera on their table through the floor-to-ceiling glass and recorded the entire conversation through a concealed microphone.

In the mid-nineties, the Manhattan District Attorney's office had gone after the bucket shops. An attorney with expertise in the subject, David Gourevitch, was hired from the S.E.C. to lead a team that began with A.R. Baron, whose principals were indicted for running a criminal enterprise. During a lull in the Baron case, the team decided to prosecute a bucket-shop crime that had the look of a short and sweet conviction—the looting of the account of Shy Glass. After winning an N.A.S.D. arbitration, Glass's attorney, Kenneth David Burrows, had been aggressive about trying to collect what his client was owed. (Burrows did eventually recover a good deal of money from the company that had acted as Beacon's clearing broker.) He also pressed law-enforcement agencies. He got in touch with both the United States Attorney's office and the Manhattan District Attorney's office. Unauthorized-trading cases are often difficult to prosecute—the broker's defense tends to be that the client did authorize the transaction in one of their many telephone conversations—but Streich had made this one easy by his forgery. The D.A.'s office called in Jeff Streich and demonstrated to him and his lawyer that it had enough evidence to put him in prison for fraud.

Whatever differences may exist between people who work in Wall Street's most prestigious securities firms and people who work in bucket shops, they are as one when it comes to their response to being caught in an offense that could mean jail time: they look for someone else to turn in. Faced with serious charges in the Glass case, Streich offered information on Beacon and said that he'd been involved in an insider-trading ring whose participants he could name. He was willing to wear a wire to a meeting with the central figure herself—Marisa Baridis. A few days after Marisa Baridis had dinner with Jeff Streich at C.S. Barrington's, she was summoned to the chief counsel's office at Morgan Stanley. Two detectives were there, and they took her to the District Attorney's office for questioning. Within a few hours, the head of the Morgan Stanley compliance department was flying home from Hong Kong to oversee a damage-control operation that included hiring a law firm, a public-relations firm, a private-investigation firm, and a team of trauma specialists to minister to the remaining members of the control group. "It was a very painful time for the firm," the leader of the compliance department said later. The press had been predictably unkind. The phrase in the newspapers which stuck in his mind was Manhattan District Attorney Robert Morgenthau's comment that at Morgan Stanley the fox had been put in charge of guarding the henhouse.

It was a painful time for Marisa Baridis, too. She spent that first night in jail. Then her father came up from Philadelphia and made bail. Her initial denial of wrongdoing hadn't lasted long. The videotape was devastating. She was actually seen accepting marked hundred-dollar bills, twenty-three of which were later found by the D.A.'s people in her apartment. On the tape, she had described the Chinese wall and said that for someone in her position to leak inside information was the most illegal thing you could do. When her lawyer, Paul Shechtman, saw the tape some days later, he told her, "There are two phases of a criminal case—the guilt-determining phase and the sentencing phase. I think we should focus on the sentencing phase."

Marisa Baridis had turned the conversation so relentlessly to every element of the crime that one senior assistant district attorney who watched the tape thought at first that she might have been wired herself by some other law-enforcement agency. The agency he would have had in mind was the United States Attorney's office, which up to then had handled insider-trading cases. In fact, the federals were so irritated at what they considered poaching that they, in effect, stole Marisa Baridis as a defendant. Even after two senior assistant district attorneys rose in protest from the spectator seats in a federal courtroom, like a couple of strangers at a wedding taking the minister up on his invitation to speak now or forever hold their peace, she was allowed to plead guilty to federal charges, which carried some tactical legal advantages and made it impossible for the state to prosecute her.

Among the conditions, of course, was that she reveal absolutely every-thing she knew about the insider-trading scheme and its participants. In other words, she had to give up somebody, too. All she had to offer was her best friend's husband.

In a court of law, someone who receives inside information is called a tippee. Of the dozen people identified as tippees by Jeff Streich only Vincent Napolitano elected to go to trial. The rest of them showed up at a cramped and well-worn courthouse on Centre Street, in lower Manhattan, to plead guilty before New York Supreme Court Judge Edward McLaughlin and to swear, in most cases, that they were both remorseful and nearly broke. Although only one of the tippees received a sentence that included jail time, Judge McLaughlin did not attempt to hide his contempt for how easily they had yielded to temp-tation and how dissolute their lives had been. "I just wonder whether there are people who actually when they get access to inside infor-mation say, 'I'm going to turn down the chance to make that thirty or forty thousand dollars,'" he said at one sentencing. "The thirty or forty thousand dollars becomes a hundred thousand or so. . . . It goes up the nose, down the toilet, and out the window."

Streich and Marisa Baridis couldn't be sentenced until they made good on their agreements to testify for the prosecution at Napolitano's trial, and, for one reason or another, that trial didn't take place until last fall, nearly two years after the videotaped dinner at C.S. Bar-rington's. At one point during the wait, Streich wrote to literary agents about the possibility of marketing his story as a book—a project that didn't go even as far as his laundromat-slash-café. "It's a story of greed, backstabbing, double-crossing, manipulation, and love, set in the high stakes, high pressure world of finance," he wrote. "This is a strong character-driven morality tale that plays out like Sleepers, Wall St., and Goodfellows, that is full of lovable losers."

Nobody who was involved in the aftermath of the insider-trading scheme had actually found Jeffrey Streich lovable, but the impression of Marisa Baridis was more complicated. "I submit to you that Marisa

Baridis is one of the strangest people any of us will ever encounter," Adam Reeves, an assistant district attorney, told the jury during the trial of Vincent Napolitano, who was ultimately convicted. Baridis was, of course, a witness rather than the defendant in that trial—a witness who sometimes seemed bewildered by the questions she was asked, and answered so quietly that she was regularly asked by the lawyers to raise her voice—but she was sufficiently central to the narrative of the case to require an explanation by both the prosecution and the defense. Both lawyers seemed to take it for granted that, to some extent, she'd been a victim of Streich's manipulation, if not exactly an innocent victim. She wanted her cut, after all, and being bedazzled by a smooth-talking scoundrel did not seem to explain the inside tips to her best friend's husband. "To suggest that Marisa Baridis is shallow and superficial I don't think is a stretch," Napolitano's lawyer, Joseph Corozzo, Jr., said to the jury, although he also said, "I submit she is smart and she is devious." Some of the law-enforcement people who worked on the insider-trading case saw Marisa Baridis as a spoiled kid looking for thrills—someone whose daddy was still paying for her apartment when she was making seventy thousand dollars a year, someone who had said in the Barrington's transcript that carrying on the insider-trading scheme was fun. But even people who felt that way did not seem completely without sympathy for her. It was not easy to put aside that breathtaking betrayal at C.S. Barrington's.

"I find in my own thinking that I come back to one word constantly," Assistant District Attorney Adam Reeves said when Jeffrey Streich appeared before Judge McLaughlin to be sentenced for his crimes against Shy Glass and his role in the insider-trading ring. "It's the word 'betrayal' and . . . it ramifies in many different ways throughout this case." Streich had undoubtedly betrayed the trust of Shy Glass, Reeves said, and there was what some saw as "a very ugly form of betrayal" at Barrington's—although that had been at the behest of the authorities. The District Attorney's office itself had been betrayed by Streich, who was at one point declared in violation of his cooperation agreement after authorities discovered that he had not been forthcoming about the participation of two people—Tina Eichenholz and Vincent Napolitano. Streich, Reeves said, even betrayed the court, in a manner of speaking, since it was apparent that he had not always testified fully and accurately in the Napolitano case.

The previous day, Reeves had asked the judge to impose a stiff prison sentence on Vincent Napolitano—charging, as the prosecution had charged from the start when the jury was out of earshot, that he was a loan shark and a bookie who had threatened Streich and others by claiming a connection to organized crime. (Judge McLaughlin gave Napolitano two-to-six.) But Streich's case, Reeves said, was much more complicated. Acknowledging that the crime against Shy Glass had been monstrous, Reeves argued that such monstrousness had to be weighed against coöperation that had been instrumental in the successful conclusion of two major investigations. Giving Streich a sentence that was as severe as the one given Napolitano, Reeves said, could have a chilling effect on the inclination of criminals to come forward with information on crimes that would otherwise go unprosecuted. "The dignity of our criminal justice system is dependent on offering fair outcomes to people who do many unfair things," Reeves said.

There really wasn't much left for the defense lawyer to add. Reeves had even reported detecting remorse in Streich, and had not drawn attention to the fact that the principal criminal scheme Streich's coöperation had brought down would not have existed if he himself hadn't concocted it. "I have radically changed my life," Streich said. "I am no longer involved with drugs and gambling. I no longer take shortcuts that have plagued my whole life." Judge McLaughlin noted that Streich's "active, potentially dangerous coöperation" had produced convictions, but he also said, "There is no rational system that absolves entirely the conduct that you did." To use financial terms, Judge McLaughlin said, the sentence was deeply discounted—one and a third years to four years in state prison.

Marisa Baridis's friends are less likely than the district attorney to find any mitigating factors about Streich's betrayal that night. He had used her, as well as her inside information. Rather than spare her as much pain as possible, he had seemed to lead her gratuitously into a discussion of embarrassing personal matters while Investigator Alexander dutifully recorded the conversation from his van. In fact, Marisa's friends say they're astonished at how little anger she seemed to feel after she realized what Streich had done—almost as if his behavior were just an extreme example of how relationships often end.

By the time Jeff was sentenced, Marisa had already appeared before Federal District Judge John Keenan for sentencing. A dozen people had shown up to be with the defendant. Her father was there. So was her new fiancé—someone she had met at the real-estate firm she now works for, and someone her friends judge to be a welcome change from the sort of men she'd been attracted to in the past. Four of her girlfriends were there, dressed so much alike, in black pants suits, that they appeared to be members of some sort of team. Her lawyer, Paul Shechtman, said the case had "destroyed her human capital"—her closest friendship, her career in the financial industry. Describing his client as someone whose psychological vulnerabilities made her an easy mark for Streich, Shechtman said, "We wouldn't be here today if Ms. Baridis hadn't met Jeffrey Streich in the summer of 1996."

In the interpretation of the case which Shechtman favors, money was not a serious motivation for what his client did—unless it was making money for Jeffrey Streich so that he could buy bracelets for her instead of for Tina Eichenholz. Even the leaks to her best friend's husband could be interpreted as a way of making Jeff jealous that she could deal with somebody else, although that interpretation suffers from the fact that she'd waited nine or ten months to tell Streich that there was another tippee. She did say to Streich at Barrington's that she had tipped someone else, and that the unnamed other person paid her with "no ifs, ands, or buts." As it turned out, she was mistaken: her best friend's husband had also been cheating her on the split.

There was no sign of anger when Marisa Baridis made her statement to Judge Keenan, in a barely audible voice. "My friends blame Jeffrey Streich for what has occurred," she said. "I see it differently. He was no friend but I only blame myself. I have tried to understand why I acted the way I did and to deal with the pieces of my life that are left." The probation report had recommended that she not be sent to prison, and the federal prosecutor did not quarrel with that recommendation. Judge Keenan gave Marisa Baridis two years' probation. The general counsel of Morgan Stanley had sent a letter urging the opposite—a particularly stiff sentence. Morgan Stanley, of course, had also been betrayed, and, in an indication that old-fashioned manners are still valued somewhere on Wall Street, its general counsel pointed out, among other things, that Marisa Baridis had never apologized to the firm.

Jeffrey Streich is now in prison. Although he's pleased Marisa Baridis got off without jail time, he said during a recent conversation in the prison visiting room, the notion that her insider trading was driven by an infatuation with him is nonsense—simply a convenient way to present her as a victim. In his version of what happened, insider trading had the same attraction for her as for anyone else—the power that comes from being the source of information and the money that could help support a style of living he summed up as "Prada and two dogs." He said that Marisa was simply a friend, and that he'd done nothing to woo her. He described their interlude in Las Vegas—an occasion for her to send elated E-mails back to friends in New York—as nothing more than two people who'd had too much to drink going to bed together.

Streich expressed regret for betraying his friends in the insider-trading scheme but much more regret for betraying the customers who trusted him as a broker. Although he is certain that his bucket-shop days are behind him forever—he intends to make his living in the construction business—he still seems proud of how good he was at selling stock over the phone. When other brokers had difficulty closing, he said, they'd often ask him to come on the line. In the entire time he was a broker, of course, he didn't sell one share of legitimate stock, but it occurred to him that he might have been good at that, too, if he had learned the business somewhere other than in the Hirsch group. Musing on that as he sat in the visiting room, he said, "If I had started at Lehman Brothers, I would have been all right. Maybe."

The Shit-Kickers of Madison Avenue

by Lillian Ross

Lillian Ross (born 1927) has written eleven books, including Picture and Portrait of Hemingway. This short piece appeared in The New Yorker in 1995.

The tenth graders heading up Madison Avenue at 7:30 a.m. to the private high schools are freshly liberated from their dental braces, and their teeth look pearly and magnificent. They are fifteen years old. During the week, they arrive, by bus or on foot, singly or in pairs or in clusters, and they make their way up the west side of Madison—they call it the "cool" side—toward their schools: Dalton, on East Eighty-ninth; Sacred Heart and Spence, on East Ninety-first; Nightingale-Barnford, on East Ninety-second; the Lycée Français, on East Ninety-fifth. Brearley and Chapin are farther east; Collegiate, Columbia Prep, and Trinity are in the west; Browning is south; Horace Mann, Riverdale, and Fieldston are in the north. On the weekends, the tenth graders from all points will find a way to get together. Today is only Tuesday.

Boys and girls spill out of the Eighty-sixth Street crosstown buses at

Madison Avenue and join the flow of their counterparts heading north. The walking tenth graders greet one another in soft, kindly rhythms, in polite, gentle tones. The boys greet one another with high fives. Girls with girls and girls with boys bestow quick, sweet kisses on one another's cheeks—some cheeks still not completely rid of hints of baby fat. No routine air kisses from these kids. Their kisses are heart-felt, making their unity, their devotion to and trust in one another, pal-pable. Kisses from their mouths are like the cool little first nippy smacks of a very young baby.

Most of the tenth graders are in the habit of leaving home without eating any breakfast. Still in clusters, with fifteen minutes to get to school, they pause in doorways. One girl in a cluster of five takes out a pack of Marlboro Lights—the brand favored at the moment—and each member of the cluster participates in lighting the cigarette, striking the match, guarding the flame, offering a propane lighter. They share. The lighted cigarette is passed from mouth to mouth. They all inhale, the girls twisting their mouths like tough pros, exhaling the smoke from a tiny corner opening on one side of the lips.

One angelic-looking blond beauty with raw, red nostrils takes a puff, inhales deeply, and says wearily, "I've like got the fucking flu or something."

"Fuck the you know fucking germs," another one says smoothly, reassuringly, a positive reinforcer.

"I got home like three?" another member of the cluster says, making her statement in the form of a question. "I sweat Henry? Who you sweat? Anybody?"

The others regard her skeptically. "Nobody," one says.

"I sweat the shit out of Henry," the one who got home at three says mildly.

On the feet of all the members of this cluster are boots, not quite Timberland. The girls, some wearing black panty hose or black kneesocks, have on chic black laceups, all with Vibram soles, all with steel tips. One girl wearing laceups two feet high lifts a knee, turning the booted foot this way and that. "New shit-kickers!" she squeals, but in subdued, ladylike tones.

"Cool," the angelic-looking one with the flu says. "Cool shit-kickers."

They crush out their shared cigarette with the heels of their shit-kickers, and they go to school.

Whenever the tenth graders have a break in their school program, and daily at 12:35 p.m., they head for one of their hangouts. The second floor of Jackson Hole, at the southwest corner of Ninety-first and Madison, is in at the moment. On this Tuesday, at 12:36 p.m., six four-place tables and a couple of two-place tables, accommodating twenty-eight customers, are filled. Ketchup bottles absolutely full are at the ready on every table. A teen-age Al Pacino–look-alike waiter serves them their first meal of the day: lone platters of ketchup-doused French fries or fried onion rings, or combo French fries and onion rings, and Cokes. A late arrival, dark-eyed, and smaller and chubbier than the ones settled in, turns up, and a place is found for her. Tearfully, she reports that her French teacher sprang a surprise test on her class, and she thinks she did badly on it.

"Don't like get fucking stressed out," a girl says, offering that same kindly positive reinforcement.

"Fucking teachers," a companion says, chewing on a fry and simultaneously taking a drag on a cigarette and passing it on. "I'm on my way you know to lunch, and the fucking teacher asks where I'm going?" The statements continue to sound as though they were questions. "I don't want teachers being like into my you know business?"

"I miss the teacher who used to be a model and then left the school and went to Africa to be a nun?" someone says. "She would like talk you know about her experiences? She was very like open to everybody?" The others at the table and the girls at all the other tables agree that they miss the teacher who went to Africa to be a nun.

One of the girls, very pretty, with long dark hair, is "presenting" a party and hands out printed invitations. She has dark glasses pushed up on top of her hair. She wears silver loop earrings, a double in the left ear, a single in the right. At her throat hangs a large wooden cross. The invitation shows a picture of Stonehenge on one side, and the other side has a long list of names of people supporting the party, which has a title: "The Farside."

"I can't go to the party?" one of the fifteen-year-olds says. "My father grounded me? Because I was smoking?"

"My mom is trying to like ship me off to a fucking school in fucking Spain?" another girl says. "Unless I you know quit smoking?"

"I want to quit, but I can't? I don't have a choice? It's too late?" one fatalist says.

The party entrepreneur explains that she is working with six other presenters to spread the invitations around, to telephone friends at the schools to the east, west, north, and south, and to obtain the services of a really topnotch d.j. They are working with a well-to-do party producer, whose take of the proceeds will be forty per cent, the balance to be divided evenly among the seven presenters. Admission to the party will be twelve dollars per person.

"This rich, older guy is like experienced you know?" she says. "He's twenty-nine?"

The mention of the number draws forth gasps.

"Fucking twenty-nine," one of the girls says. "That's the age of those actors in that mindless '90210' or that mindless 'Melrose Place.' They're twenty-nine, and they're like playing our age."

At any rate, there are plans to be made. The party is going to start at 10 p.m. The girls will spend the afternoon before in preparations.

"Here's what we'll do," the entrepreneur says. "We need five hours. You three come to my house you know at five? You bring all your clothes? I take everything out of my closet and spread everything out on the floor? We try on all the stuff? Depending on what kind of mood we're in, we make our selection?"

"We have to be fucking blunt," one of the potential guests says. 'About what like looks good on us."

"Then we take showers? Half an hour? Then we like shave our legs? Half an hour? Then we like put cream on our legs? Half an hour? Then we call up everybody who's been like grounded? We talk to them for at least an hour? Maybe we give them an hour and a half? Then we go out and buy a quart of vodka and some orange juice and cranberry juice? Then we go to somebody else's house and drink vodka with orange juice or vodka and cranberry juice? Then we get dressed? Then we get another quart of vodka and go to somebody else's house? We become like outgoing? And we make calls to friends and invite them over? By then, we'll be ready to go?"

On the first school day after the weekend, promptly at 12:36 p.m., the tenth graders are back in place at Jackson Hole, smoking, chewing gum, eating fries and onion rings, and reviewing the party. "I like feel real ripped off?" the young Farside presenter-entrepreneur is saying, "Too many people came to the party, which was at this nice club on West Forty-seventh Street? There were hundreds pushing and shoving and clogging the street, and the police came? And they said we had to be carded, because they had a bar? And we you know didn't like have cards, so this twenty-nine-year-old rich guy said the fee for getting the club had to be raised from three thousand dollars to eight thousand dollars, because they had to close the bar and were not allowed you know to sell us drinks? And everybody had to pay twenty dollars instead of twelve dollars just to get in? So, but even so, nobody like wanted to leave? And it was so crowded you couldn't even dance? And at the end of it the twenty-nine-year-old rich guy took forty per cent, and all I got was about fifty fucking dollars, after I did all the fucking work and made a million phone calls?"

She chews on a French fry, accepts a glowing Marlboro Light from the girl beside her at the table, and takes a quick puff. The chubby, dark-eyed girl who was stressed out by her French teacher comes over from another table and gives the entrepreneur a soft, comforting kiss on the cheek, and one by one all the other tenth graders in the area come over and do the same.

acknowledgments

Many people made this anthology.

At Thunder's Mouth Press and Avalon Publishing Group:
Thanks to Ghadah Alrawi, Tracy Armstead, Will Balliett, Sue Canavan, Kristen Couse, Maria Fernandez, Linda Kosarin, Shona McCarthy, Dan O'Connor, Neil Ortenberg, Paul Paddock, Susan Reich, David Riedy, Simon Sullivan, and Mike Walters for their support, dedication, and hard work.

At The Writing Company:
Nate Hardcastle and Nathaniel May helped with research. Nathaniel May also oversaw rights research and negotiations. Mark Klimek, Taylor Smith, March Truedsson, and Kate Fletcher took up slack on other projects.

At the Portland Public Library in Portland, Maine:
The librarians helped collect books from around the country.

Finally, I am grateful to the writers whose work appears in this book.

p e r m i s s i o n s

b i b l i o g r a p h y

The selections used in this anthology were taken from the editions listed below. In some cases, other editions may be easier to find. Hard-to-find or out-of-print titles often are available through inter-library loan services or through Internet booksellers.

Asbury, Herbert. *All Around the Town.* New York: Knopf, 1934 (for "The Persecution of the Reverend Dr. Dix").

Asbury, Herbert. *The Gangs of New York.* New York: Thunder's Mouth Press, 2001.

Berger, Meyer. *The Eight Million.* New York: Columbia University Press, 1983 (for "Mom, Murder Ain't Polite").

Byrnes, Thomas. *Rogues' Gallery: 247 Professional Criminals of 19th Century America.* Secaucus, New Jersey: Castle, 1988.

Hamill, Pete. *Piecework.* New York: Little, Brown & Company, 1996 (for "Notes From Underground").

Jacoby, Richard. *Conversations with the Capeman.* New York: Painted Leaf Press, 2000.

McKelway, St. Clair. *True Tales from the Annals of Crime and Rascality.* New York: Random House, 1951 (for "The Wily Wilby").

Riordon, William L. *Plunkitt of Tammany Hall.* New York: E.P. Dutton & Co., 1963.

Ross, Lillian. *The Fun of It: Stories from the Talk of the Town.* New York: The Modern Library, 2001 (for "The Shit-Kickers of Madison Avenue").

Sager, Mike. "The High Life and Strange Times of the Pope of Pot." Originally appeared in *Rolling Stone,* June 13, 1991.

Sante, Luc. *Low Life: Lures and Snares of Old New York.* New York: Farrar, Straus and Giroux, 1991.

Trillin, Calvin. "Marisa and Jeff." Originally appeared in *The New Yorker,* July 10, 2000.

Wall, Patrick M. "The Annals of Manhattan Crime." Originally appeared in *New York* magazine, November 14, 1988.

Wodehouse, P.G. *The World of Jeeves.* New York: Harper & Row, 1967 (for "Jeeves and the Unbidden Guest").